VISIONS FOR THE MASSES

VISIONS
FOR THE
MASSES

Chinese Shadow Plays
from Shaanxi and Shanxi

Fan Pen Li Chen

East Asia Program
Cornell University
Ithaca, New York 14853

The Cornell East Asia Series is published by the Cornell University East Asia Program (distinct from Cornell University Press). We publish affordably priced books on a variety of scholarly topics relating to East Asia as a service to the academic community and the general public. Standing orders, which provide for automatic notification and invoicing of each title in the series upon publication, are accepted.

If after review by internal and external readers a manuscript is accepted for publication, it is published on the basis of camera-ready copy provided by the volume author. Each author is thus responsible for any necessary copy-editing and for manuscript formatting. Address submission inquiries to CEAS Editorial Board, East Asia Program, Cornell University, Ithaca, New York 14853-7601.

Number 121 in the Cornell East Asia Series
Copyright © 2004 by Fan Pen Li Chen. All rights reserved
ISSN 1050-2955
ISBN-13: 978-1-885445-21-6 pb / ISBN-10: 1-885445-21-0 pb
Library of Congress Control Number: 2004102513
Printed in the United States of America
20 19 18 17 16 15 14 13 12 11 10 09 08 07 06 04   9 8 7 6 5 4 3 2 1

"The Temple of Guanyin" was originally published in *Asian Theatre Journal* (Volume 16, No. 1, Spring 1999, pp. 60-106). Cover design by Karen K. Smith

⊗   The paper in this book meets the requirements for permanence of ISO 9706:1994.

To My Family and Friends

Contents

Plates

1, 2: *The Temple of Guanyin.* Photos from an actual performance: Bao Chengjie 包
承洁.

3: Anxious village audience for *The Temple of Guanyin*. Photo: author.

4: A sun-lit performance found only in Qishanxian 岐山縣, Shaanxi. Photo: author.

5: The backstage orchestra of a troupe in Liquanxian 禮泉縣, Shaanxi. Photo: author.

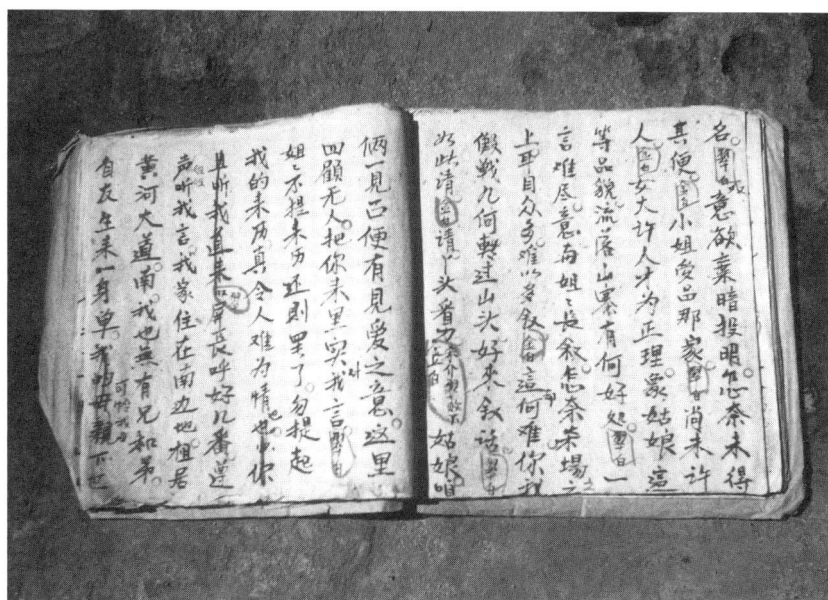

6. A Shaanxi playscript. Photo: author.

Introduction

Combining design, carving, and painting with music, song, dialogue, and manipulation of the shadow figures, [1] Chinese shadow theatre, *yingxi* 影戲, was already highly developed by the Song dynasty (960–1280). [2] More than a dozen Song sources mention the shadow theatre, [3] one of which inventories the impressive contents of a trunk belonging to a single troupe. According to *Baibao zongzhen* 百寶總珍 (Complete inventory of a hundred treasures), this particular trunk contained 1,760 heads, bodies, props, and weapons for

---

1. I use the word "figure" instead of "puppet" because shadow puppeteers insist that "in no language except English are they referred to as 'puppets' (which derives from a word meaning 'doll,' indicating 3-dimensions)" (Humphrey 1981, 144).

2. Although scholars have tried to trace the origins of shadow theatre to a Han Dynasty Daoist adept's attempts to conjure up the likeness of a deceased consort of Emperor Wudi 武帝 (r. 140–86 b.c.) behind a curtain, we have yet to find a concrete reference to shadow theatre before the Song. I discuss the history and various myths about Chinese shadow theatre in detail in my forthcoming book, *The Chinese Shadow Theatre and Popular Religion and Women Warriors*.

3. Namely, "yingxi" (shadow theatre) in Gao Cheng's 高承 (fl. ca. 1068–1086) *Shiwu jiyuan* 事物記源 (Origins of things); Zhang Lei's 張耒 (1052–1112) *Mingdao zazhi* 明道雜誌 (Miscellany to enlighten the way; written 1032–1033); "washe zhongji" 瓦舍眾伎 (performing artists in the tile district) in Nai Deweng's 耐得翁 (1122–1279) *Ducheng jisheng* 都城記勝 (Records of the beauty of the capital; written1235); "baixi jiyi" 百戲伎藝 (art of the hundred types of performances) and "fencha jiudian" 分茶酒店 (tea and wine shops) in Wu Zimu's 吳自牧 *Meng liang lu* 夢梁錄 (Record of dream of [Bian] liang 汴梁); "yingxi" (shadow theatre) by an anonymous author in *Baibao zongzhen*; "yuanxi" 元夕 (night of first full moon of the year), "zhuse yiren" 諸色藝人 (various performing artists), "shehui" 社會 (guilds), "dengpin" 燈品 (lamps), "feiza" 杷鮓 (an exotic food), and "xuanyingxi" 鏇影戲 (turning shadow plays) in Zhou Mi's 周密 (ca. 1290) *Wulin jiushi* 武林舊事 (Tales of martial artists) and *Xihu laoren fansheng lu* 西湖老人繁勝錄 (Records of scenic attractions by the Old Man of the Western Lake); "jingwa jiyi" 京瓦伎藝 (performing arts in the tile district of the capital) in Meng Yuanlao's 夢元老 *Dongjing menghua lu* 東京夢華錄 (Record of the dream of prosperity in the eastern capital, written ca. 1131–1161); and Yue Ke's 岳柯 *Chengshi* 程史 (Cheng's history). See Jiang 1992, 24–42, for the most comprehensive descriptions of the above sources except for the last item which is quoted in Wang (1995, 9). Chang (1982, 16–24) contains translations of some of the sources.

enacting historical romances (Jiang 1992, 30–31; also translated in Chang 1984, 22). Sources on the shadow theatre during the Yuan and Ming dynasties are much less numerous. By the Qing, however, this form of theatre once again exploded in popularity and developed to great heights of sophistication and variety.[4]

Traditional Chinese figures are made of translucent parchment (donkey, water buffalo, goat/sheep, or cattle/calf hide, depending on locality) and painted in colors. The heads are detachable, and most of the human figures consist of eleven separate pieces. They are manipulated by a central control rod attached to the neck and two arm control rods attached to the hands. The puppeteer holds the central rod in one hand and manipulates the other two in the other hand—one rod between his thumb and index fingers and the other between his middle and ring fingers (some place this rod between the middle finger and the little finger).[5] The characters usually move one arm when speaking. Sometimes puppeteers work with several figures in each hand. The amount of intricate movement is reduced, of course, when a number of figures parade across the stage or engage in combat. The sizes of the screens and shadow figures vary in the different traditions of shadows. Traditionally, oil lamps were used as the source of lighting, but nowadays only electric lights can be found.

---

4. The famous ethnologist and museum curator, Berthold Laufer, even pronounced: "If we have a right to say that the home of an art is where it has developed to its highest technical perfection, then the Chinese shadow plays are proof of the origin of the idea in China" (Wimsatt 1936, xiv). Although the immensely popular Western European shadow shows during the latter part of eighteenth century were known most commonly as "Ombres Chinoises" "Chinesische Schattenspiele," "Chinese shadows," and "Sombras Chinoises" (And 1979, 40), the "Chinese" part of these terms probably reflects an attempt to cash in on the vogue for chinoiserie in Europe rather than the direct influence of Chinese shadow theatre. The European figures were black silhouettes of European style and depicted European stories (Blackham 1960, 65-112). European shadow theatre most likely arrived from Turkey via Italy—the earliest performers of Ombres Chinoises were all Italian showmen. The ancestry of shadow theatre is controversial, but scholars all agree that it originated in Asia.

5. For information on making and manipulating Chinese shadow figures, see Lily Chang (1982, 45–96) and Chen-an Chin (1993, 76-122 and 134-140). Chin's historical accounts contain numerous inaccuracies, and his attacks on Lily Chang and a shadow theatre artist are vicious and often unfair. Moreover, the Luanzhou tradition has never been the "mainstay" of Chinese shadow theatres. Chin's sections on the manufacturing and manipulation of Luanzhou-style figures are, however, very instructive. The cited version of his book is in English and can be obtained from Chen-an Chin at 4319 Spellman, Houston, TX 77035. Chinese Theatre Works, the umbrella organization for the Arts Education Program, Chinese Theatre Workshop, Gold Mountain Institute, and Yueh Lung Shadow Theatre gives a course on making very simple shadow figures. The course includes a handout with directions for making a shadow screen. This non-profit institute can be reached at: 34-17 Steinway Street, Box 241, Long Islang City, NY 11101. Phone/fax: (718) 392-3493; email: Chinesethtrworks@aol.com.

In his *Zhongguo yingxi* (Chinese shadow theatre), Jiang Yuxiang (Jiang 1992, 191–247)[6] categorizes the Chinese shadow theatre into seven main traditions: Qin 秦 and Jin 晋 shadows; Luanzhou 滦州 shadows; Shandong shadows; Hangzhou 杭州 shadows; Sichuan, Hubei and Yunnan shadows; Hunan and Jiangxi Shadows; and Chaozhou 潮州 shadows.[7] I would like to add to these traditional shadows the category of Modern shadows, which began during the 1950s. The traditions differ in terms of dialect, music, mode of performance, and style of the shadow figures. Shadow theatre is basically an operatic form; all the traditional troupes consist of at least one master puppeteer and an orchestra ranging from three to seven musicians. The most sophisticated traditions tend to use playscripts and employ different performers to manipulate the figures and do the singing and dialogues or narrations. The simpler traditions have one master puppeteer, who performs from memory and is in charge of both the oral and the figure-manipulating aspects of the show. The musicians in the orchestra are considered secondary. They are usually invited to participate in performances according to need, and some may perform for several different troupes. The troupe I saw in Qishan 岐山, Shaanxi, hired musicians from an opera troupe that had virtually disbanded. Privately sponsored troupes of these traditional shadow shows perform for supplementary income. In rural areas, village performers such as the ones I saw in Shaanxi are all farmers.

With the exception of performances in theatres such as in the entertainment quarters during the Song dynasty and in theatres or parks of Modern shadow shows, traditional style shadows have always been sponsored mainly to entertain the gods in order to elicit blessings or to express thanksgiving. While entire communities or several villages might sponsor shadow shows during major festivals (all Chinese festivals have religious significance), temple fairs, and sowing and harvest celebrations, private families also hired shadow performers to entertain their friends and relatives during celebratory occasions. Such events as weddings, birthdays of the aged and one-month birthdays of newborns, establishment of new houses/businesses, passing of college entrance examinations, and funerals are still affordably celebrated with shadow performances.[8] Vestiges of certain religious cere-

---

6. Chinese characters for books listed in the bibliography and for the names of the provinces are not inserted.
7. See Appendix III of my book, *The Chinese Shadow Theatre and Popular Religion and Women Warriors*, for a list of subgenres within these traditions, their characteristics and most popular plays.
8. Funerals were traditionally considered a type of celebratory event, as the "white" part of the "red and white celebratory events" (*hongbai xishi* 红白喜事; i.e., weddings and funerals).

monies such as the waving of deities across the screen at the beginning of the shows indicate the original primarily religious function of such shows.[9] For example, in the county of Qishan, Shaanxi, where shadow theatre is the most popular form of operatic entertainment, shadow plays are performed during the day as well as at night. When one hires a troupe for a session (*yitaixi* 一台戲), it consists of shows for three days and four nights and costs around one thousand *yuan*.[10] Two performances of about three hours each are given during the day—one around noon and one in the afternoon. I watched some plays performed during the day, when the semi-transparent gauze screen was lit by the sun. The master puppeteer alternated episodes from vigorous martial (fighting) plays with slower civil (romantic) plays; when he got very tired, he would set up an elaborate scene on the screen and leave it there while secondary singers sang to music from totally different plays. During the past five years shadow theatre has become even more popular in this region than the government-sponsored human actors opera troupe. The Seventh, Eighth, and Ninth months (about the end of August to early November) are the most popular months for shadow theatre in this region of Shaanxi, with the Seventh Month (particularly the 7th, 12th, 15th, 20th, and 23rd) being the most important.[11]

Aside from traditional shadow troupes in certain rural communities, a few cities still have government-sponsored troupes performing mostly Modern shadows. Instead of performing traditional dramas and using the parchment figures found elsewhere, such troupes use large cartoon-like figures made of celluloid to tell very short (about 10 minutes), mostly pedagogical animal fables to prerecorded music and dialogue/narration. Unlike traditional shadow theatre, in which characters sing as they do in operas, these "modern" animal characters do not sing. Usually a narrator starts the story, and the characters continue it through dialogue and action. Although the shadow characters do not sing, music and other sound effects accompany the show.

Of the main traditional shadow traditions mentioned, only those of Luanzhou shadows, Sichuan, Hubei, and Yunnan shadows, Taiwan shadows,[12] Shaanxi shadows, and Modern shadows survive. Hangzhou shadows, which may have been a descendent of the shadow theatre described in Song

---

9. See the chapter on the role of religion in my book, *The Chinese Shadow Theatre and Popular Religion and Women Warriors*, for a detailed discussion of this topic.
10. Around US \$120 in 2003.
11. The Seventh Month is the Month of the Spirits and has always carried great significance within the popular religious realm.
12. Jiang includes Taiwan shadows in the Chaozhou tradition, although Piet Van der Loon shows that Taiwan shadows could have originated in either Chaozhou in Guangdong province of Chaozhou migrated from Fujian to Guangdong during the Ming dynasty may account for the cultural similarities found between those of Chaozhou and those of Fujian.

dynasty sources, is practically extinct. I was able to find only one semi-defunct, low-caliber troupe in rural Shanghai. Aside from Modern shadows performed by government-sponsored troupes in a few large cities such as Beijing, Changsha 長沙, and Chengdu 成都, the shadow theatre exists in fairly remote rural villages. Luanzhou shadows are found in Hebei, Liaoning, and Heilongjiang; Sichuan, Hubei, Yunnan, and Taiwan shadows in those respective provinces. Shaanxi shadows spans the widest area of influence and features the largest number of minor traditions. Found in the provinces of Shaanxi, Shanxi, Gansu, Qinghai, (western) Henan, and (northern) Sichuan, it consists of at least eighteen different minor styles. Despite its prominence, this form of Chinese shadow theatre has been neglected in Western language sources. All the plays in this book belong to the Shaanxi shadow tradition.

The most sophisticated and renowned traditional styles such as the Leting shadows 樂亭 (pronounced *laoting* by the locals and people in Beijing; and also known as Luanzhou shadows; Eastern Hebei shadows, and Northeastern shadows) of the Luanzhou tradition and the *wanwanqiang* shadows 碗碗腔 of the Shaanxi tradition seem to have developed during the Qing dynasty.[13] Leting shadows uses playscripts ranging mostly from three to almost twenty volumes.[14] Each volume constitutes the content for one evening. Influenced by Peking opera other forms of performing arts, the Luanzhou shadows performed in Beiping 北平[15] in the early twentieth century put on mostly popular episodes from serial plays rather than entire plays, as well as short, oftentimes comical playlets adopted from minor operatic performing art genres. Playscripts from Taiwan also show a combination of serial plays, individual plays derived from episodes of serial plays, and totally independent short plays. The performance I watched in rural Sichuan did not use playscripts, but a collection of one-volume playscripts once used in its provincial capital, Chengdu, indicates a close similarity with the local human actors' Sichuan opera.

The styles of Shaanxi shadows are most varied, and more troupes survive in this province than in any other. Compared with the serial plays in Luanzhou and Taiwan shadows, Shaanxi shadows tend to be fairly short—about two to three hours in length in single-volume playscripts (when applicable). They are either totally independent plays or episodes from historical

---

13. See the chapter on history in my book, *The Chinese Shadow Theatre and Popular Religion and Women Warriors* for a detailed discussion of the controversies concerning the histories of the genre as well as some of its traditions.
14. I have forty-five volumes of an incomplete script of *Fengshen yanyi* 封神演義. For lists of my shadow play collection and others, see Appendix II of *The Chinese Shadow Theatre and Popular Religion and Women Warriors*.
15. Peking; Beijing was called Beiping during the Republican era.

sagas presented as independent plays. Traditionally, two such plays would be performed during one evening-to-early-morning session. Nowadays, one play seems to suffice. Sometimes a post-midnight skit (*houbanyexi* 後半夜戲) would be performed after the main play when the women have gone home with the children.

Although the shadow theatre traditions in Shaanxi were among the most prominent during the Qing dynasty and are probably the best surviving traditions at present, practically nothing has been written about this genre in non-Chinese sources. The Beijing /Beiping, Sichuan, and Taiwan shadows have been the most popular in the West. Foreigners who collected shadow figures and playscripts and who watched shadow plays early in the twentieth century, resided in and visited the major cities of Beijing/Beiping and Chengdu. As a consequence they wrote only about those traditions. And since 1950, the Taiwan shadows have been studied more intensively because Taiwan is accessible and because an extensive collection of traditional Taiwan Shadow playscripts is owned by the University of California in Los Angeles.

The short, episodic shadow plays popular in Beijing/Beiping from the end of the Qing to 1950 have been translated the most. Kate Stevens has translated *A Leather Trunk Pawned*, *A Basket is Thrown*, *Sacrifice to a Stone Figure*, and *Gao Family Village* from the Beijing/Luanzhou shadow play collection of the Yenching Library at Harvard University.[16] Genevieve Wimsatt has translated *Lotus Flower Temple* in her *Chinese Shadow Shows* (1936), and Benjamin March has translated three episodes from *The Chaos Box* (*Visiting Li Er Ssu*, *Fox Bewitchment*, and *The Exorcism*) as *A Trilogy of the Shadow-figure Theatre* in his *Chinese Shadow-figure Plays and Their Making* (March 1938, 30–52). Mary Hirsch has translated *Borrowing a Headdress* and *A Few Wrong Words* in her M.A. thesis, *Chinese Shadow Theatre Playscripts: Two Translations* (1998). Pauline Benton gives synopses of nine shadow plays in *The Red Gate Players* (1940). Wilhelm Grube and Emil Krebs have translated sixty-eight similar Beijing shadow plays into German in their *Chinesische Schattenspiel* (1915). And Sven Broman has translated ten episodes and complete plays (*The Temple on the Golden Mountain*, *The Broken Bridge*, *The Almsbowl*, *The Sacrifice in the Pagoda*, *The Immortal of Heaven Brings a Son*, *The Lesser Insult at the City-wall*, *The Execution of Tou O*, *Beating the Sack*, *The Pavilion*, and *The Rice Tribute*) in his *Chinese Shadow Theatre Libretti* (1995). I have translated the only shadow play not from Beijing, a Shanxi work entitled *The Temple*

---

16. These unpublished translations are collected at the Gold Mountain Institute for Traditional Shadow Theatre, presently a branch of Chinese Theatre Works on Long Island City, New York.

of Guanyin (1999, 60–106).[17] Conrad Young has made synopses of fifty plays from Taiwan shadow playscripts in his dissertation, *The Morphology of Chinese Folk Stories Derived From Shadow Plays of Taiwan* (1971, Part II).

Enjoying a richer variety of shadow theatre styles than any other province in China, Shaanxi offered more than ten different styles as late as the 1980s,[18] of which the main ones include the *wanwanqiang* 碗碗腔, *laoqiang* 老腔, *xianbanqiang* 弦板腔, *agongqiang* 阿宫腔, and *qinqiang* 秦腔. The most famous is the *wanwanqiang*. The surviving shadow performers who participated in the filming of *To Live* reside in Huaxian 華縣, Shaanxi, where *wanwanqiang* shadow theatre is still routinely performed to celebrate birthdays, funerals, completion of new houses, and other festivities.

Four styles of *wanwanqiang* spread throughout Shaanxi: the Eastern style (*donglu* 東路), the Western style (*xilu* 西路), the Southern style (*nanlu* 南路), and the Northern style (*beilu* 北路). Found in Huaxian, Huayin 華陰, Weinan 渭南, Lintong 臨潼, Dali 大荔, and other counties,[19] the Eastern style *wanwanqiang* is the most popular and refined. Tradition has it that this style of *wanwanqiang*, also known as Gauze Screen shadows (*shachuangying* 紗窗影) in Shanxi, was imported there by refugees from Shaanxi during the Guangxu 光緒 reign (1874–1908) (Yu 1993, 91). It apparently took the province by storm and eventually displaced the indigenous *piqiang* 皮腔, also known as Paper Screen shadows (*zichuangying* 紙窗影). *The Temple of Guanyin* (*guanyintang* 觀音堂) included in this volume is an orally transmitted *wanwanqiang* from Shanxi.

Wanwanqiang shadows is generally recognized to have begun around the Qianlong reign (1736–1796) approximately when the *juren* 舉人 (select or second degree) scholar, Li Fanggui 李芳桂 wrote its most famous ten plays (Jiang 1992, 201; Yu 1983, 90). Even now it is known as the "Contemporary New Tune" (*shiqiang xindiao* 時腔新調), in contrast to the "Old Tune" shadows (*laoqiang* 老腔). The namesake of the tune, the *wan* 碗 (bowl) is in fact a small, three-inch-high bell-shaped inverted brass bowl which is struck by a musician in the orchestra. Lily Chang calls it Bell shadows in her dissertation. Unlike most of the other Shaanxi shadow traditions, *wanwanqiang* is dominated by romantic, "civil" plays. The participation of a *juren* caliber scholar in the creation of its repertoire must have helped *wanwanqiang's* bid for prominence. In this, one of the most sophis-

---

17. This translation is reprinted in this book.

18. This is based on Jiang Yuxiang's research during the 1980s (Jiang 1992, 198); a few of them may no longer exist.

19. *Shaanxi xiqu juzhongzhi* mentions fifteen-some locations (Yu 1983, 93). I note only the ones I'm familiar with.

8

ticated forms of shadow theatre, different performers take charge of the manipulation and the voice parts of the shadow show. A master puppeteer, sometimes aided by an assistant, manipulates the shadow figures, while the director-owner of the troupe would beat on a drum, play on a type of mandolin-like lute (*yueqin* 月琴), and provide the singing and dialogue for all the characters.[20]

Li Fanggui is generally also known as Li Shisan 李十三 or Li the Thirteenth (Jiang 1992, 201), although one source claims that these are the names of two different people from the same clan in Weinan 渭南 (Yu 1983, 90). His style is Qiuyan 秋岩 (Yu 1983, 90). This name is mistakenly written as Li Qiuyai 李秋崖 in Qi Rusan's paper (Qi 1962 reprint, 27). Qi's error is perpetuated in Lü Sushang's book, *Taiwan dianying xiju* (Lü 1961, 430), and in Lily Chang's dissertation (Chang 1982, 28) which bases all the information about Shaanxi shadows on this article by Qi.

Ironically, it was Li's own misfortune, his unsuccessful official career, that made it possible for him to create so many brilliant plays for the *wanwanqiang* repertoire. According to Huan Zhi 驩之, Li Fanggui was born around 1748. In 1799, he took the civil service examination in the capital (the metropolitan examination) for the second time. Although he placed 64th, he in fact failed the examination. Later he was recommended for the position of magistrate at Langao 蘭皋. But this was apparently a title without real office. Disillusioned by the official realm by now, Li returned home and spent the rest of his life teaching children and writing shadow plays. In 1810, when he was sixty-two, an imperial edict was issued prohibiting the performance of shadow plays. Shadow theatre performers and playwrights were also prosecuted. Li was deemed a criminal as a shadow theatre playwright, and he was also charged with propagating the White Lotus rebellion that raged at the time. He died among reeds in a swamp while escaping governmental forces (Huan 1992, 92; quoted in Jiang 2000, 3:1).

Sources mentioning Li Fanggui tend to emphasize his failure to pass the metropolitan examination. The fact is, however, that attaining the *juren* degree itself was a rare honor. During the Qing dynasty, only one licentiate in a hundred passed the provincial examination to receive the *juren* degree (Miyazaki 1976, 59). Well over ten thousand of the candidates who had ever passed a provincial examination (Miyazaki 1976, 64) took part in the metropolitan examination, and of these only two hundred passed in each of the three years during Li Fanggui's time (Miyazaki 1976, 67). People who did not pass the metropolitan examination were not considered failures. In Li Fanggui's case, however, it was unusual that he did not land an official post as a *juren*.

---

20. This form of performance seems to have been inherited from *laoqiang* shadows.

I have found no traces of White Lotus propaganda in his plays (Shaanxisheng Wenhuaju 1980, 212–218). However, like the numerous shadow plays created by semi-literate performers, Li Fanggui shows a certain amount of sympathy for rebels and "bravos." Although all of these rebels have grandiose reasons for carrying out insurrections—e.g., the civil courtiers are corrupt and treacherous—they are ultimately simply indigent elements of society who hope to gain wealth and power through their acts. They represent the desire of peasants and marginalized populations, many of whom did become involved in the White Lotus Rebellion, to eventually gain titles, riches, and legitimacy hopefully through government co-option. Because shadow theatre represented the rebellious desires and sentiments of the peasants so closely, Qing dynasty officials frequently associated it with the White Lotus Sect and condemned it along with sectarian religion.

A similar persecution of shadow theatre on account of another White Lotus Rebellion can be found in Hebei during the late 18th and early 19th centuries. While some shadow performers were probably members of rebellious sects, most seem to have been wrongly implicated. Government officials called the White Lotus rebels *xuandengfei* 玄燈匪 (bandits of dark illumination) and often confused them with shadow theatre performers. The problem was further compounded by the belief that shadow performers were able to create evil spirits and armies out of shadow figures (Chang 1982, 216–217; Liu 1991, 7; Liu 1986, 6).[21]

Ironically, compared with the authors of other shadow plays, Li Fanggui was distinctly a Confucian scholar. His shadow plays keep affirmation of rebellions and bandit-type figures to a minimum, although they do exist to please his audience. His complicated plots are more reminiscent of literary *chuanqi* 傳奇 operas, and his plays are more concerned with talented scholars and beautiful maidens than warrior heroes and heroines. He seems to enjoy flaunting his knowledge of literature and history, and has indeed produced the most refined and most popular plays of one of the most famous traditions of the Chinese shadow theatre.

Shadow plays with known authors are very rare.[22] And of the eleven most popular and "representative" plays in the *wanwanqiang* repertoire, ten of them are attributed to Li Fanggui. These ten plays are: *The Fragrant Lotus Pendant* (*xianglianpei* 香蓮佩), *A Match of Spring and Autumn* (*chun-*

---

21. Jiang Yuxiang, however, proves that the influence exerted by the persecution of the White Lotus Society on the shadow theatre as a whole was minimal (Jiang 1992, 92-101).

22. In Leting 樂亭, an area in Luanzhou 灤州 (pronounced Lanzhou locally), Hebei, a licentiate (*xiucai* 秀才) by the name of Gao Shuyao 高述堯 wrote six famous plays during the Daoguang 道光 reign (1821–1851), and a *juren*, Gao Keting 高可亭 wrote a dozen plays beginning from the Guangxu 光緒 reign (1875–1908). Others like Liu Huanting 劉煥亭 and Li Dazhao 李大釗 from the same region also wrote during this century (Wei 1990, 17–21).

qiupei 春秋配), *Shrine of the Ten Gods* (*shiwangmiao* 十工廟), *The White Jade Hairpin* (*baiyudian* 白玉鈿), *The Jade Swallow Hairpin* (*yuyanchai* 玉燕釵), *The Purple Cloud Palace* (*zixiagong* 紫霞宮), *The Lotus of Ten Thousand Felicities* (*wafulian* 萬福蓮), *Matched by Butterflies* (*hudiemei* 蝴蝶媒), *The Flame Stallion* (*huoyanjü* 火餤駒), and *The Convent of Purity and Simplicity* (*qingsu'an* 清素庵). So renowned are they that they are also known by the acronym of *peipeimiaochaidian, gonglianmeiju'an* 佩配廟鈿釵, 宮蓮媒駒庵 (Yu 1983, 95). Translations of *The White Jade Hairpin* and *The Jade Swallow Hairpin* by Li Fanggui are hence intended to showcase two of the best plays of this genre.

I have also included a less refined, anonymous *wanwanqiang* play, *The Coral Pagoda* (*shanhuta* 珊瑚塔), and a *xianbanqiang* play, *Yang Long Draws the Bow* (*yanglong kaigong* 楊龍開弓). Unlike the more literary and refined *The White Jade Hairpin* and *The Jade Swallow Hairpin* in which the objects that gave the plays their titles play an important role in the development of the storyline, the coral pagoda in *The Coral Pagoda* hardly appears at all. But these two anonymous plays reflect many of the most popular motifs found in shadow plays: the preference for "military" over "civil" content, the fondness for independent, bandit-like male and female warriors, the distrust of muddle-headed emperors and evil courtiers (i.e., the prime minister), the penchant for violence and bloodthirstiness, and the desire to obtain titles, wealth, and marriage into the imperial family through raising a rebellion. The playwright invariably legitimizes plans for rebellion by having a victimized general and members of his clan rebel nominally against the prime minister who is the arch enemy of the general and who is designated as an evil "traitor" in the play. Rebels pose as protectors of the state and the emperor, rather than as overthrowing the system. The rebellion itself is usually couched in grandiose terms such as helping to "revitalize the state," "eliminate the evil traitor," and "save the emperor." Young men of the victimized clan typically collect many beautiful martial wives who are the sisters or daughters of marginalized groups indispensable to their final victory.[23]

Yang Long Draws the Bow also portrays the classic power struggle between the civil and military officials of the court. While the court depends on the military to protect the state from foreign invasions and internal rebellions, the powerful generals themselves are also potential threats to the state. While historical accounts written by intellectuals typically present this power struggle from the point of the view of the courtiers, this play takes the side of the generals and rebels. In shadow theatre the prime minister is

---

23. See the chapter on women warriors in my book, *The Chinese Shadow Theatre and Popular Religion and Women Warriors*, for an elaboration of this theme.

always a treacherous manipulator who must be destroyed. The emperor is often a muddle-headed, whimsical figurehead easily swayed by the prime minister. The general and his family are always victims, driven to rebellion but destined for victory. They win by raising a rebellion that forces the emperor to punish the prime minister and confer them with titles.

Possibly influenced by skits performed in human actors' minor operatic performing art forms, comical playlets emerged in the repertoires of many styles of Shaanxi shadows. Usually performed after midnight, when women, children, and older people have left, these playlet are known as post-midnight plays (*houbanyexi* 後半夜戲), extra or additional plays (*shaoxi* 稍戲), and ribald plays (*saoxi* 騷戲). In *wanwanqiang* shadows, these highly entertaining but unseemly skits are frequently performed by secondary performers, the musicians of the orchestra of the troupe, rather than by the main singer or the master puppeteer. The skits provide light-hearted entertainment that helps lift the spirits of audience during the wee hours of the morning before the serious main play recommences. They also afford a rest to the main performers.

This type of comical skit based on everyday life apparently became popular during the late Qing and early twentieth century. The skits may have originated in other minor performing arts, such as drum songs and the various minor human actors theatres (*xiaoxi* 小戲). They exist profusely among the shadow playscripts collected during this century from Beijing/Beiping but not among the scripts found in Luanzhou whence the shadow theatre in Beijing was supposed to have derived. The performance of such trivial plays may have also been a fairly recent phenomenon (less than a hundred years) in Gansu and Shaanxi. They are not found in any of the traditional hand-copied playscripts found in Gansu[24] and Shaanxi; and I was told by the troupe I visited in Lingbao, Henan, that such plays were a fairly recent addition to their repertoire.

Unlike the main plays, these skits are very short, lasting no more than fifteen minutes each. They are transmitted orally and are performed without playscript. The audience, mostly young and middle-aged men, obviously enjoy sarcasm, exaggeration, and scatological and lewd jokes. Given the puritanical influence of the official regime, the skits I have been able to collect tend to be more comical than lascivious. Performers may have felt uncomfortable with having lewd plays transcribed. But the skits in this volume are otherwise indicative of the tastes and mentality of their audience.

The post-midnight play is different from regular formal plays in that the clown role is allowed to sing. The scripts for *Henpecked Zhang San* (*zhang-*

---

24. The modern troupes in Gansu don't seem to use playscripts any more. Most the playscripts collected by Prof. Zhao Jianxin are from the Qing dynasty (Zhao 1996).

san paqi 張三怕妻) and *Rotten-kid Dong Sells His Ma* (*donglanzi maima* 董爛子賣媽) translated here are still being used by the Provincial Theatre for Folk Dramas (*shengminjian yishu juyuan* 省民間藝術劇院) in Xi'an 西安, Shaanxi. They are by far among the best post-midnight shadow plays I have been able to collect. Farce, however, prevails beyond the post-midnight skits. Comic characters seem to play a larger role in shadow theatre than in human actors theatre. Many significant secondary roles are intentionally hilarious, and so colloquialisms, farcical language, and double entendres are common even in the most refined pieces of this genre.

In this volume I present both the most refined and the highly popular though less refined plays of this genre. With the exception of the elegant plays by Li Fanggui, all the others are rare transcriptions of orally transmitted plays. These "visions for the masses" will hopefully provide us a window into the mentality of the common people, at once the largest audience of these plays and the largest social group in China.

The Search for a Dying Art

The decline of traditional Chinese culture since the early 1900s has meant the gradual demise of this fascinating form of theatre as well. When Berthold Laufer, curator of the American Museum of Natural History, purchased a trunk of shadow figures for the museum in 1913, he sincerely thought that he had purchased the last set in China.[25] In fact, however, more than twenty shadow theatre troupes were active into the 1920s in Beijing (Guan 1959, 5–6), but after 1949 only one, government-sponsored troupe survived there.[26] Like many cultural activities, shadow theatre enjoyed something of a revival during the 1950s and early 1960s, mainly under government auspices, but it was banned during the Cultural Revolution from 1966–1976.[27] Private shadow troupes sprouted in the countryside during the 1980s, but this revival declined during the 1990s. Old masters have been

---

25. In 1901 Franz Boas, a curator at the American Museum of Natural History, sent Laufer to China for three years to collect cultural artifacts. Laufer wrote to Boas: "This [shadow theatre] company was the only one in Peking to have the *ying-hsi*, and there is only one living man who is able to make the figures" (Stalberg 1983, 35).

26. This troupe changed its name from Deshun Shadow Theatre Troupe (*deshun piying xishe* 德順皮影戲社) to Beijing Shadow Theatre Troupe (*beijing piying jutuan* 北京皮影劇團) soon after 1949 when government sponsorship began. Although another troupe was known to have performed in Beijing until 1955, the Beijing Shadow Theatre Troupe has been the sole troupe there since then (Guan 1959, 6).

27. Like all traditional theatres, shadow shows were banned during the Cultural Revolution. A few troupes made new shadow figures and managed to continue longer by putting on plays that depicted scenes from the "Model Plays" (*yangbanxi* 樣板戲). They all eventually disbanded and the majority destroyed their equipment as well.

dying, and younger people appear to prefer the ubiquitous television. Until 1998, tourist shops were selling the beautiful transparent parchment figures of disbanded troupes in alarming quantities. By 2002, few of the older figures can be found.

Following the fortuitous acquisition of about 1,600 shadow figure pieces, which I now co-own with my sister, Sen Pen Pu, and seventeen fascicules of shadow playscripts that accompanied them, I began research in this neglected form of Chinese theatre. During three separate research trips to China from 1996 to 1998 in search of shadow playscripts and troupes, I videotaped more than thirty plays whole or in excerpt. The collection of Chinese shadow plays presented here in translation is one result of the project; the other is a forthcoming book entitled, *The Chinese Shadow Theatre, Popular Religion, and Women Warriors*.

I found three troupes during my first trip. The Beijing Shadow Theatre Troupe is the most modern in terms of production techniques, style of shadow figures, and dramatic content. This Beijing troupe performed almost daily from a permanent stage at the Minsuguan 民俗館 (Gallery of Folk Culture) at the Liulichang 琉璃廠, a tourist center. The innovative repertoire appears to be versions of modern shadow plays popular in cities like Beijing and Changsha 長沙 during the 1950s and early 1960s. Unlike traditional shadow theatres in the countryside, which play to adults, the Beijing theatre seems to consider children to be their target audience. But so many types of entertainment are available to city dwellers nowadays, that business was very poor. Aside from the children of the performers, my daughter and I were the only members in the audience the two times we visited. By summer 1997, the entire Gallery had closed down. Members of the troupe receive a small salary from the government and now perform only occasionally in city parks at publicly funded festivities.

The building of a new Mu'ou Piyingxi Bowuguan 木偶皮影博物館 (Puppet[28] and Shadow Theatre Museum) led me and two associates to the small city of Xiaoyi 孝義 about two hundred kilometers southwest of Taiyuan 太原, the provincial seat of Shanxi.[29] Anxious to re-establish designated traditional folk arts, among which shadow theatre has been included, the local Cultural Bureau is once again supporting a group of shadow artists. The

---

28. *Mu'ou* 木偶 refers to three-dimensional puppets which are manipulated variously by rods, strings, or fingers. In Shanxi and parts of Shaanxi, many troupes perform rod puppetry by day and shadow shows at night.
29. I was accompanied to Taiyuan and Xiaoyi by my researcher friends, Cai Yuanli and Bao Chengjie.

need for them to work in different trades since 1985,[30] however, has meant they have abandoned much of their theatrical equipment. As a consequence this government-sponsored puppet and shadow theatre troupe can perform only two shadow plays at present. More shadow figures will have to be made before they can expand their repertoire.[31]

After some inquiries, we discovered the existence of a peasant troupe in a small village, Bidu 必獨, about half an hour from Xiaoyi by jeep. There I was finally able to watch a traditional shadow play, *The Temple of Guanyin*.[32] This Bidu troupe serves a large geographical area by traveling wherever its services are engaged. The director of the troupe, Wu Haitang 武海棠, is a sixth-generation puppeteer—his son, a shadow theatre musician—is a rare seventh generation performer. Most of the members of the troupe are invited artists. The director typically travels to different villages as well as to the city of Xiaoyi putting together a troupe as the need arises. I had to wait while he tried to locate a septuagenarian drummer—the only person in the area said to be capable of performing the drum and gong accompaniment for *The Temple of Guanyin* [also known as *Twice Pacifying the North Sea* (*erzheng beihai* 二征北海) and *Apotheosis of Five Celestials* (*wutong guitian* 五同歸天)], the woman warrior play I had requested. Apparently, the drummer was on tour with a local opera troupe at the time. The wait was worth it, however. A simple stage was set up in the courtyard of the home of the troupe's director, who was also the proud inheritor of the only trunk of figures and props in the area. The director performed an excerpt of an older form of shadow theatre before the master puppeteer, Liang Quanming 梁全明, three assistants, and five musicians enacted *The Temple of Guanyin* in its entirety. *The Temple of Guanyin*, which I videotaped, lasted about two hours and ten minutes. The show began after dark (after 9 p.m.), and did not end until after midnight. The music was loud, but the singing and dialogue overpowered it with the aid of an old microphone. What seemed like half of the population of the village crowded around the stage with us.[33]

---

30. Many Cultural Bureaus ceased to support the troupes under their auspices during the 1980s, after implementation of the Open Door Policy with its accompanying adoption of a market economy. Many members of such troupes were therefore forced to ply other trades.
31. In 1998 I met Chen Zengli 陳增禮, a rare shadow artist who is able to design shadow figures as well as manipulate them for performance—he has a one-man troupe which makes use of prerecorded music and singing—in the remote village of Beixiaocun 北肖村, Guanbeixiang 觀北鄉, Huayin 華陰, Shaanxi. At the time of my visit, Chen Zengli was painting a large group of traditional shadow figure designs for people in Xiaoyi, Shanxi. Chen painted directly on rice paper with a very fine brush without making prior sketches.
32. I have also produced a videotape of *The Temple of Guanyin*, with both English and Chinese subtitles, which can be obtained for a nominal fee by contacting me at: fannchen@albany.edu.
33. I was accompanied by fellow researchers, Cai Yuanli, Bao Chengjie, and my teenage daughter.

The stage consisted of a rectangular, semitransparent gauze screen about six feet wide by four feet high framed by curtains fashioned out of faded turquoise cloth.[34] This screen rested on two tables. While the tables were not visible to the audience, they provided space on the performer's side for storing figures which were ready for entrance or had already made their exits, as well as an old sound system, a playscript, and pegs to secure figures which were not moving on stage. A coarse goat hair rug lined the tables and added extra traction for propping up immobile figures on stage. Ropes extended from the top of the two sides of the screen to about twelve feet behind the stage. Shadow figures were hung on these ropes, their placement determined by the requirements of the show. As in classical Chinese theatre with human actors, the left side of the stage to the audience represented the entrance from the outside and the right side represented either the exit or door to the inside of a room or a city. Thus, most of the shadow figures moved from left to right and consequently were hung to the right of the puppeteers. The area behind the stage was covered on the two sides by a material made out of woven thin plastic strips.[35] A bare light bulb[36] hung between the screen and the master puppeteer, who performed the entire show standing up. The drummer sat to the left of the puppeteers[37] while the rest of the orchestra sat behind them.

Because the master puppeteer ruined his voice in the 1960s, he invited three women assistants to do most of the singing and dialogue, with the aid of his script. Aside from providing different voices, the assistants helped with moving figures to and from the stage. The actual manipulation of the figures was done almost entirely by the master puppeteer. The master puppeteer and his assistants were accompanied by six musicians.

Compared with many of the elaborate shadow shows I later saw in Shaanxi (the troupes of which had new figures made for them), the props used by this Bidu troupe were somewhat spartan. Items such as horses and banners were absent. The old figures imparted a feeling of rusticity and age,

---

34. The size of the screen and figure, as well as other details, vary greatly from location to location. What I describe here is representative only of a rustic show in rural Shanxi.

35. A troupe I saw later at Huayin 華陰, Shaanxi covered all three sides of the backstage with heavy, quilted blankets. The same is true with a troupe in Zhangxian 漳縣, southern Gansu.

36. "Borrowing" electricity from the electric pole in the director's courtyard was the most challenging event of the evening. At least five young men from the neighborhood climbed up and down, trying out different options and giving advice. The circuit shorted continuously. I was getting quite worried until the problem was finally solved about an hour later and after it had become very dark.

37. In Huaxian, Shaanxi, where the *wanwanqiang* shadow plays originated, the drummer who also plays a lute-like instrument called *yueqin* 月琴 sings all the arias and dialogue (like all forms of Chinese opera, the dialogue is performed in a stylized singsong manner by all the characters except for the clown—as does the tutelary god in my translation.) The drummer-singer of *wanwanqiang*, moreover, is usually director of the troupe and owner of the trunk.

though they still reflected the intricate carving style of the Shaanxi tradition. The trunk had an impressive piece of palace scenery made of eight pieces of cowhide. My favorite was the special effect created by the simple cloud which carried immortals to and from their mountains. The patterns on this cloud cast a beautiful shadow that changed in size and clarity depending on the distance of the piece to the light and the screen. Unable to appreciate all the skills involved in performing some of the scenes, I did not even notice the rapid change of figures by the master puppeteer—when the king becomes disheveled from fright, for example, and when the queen is taken to the execution ground—until I viewed the videotape later.

The master puppeteer Liang Quanming, who is now resident artist of the Puppet and Shadow Theatre Museum, kindly lent me a copy of the script of *The Temple of Guanyin*. Although he had only a fourth-grade education, the master puppeteer had done a remarkable job (with very limited use of the incorrect Chinese characters typically found in such scripts[38]) of rendering the play into writing from memory in 1991. Realizing how difficult it would later be for non-natives to follow the songs and dialogue when performed in Shanxi dialect, I decided to have both Chinese[39] and English subtitles inserted into the videotape of the production I had shot. I translated the play from the master puppeteer's script and then tried to match it to the performance on the videotape. To my great dismay, however, I discovered that not only were some of the lyrics deleted or changed, but the dialogue was often elaborated or altered for dramatic effect. Now I could understand why the drummer (the conductor of the orchestra) sat right next to the master puppeteer and his assistants. He had to watch them carefully in order to let the other musicians know when to play the appropriate music.

Although the scripts of such plays are not prescribed in the same way as plays found in the more codified theatre forms such as *kunqu* 崑曲 (Kun opera) and *jingxi* 京戲 (Peking opera) are, the codes, formulas, and conventions are so familiar to the performers that they are able to create organic theatrical presentations despite improvisations and variations.[40] Indeed, the

---

38. All the hand-copied and printed shadow playscripts as well as traditional song sheets of a popular nature that I have examined are characteristically full of homophones and other types of "wrong" characters. These are so prevalent in such popular genres that one scholar calls them *suzi* 俗字 (popular characters) as well as the more common but derogatory term, *baizi* 白字 (homophonous wrong characters; Yao 1979, 74).

39. Although Shanxi dialect is still considered to be "Chinese," people from other parts of China will probably not understand the spoken form. When the dialect is written down using Chinese characters however, most people comprehend what is being said. This applies to all dialects: people generally have trouble understanding other dialects unless they are put into writing.

40. Apparently, however, many of the codified regional operas forms, *difangxi* 地方戲, have always operated this way. A similar situation is described in the videotape, *Zeyang xinshang gezaixi* 怎樣欣賞歌仔戲 (How to appreciate the Gezai Opera) produced by Taiwan's Ministry

shadow plays in Shanxi used to be performed wholly from memory. Flexibility and adaptability are built into such performing arts. The puppeteers and musicians work with conventions which make group creativity possible. As the performers are all familiar with the conventions of the plays, a certain amount of improvisation and creativity expected. Not only were they expected to respond to each other, but the orchestra was expected to react and accompany them accordingly.

I was more fortunate in locating shadow playscripts during this first trip. By far the largest collection of serial fascicules of Luanzhou shadow plays can be found at the library of the Xiju Yanjiusuo 戲劇研究所 (Drama Research Institute) in Beijing.[41] Many of the hand-copied playscripts in fact once belonged to the renowned scholar of Chinese drama, Qi Rushan 齊如山, and the famous Beijing Opera singers, Mei Lanfang 梅蘭芳 and Cheng Yanqiu 程硯秋. This impressive collection is characterized by voluminous fascicules similar to the ones I collected from Chengde 承德, Hebei.

The Shanxisheng Xiju Yanjiusuo 山西省戲劇研究所 (Drama Research Institute of Shanxi Province) in Taiyuan has a collection of about 154 shadow plays. In the 1950s the Bureau of Culture of the Lüliang 呂梁 region southwest of Taiyuan had researchers transcribe all the shadow plays that local performers had memorized. Copies were made for the library of the Shanxi Xiju Yanjiusuo when the now-retired researcher Luo Renzuo 羅仁佐 transferred from that area to Taiyuan. The library of the Taiyuan Research Institute is closed to visitors, however, and the playscript collection was in the process of being edited for printing as *neibu ziliao* 內部資料 (publications for internal use). As a friend of Cai Yuanli 蔡源莉 and Bao Chengjie 包承洁, who accompanied me on the trip to Shanxi, Luo kindly obtained ten plays for my examination.

After more research I contacted Professor Jiang Yuxiang 江玉祥 of the Museum of Sichuan University (*Sichuan daxue bowuguan* 四川大學博物館), who is the premier scholar of Chinese shadow theatre. With his help, I was able to visit eleven shadow troupes during my second trip in 1997. The sole surviving performer in Chengdu 成都, Sichuan, was too ill to perform, but Jiang Yuxiang accompanied me to Santai County 三台縣 in Sichuan and numerous locations in Shaanxi. The sixty-five-year-old master puppeteer, Xiong Weisen 熊維森, came to the county seat of Santai with his musicians and treated us to an excellent performance. Xiong was able to manipulate

---

of Education. Traditionally, the director of a Gezai Opera troupe would tell the plot of the story to troupe members and assign them roles just prior to performances.

41. Most of the photocopies of plays in the 57-volume collection of Chinese shadow playscripts and articles on the shadow theatre at the University of Hawaii at Manoa come from this library.

five large Sichuan figures in each hand during intensive warfare scenes. Like the master puppeteer in Shanxi, he worked from memory and handled both the recitation and figure manipulation by himself. The level of artistry continued to be extraordinary as we traveled next throughout Shaanxi. Unless indicated, all the troupes consisted one or two main performers, an assistant, and an orchestra of five to seven musicians. We watched a troupe from Lintong 臨潼 led by fifty-seven-year-old Sun Jingfa 孫景發 perform excerpts of three plays in the *wanwanquiang* style. Two troupes from Hua County 華縣 led by the sixty-seven-year-old Wei Zhengye 魏振業 and the sixty-eight-year-old Pan Jingle 潘京樂 also performed *wanwanqiang* plays for us. We also watched a troupe at Huayin 華陰 County led by the fifty-year-old Zhang Ximin 張喜民 perform *laoqiang* 老腔 plays. At Liquan 禮泉 County, the forty-five-year-old Cheng Youcai 程有才 performed *xianbanqiang* 弦板腔 plays for us. At Qishan 岐山 County the fifty-seven-year-old Wang Yunfei 王雲飛[42] hired musicians who were members of a disbanded human actors opera troupe and performed *qinqiang piying* 秦腔 for us in his courtyard.[43] There was even a one-man troupe using recorded music as a tourist attraction near Banpo 半坡 Museum. Chen Zenli 陳增禮 is a sixty-six-year-old who performed *wanwanqiang* plays. Chen began his one-man troupe before he came to Banpo.[44] The cost-effectiveness of his operation made him popular with poorer villagers. It seems that the more remote and less developed the village, the better chance its shadow troupes have for survival. Even then, according to Professor Jiang, more than 85 percent of the village troupes he had visited when he did fieldwork in the 1980s are no long in existence.

My subscription to a service at the People's College (*renmin daxue* 人民大學) that collected recently published newspaper and magazine articles on specified topics enabled me to find a shadow theatre troupe in Shanghai. Ma Yu 馬玉, my cousin in Shanghai made arrangements and accompanied me to Qixianzhen 齊賢鎮, Fengxianxiang 奉賢鄉, in the countryside of Shanghai. Possibly the only surviving troupe in Shanghai, Jiangsu, and Zhejiang, this troupe is led by the eighty-two-year-old master puppeteer, Tang Baoli-

---

42. Wang Yunfei had the most exquisite trunk of old shadow figures—they were the most beautiful I've ever seen. When I mentioned that fact to Yang Fei a year later, I was informed that the entire trunk landed in a river a few months after I'd seen it. Apparently Wang's son was driving a small truck carrying the trunk from a performance when the truck backed into a river on its way up a bridge. All the figures were destroyed.

43. The style/subgenre of shadow theatre of Wang's troupe is not clear. The music is probably similar to the local human actors opera. This is the only type of shadow play which is performed during both day and night and made use of the sun as its source of light for casting shadows during its day performances.

44. When I visited in 1998, Chen had already moved back to his village of Beixiaocun 北肖村 at Guanbeixiang 觀北鄉 in Huayin.

ang 唐寶良. Tang is a tailor who draws many of the plots and inspiration for his shadow plays from storytellers at teahouses. All his plays are stories about the Xue 薛 family or about Fan Lihua 樊梨花 of *Shuotang sanzhuan* 說唐三傳 (Three tales on the Tang), a traditional novel, episodes of which have become mainstays of operas and other performing arts. The figures he uses are about two feet tall, made mainly of clear plastic and cardboard, painted in the same tradition as Jiangsu and Zhejian shadows used to be painted. The performance of Tang's troupe was characterized by simplicity—the figures did not move extensively, and the music consisted of one repeating tune. It represents an unsophisticated form of the genre which has survived because of the persistence and enthusiasm of one elderly man. Tang's is probably the sole surviving troupe of the Hangzhou shadow tradition.

I went to Tangshan 唐山 and Leting in Hebei with my researcher associate, Cai Yuanli. This area is known for Luanzhou shadows which traditionally used donkey parchment figures. The Tangshan Shadow Play Theatre[45] troupe (*tangshanshi piying jutuan* 唐山市皮影劇團), directed by the playwright Yao Qigong 姚其鞏, is a government-supported troupe with forty-one permanent and a few temporary positions. It is the largest and most prosperous shadow troupe in China. While much of their income derives from performances abroad—a group was in Japan while another was in Spain when I visited—the demise of most private troupes in that area have made this troupe also immensely popular at local village festivals. As many as 10,000 people might gather around their huge screen (6 x 2.1 meters), usually to watch their favorite serial play, the traditional *Wufenghui* 五鋒會 (Meeting of the five swords) during local festivals. Performances last from ten to eighteen nights, depending on whether the shortened or complete version is selected. Their three-feet-tall figures are made of celluloid and manipulated by several puppeteers.

Cai Yuanli and I also visited a troupe in Luannan 灤南, Leting County in Hebei, nominally sponsored (with minimal financial support) by the local Cultural Bureau. It had just built a larger screen (3.3 x 1.3 meters) to accommodate larger audiences. They performed *Baishezhuan* 白蛇傳 (Story of the snake) for me. While I was impressed by their ingenious homemade mechanisms for creating special effects—marine-animal soldiers moved in shimmering blue waves—I was disappointed by their use of scenery painted on clear plastic. They have apparently discarded their traditional shadow figures and small screen in the hope that they too will be invited to perform abroad like the Tangshan Shadow Play Theatre troupe. Despite innovations by these government-sponsored troupes involving shadow figures, the

---

45. Their own translation.

screen, and lighting, the music, mode of singing, and traditional plays continue in accordance with the old Luanzhou tradition.[46]

During my third research trip to China in 1998, the liturgical and ritual significance of shadow theatre became apparent to me. Professor Zhao Jianxin 趙建新 of Lanzhou 蘭州 University in Gansu accompanied me to the mountainous region in southern Gansu to visit a small traditional family troupe. Located in Wujiamen Village 吳家門, Sanchaxiang 三岔鄉 of Zhangxian 漳縣, about two hundred kilometers due south of Lanzhou, this family troupe is headed by Zhu Tingyu 朱廷玉, a seventh-generation member of the troupe. The village was pitch black by the time we reached it, but Zhao Jianxin's local contact took us to Zhu's home anyway and woke all the adults out of their sleep. Amused by our interest in shadow theatre, an older relative who was staying with the family laughed and said, "What's there to see?" I soon found out that few people actually watch the performances, particularly during the cold nights common to this area. Troupe members would surround the backstage with heavy quilts and warm themselves at a coal stove while they performed *for the gods*.

Zhu's troupe consists of himself and four invited musicians. He claims that a troupe can be established with as few as three performers. His father used to know more than thirty plays, but Zhu can perform only about a dozen. The family used to possess playscripts, but they were taken by the Provincial Cultural Bureau during the Cultural Revolution and have never been seen again. Many performers have mentioned the loss of shadow figures, scripts, and equipment during the Cultural Revolution. Nevertheless, much material has survived either because it was hidden or because there were fewer "avid" revolutionary villagers and officials in some remote regions.

I returned to Shaanxi next and was accompanied by Yang Fei 楊飛, a famous shadow figure collector in Xi'an 西安 and retired member of the Provincial Folk Art Theatre (*shengminjian yishu juyuan* 省民間藝術劇院) to Huaxian 華縣 and Huayin 華陰 in Shaanxi, and Lingbao 靈寶 in western Henan near the border of Shaanxi. We visited four shadow figure carvers and videotaped the twenty-some steps involved in the making of shadow

---

46. According to videotapes of the shadow plays performed at the Third Liaoning Provincial Shadow Theatre Festival (*liaoningsheng disanjie piying yishujie* 遼寧省第三屆皮影藝術節) in 1998, the shadow troupes which participated in this festival also made innovations in their figures, such as using gauze and silk for the sleeves of female characters. I thank Bao Chengjie for making the trip and for videotaping all the plays at the festival using a video camera I left with him. The shadow theatre of Northeast China (Liaoning 遼寧, Jilin 吉林, Heilongjian 黑龍江) belongs to the same tradition as the Luanzhou shadows of Hebei, but writers from that region prefer to call them Northeastern shadows (*dongbei piying* 東北皮影).

figures, starting with the soaking and scraping of the fresh cattle hides.[47] Due to tourism around Xi'an and its vicinity, Shaanxi is the only province where the intricate art of making parchment shadow figures still thrives. Unfortunately, the workmanship of most figures produced for tourists is shoddy.

My request to see a locally hired shadow play—one hired by locals for a specific occasion rather than performed just for me—led me into many homes of shadow performers and related people. Yang Fei and I stayed with various performers and shadow figure carvers until Zhang Qi 張琪,[48] father of the shadow figure artist, Zhang Huazhou 張華州, located a troupe which was to perform at a funeral in Huayin. The *wanwanqiang* shadow troupe directed by Wei Xingbao 衛興保 performed at this village funeral because the deceased was very fond of shadow theatre. Other types of entertainment had also been hired for the occasion; including a film shown on the wall of a large building in an open space outside the village, a video screen placed in the narrow street outside the home of the deceased, and a traditional band and singers who were also in the lane along with the *lingwei* 靈位 (spirit tablet with portrait and offerings) and coffin of the deceased. The shadow play was the least popular of the entertainments. Little over a dozen elderly men and women, and a child under the care of his grandmother came, while the film from Hong Kong drew by far the largest and youngest crowd.

Yang Fei and I also visited a Daoist shadow troupe in Xiche Village 西車村, Yinzhuangzhen 尹庄鎮, Lingbao, Henan. Headed by Suo Xinyou 索辛酉, members of this Daoist troupe consider themselves proselytizers of Daoist tales and thought, and performers of Daoist rituals (e.g., during celebration of the completion of a new house). The musical instruments of the orchestra correlate with special items associated with the Eight Immortals, and the troupe dress and behave with a stronger sense of decorum during performance in comparison with the other troupes I saw. According to Suo, a few generations ago the troupe used to perform Daoist tales mostly about the immortal Han Xiangzi 韓湘子, using both puppets and shadow figures. Now, however, only the orchestra and rituals remain. He obtained shadow figures from nearby Shaanxi and revived shadow theatre, and now he plans to reintroduce three-dimensional puppets for the Daoist tales. To enhance the appeal of the troupe, he has also included some comical skits, like the two translated in this book.

My final stop was Lufeng 陸丰 in Guangdong 廣東. I was accompanied by Fei Shixun 費師遜, a senior researcher at the Institute of Music in

---

47. Zhang Huazhou 張華洲, the artist I videotaped, lives in Liuzhizhen 柳枝鎮, Fengliangcun 馮梁村 of Huaxian. I deeply appreciate the cooperation of this talented artist.
48. Zhang Qi had to ride his bicycle to several villages before he obtained the information.

Guangzhou. The government-sponsored shadow theatre troupe in Lufeng was no longer active. Its members, now engaged in business, were very unhelpful. Fortunately we were able to visit Zhuo You'er 卓幼兒, shadow master of the only surviving private troupe of the region, at Huanlin Village 環林村 of Nantangzhen 南塘鎮, Lufeng. An eighty-seven-year-old, Zhuo You'er was ill and hence unable to perform, but he received us warmly, showed us his shadow figures, and manipulated some for us. I asked Fei Shixun to videotape a performance by Zhuo You'er when he recovered, but was told that he died a few months after my visit. Since the people in this area of Guangdong migrated from Fujian 福建, Zhuo's troupe may have been the only contemporary shadow troupe in China which shared the same roots as those in Taiwan.

Hao Bingli 郝丙黎, the most famous *wanwanqiang* female-role manipulator/performer in Shaanxi and a friend, also died a year after I last met him in 1999. The list goes on. A performer who dictated some post-midnight skits to Yang Fei died a few months later. The shadow figure manipulator/performer in Zhang Yimou's 張藝謀 film, *To Live* (*huozhe* 活著; Zhang 1994), is also no longer with us. The shadow theatre is indeed a dying art in China.

VISIONS FOR THE MASSES

7: Zhang San, the clown in *Henpecked Zhang San*. This figure is made by Zhang Huazhou 張華洲. Photo: Zhang Qi 張琪.

Henpecked Zhang San
張三怕妻

Introduction

Henpecked Zhang San is a *houbanyexi*, or post-midnight play, also sometimes called *shaoxi* (extra play) or *saoxi* (ribald play), from Shaanxi. Television, movies, and other contemporary entertainments have more appeal
nowadays for most young and even middle-aged men, but in the past they
thoroughly enjoyed watching the argument between foolish Zhang San and
his completely incompetent wife. Ordinary though the men in the audience
might have been, they must have felt superior to Zhang San, and they must
have considered their wives infinitely better than the childless bungler
Zhang San is stuck with. It was probably a comfort and a relief to be able to
laugh at people definitely worse off than they themselves were. Indeed, the
ridiculing of inconceivably "bad" housewives seems to have been so popular with the men that some of the antics of Zhang and his wife gained wide
circulation and were readily plugged into different plays.

The wife in a skit called *The Disgusting Wife* (*zangponiang* 髒婆娘),[1] for
example, makes the same unconventional outfit for her husband for the
same ridiculous and greedy reasons as Zhang San's wife does. In fact, the
details for this particular fault are so much more clearly elaborated in *The
Disgusting Wife* that a transcription of it helped me understand this part of
Henpecked Zhang San. However, unlike Zhang San's wife, the "disgusting
wife" is so unkempt and lazy that her dirty habits grossly exceed the bound-
ary of decent humor. For example, when she cooks, mucus from her nose

---

1. This is one of a set of nine *shaoxi* plays Mr. Yang Fei arranged to have Ding Jilong 丁吉龙
transcribe for me. Ding wrote one of the skits and transcribed the rest from oral recitations
done by an old performer in 1998 at Village Wangdu 王都村, Township of Shide 史德鎮,
County of Liquan 禮泉縣 in Shaanxi.

and eyes, as well as the contents of her chamber pot, are all mixed in with the food; in her cooking pot, black beans and rat droppings coexist happily. Her husband can't even beat her, for, as she reminds him, she has fifteen tough brothers, seventeen paternal uncles, and an elected village headman for a father. Woe to the unsatisfactory wife without such a strong male protection from her own family! Bad as such wives may be, however, they are not adulterous, and in other ways as well they are more realistic than the paragons of virtue or embodiments of evil found in the conventional plays of both the shadow theatre and the human actors theatres. Nor do skits advocate that husbands divorce their wives. No matter how unfit wives may seem, the sanctity of marriage is never questioned.

The theme of henpecked husbands was as popular as the bashing of bad wives. Two different troupes, one in Zhangxian 漳縣, southern Gansu, and one in Lingbao 靈寶, western Henan (near Shaanxi),[2] each voluntarily selected the play *All Three Fear Wives* (*sanpaqi* 三怕妻) for me. In this skit the mother faults her son for doting on his wife when he really should beat her until the wife comes to her senses. We find out, however, from the son's father that he and his father had exactly the same problem. All the men and women in this skit are pathetic, comical figures. The young man is a good-for-nothing whose only way to make extra money to buy things for his wife is what he hopes to win by gambling. The young wife is a stubborn, lazy loafer who enjoys gossiping with the neighbors. She threatens to commit suicide to get her way. When the mother, who is unable to beat the daughter-in-law herself because the young wife has locked herself in her own bedroom, overhears how her son is trying to please his wife, the mother also threatens to commit suicide. Alarmed, the father scolds the son for being as fearful of his wife as he himself and the young man's grandfather were. The father wants to hire a geomancy specialist to improve their lot by repositioning their ancestral cemetery and house. The son, however, wants to have their property divided and move out to establish his own household. He ends the argument by throwing excrement into the father's face.

Although the characters are caricatures, their behavior nevertheless indicates something of the complexity within the marital relationships of traditional Chinese peasant families. These plays suggest that wives exercised a certain amount of control and power within their households. A husband couldn't even enter his own home or bedroom if his wife decided not to open the door for him. On the other hand, traditional women might have disagreed that they exerted any power, since many husbands did beat their wives, and wives were dependent upon their husbands for food and money.

---

2. I thank the Daoist troupe in Lingbao, Henan for sending a transcribed copy of the play to Yang Fei to send to me.

But in the minds of the men, women must have exerted a certain amount of influence. The popularity of *Henpecked Zhang San* and *All Three Fear Their Wives* probably lies in the fact that the skits recognize this anxiety and alleviate it.

The following translation of *Henpecked Zhang San* is based on a script used by the Provincial Theatre for Folk Dramas in Xi'an. Originally transmitted orally, this play has been transcribed and edited by the folk theatre institute. It is one of the best *houbanyexi* plays in my collection.

Cast

WIFE: *Zhang San's wife.*
ZHANG SAN: *a peasant.*

ZHANG SAN: (*Enters and recites.*)
    No fear of Heaven,
    No fear of Earth,
    I fear only that tigress-mother of my child.[3]
    The minute I come home, before I can utter three syllables
    My head and face are already bashed numb by her.
    (*Speaks.*) I am none other than old Zhang San. Nine husbands out of ten in my village are henpecked. (*Offstage: Who is the brave one?*) Ah, just good old me! (*Offstage: So, you're not afraid of your wife?*) Aye, I'm not henpecked. She's beaten me so much that you may consider her not to be afraid of me. (*Offstage: Doesn't that mean you're henpecked?*) Well, let me give you an update. I was walking around the block this morning when I ran into a fortuneteller. He said, "Ah! My good brother! Give me a few pennies and I'll fix you up with a Bravery Charm.[4] When you go home with this charm, your wife will be so scared that she'll tremble and pee at the very sight of you." I took his words, gave him twenty coppers, and got myself this strip of paper two fingers wide. It's tucked away here in my bosom. I'll give it a try at home. As I speak, I'm already here at my own house. Let me knock at the door. (*He knocks.*) Childless mother, open the door!
WIFE: (*Offstage.*) Who's calling me a "childless mother"?
ZHANG SAN: See how old I am and I still don't even have a single child. If that's not childless, what is? Childless mother, open this door!
WIFE: (*Offstage.*) Try to be nice.
ZHANG SAN: Open the door, your old mate is back.
WIFE: (*Offstage.*) Nicer!
ZHANG SAN: Your man's back.
WIFE: (*Offstage.*) Nicer yet!
ZHANG SAN: Your darling husband's back. Oh, I'm going to blush—calling myself a darling husband at my age!
WIFE: (*Recites offstage.*)

---

3. It is common for peasants to refer to their wives as the mother of their children, even though in this case Zhang San and his wife do not have any children. Humor, rather than logic, takes precedence.
4. The name of the charm is literally, a "Bone-Hardening Charm," *yinggudan* 硬骨丹.

I was just binding my feet in the room,
When I heard someone calling for me outside the door.
If it's not Mother Wang next door,
Then it must be that jackass old robber of mine.[5]
(*Enters and speaks.*) Let me open the door. Oh! It's you, old robber—
so you've decided to come home!

ZHANG SAN: Ah! Damn you, you rotten old bitch. I, your old man, have just stepped into the door. Instead of asking whether I want to eat or drink, you poke those fat fingers of yours right into my eyes. If you blind me, who'll keep you alive?

WIFE: Lots of people will keep me alive!

ZHANG SAN: Oh you trash! So, lots of people will keep you alive? I don't know what kind of shameless things you've been up to—I won't even bother to ask. You were fine when we first met, but now your face disappears behind your ears as soon as you see me.[6] Just look at yourself! Look at her, everyone! Look at your head—it looks like a sprouted potato. Your hair is a mess, and it sits on your head like a chicken nest. Your face is never washed—it's as black as a cooking pot. I don't even know where you found those awful shoes from—and what's with those purplish flowers you fastened on them? When visitors come, you strut around on purpose. I don't know whether you want to make a fool of yourself or a jackass of me!

WIFE: (*Begins to sing.*) Ah—ee—[7]

ZHANG SAN: No problem, I've got the Bravery Charm on me!

WIFE: (*Sings.*)

I don't comb my hair because I don't have a comb,
I don't wash my face to avoid fetching water.
I don't play the male role, and I don't act the female part,[8]
I, your old lady, have no need to dress up.

ZHANG SAN: When you bear a son, you can be your son's old lady. You're not my old lady! I'll say no more. But that day, on that other day—

WIFE: What other day?

ZHANG SAN: Oh yes, it was on that other day. That day you did that most shameless thing, don't you remember?

WIFE: Aiyaya! When have I ever done anything shameless?

ZHANG SAN: Oh yes, you've done plenty of shameless things! When our

---

5. The wives are always calling their husbands "robbers" in such skits.
6. I think this refers to her turning her head away from him whenever she sees him.
7. These represent the notes she sings before she would plunge into an extensive retort in song form.
8. She is not an opera singer.

stove was out of firewood, Dog Under next door—

WIFE: Dog Fart!

ZHANG SAN: Dog Under's brother is called Dog Fart. Anyway, Dog Under and I went up the mountain to cut some wood. I told you that woodcutters have got to have unleavened bread. I told you that I'd get a few buns down the street, but you wouldn't hear of it. You had to bake them for me—those awful thick things you made for me!

WIFE: What was wrong with them?

ZHANG SAN: What was wrong with them? One side was brown, the other side black. That aside, when I got hungry on the mountain, I brought out those fine buns of yours. I took a bite in one place, my teeth couldn't sink in. I tried gnawing it in another, nothing came off. Finally, I took out my woodcutting ax, put the bun on a rock, and went for it. Ka-cha-pun! The bun finally split into two. It was so thick that there were still big chunks of raw dough in it and something was moving in there. So I took a closer look: two huge female lice the size of hammer heads were butting horns in there! Now were you planning to let your darling Zhang San swallow those into his stomach? When they started biting me in the intestines, did you expect me to put my fingers up my ass to catch them?

WIFE: (*Begins to sing.*) Ah—ee—

ZHANG SAN: You don't scare me!

WIFE: (*Sings.*)

> Burnt buns brighten your eyes,
> Blackened buns cure your headaches.
> If they're not cooked through, your tummy can steam them.
> If your tummy can't steam them, the lice can digest them.
> If the lice can't digest them, we'll get a gravedigger.
> And the gravedigger can bury you right here!

ZHANG SAN: Listen to this, everyone! This rotten bitch is always trying to end my life! I'm willing to forget about that for now and talk about what you did the other day.

WIFE: What other day?

ZHANG SAN: That other day when you did that shameless thing, don't you remember?

WIFE: What shameless thing was that?

ZHANG SAN: Shameless things you've done aplenty! When I went to the City of Xi'an, I brought back an expensive piece of cloth[9] for my outfit. I wanted to have it made at a tailor, but you insisted that you could make it for me. So I said, "If you want to do it, then do a good job."

---

9. This cloth, known as *yindan shilin* 陰丹士林 was an imported material of dark blue color.

What a jackass fine job you did!

WIFE: What was wrong with what I did?

ZHANG SAN: What was wrong? The front was longer than the back, the waist was narrower than the trouser legs. Even if we ignore these minor details, there was still the collar problem.

WIFE: What was wrong with the collar?

ZHANG SAN: Oh—still pigheaded about it, aren't you? The left sleeve was too long, the right sleeve was not even there, and the collar reached all the way to the armpits!

WIFE: It's known as the long-collar style.

ZHANG SAN: Okay, stubborn old bag! Monks' and priests' robes have long collars, but why would I wear a long collar? Let's overlook that and talk about the buttons. Remember where you put the buttons?

WIFE: Where did I put the buttons?

ZHANG SAN: You sewed buttons over my ass so my legs showed when I walked, gas came right out when I farted, and my behind was bound so tight that I tripped whenever I tried to walk fast.

WIFE: (*Begins to sing.*) Ah—ee—

ZHANG SAN: I am not scared!

WIFE: (*Sings.*)

> The front was cut long to allow you to steal and hide food,
> The back was cut short so you won't need to tuck it in.
> The waist is narrow to keep you warm,
> The sleeves are short so you won't have to roll them up.
> Your old lady dresses you up ever so smartly,
> How can you criticize me for lacking in skills?

ZHANG SAN: Aren't you full of it—you're as full of skills as the virtuous chastity of a thousand-year-old widow who can't get remarried![10] But let's move on. Slut, oh you slut—do you remember that other day?

WIFE: What other day?

ZHANG SAN: That day when you did that shameless thing. Don't you remember?

WIFE: What other shameless thing on what day?

ZHANG SAN: What other shameless thing? Well, your shameless acts are so many, you can't even remember which one! Remember the time when my friends came to visit me, together with my friends' friends and all my relatives' relatives. Back then I filled a five-liter vat with wine and spent five *yuan*s on five pounds of cooked meat. I told you that my friends were visiting and I wanted to take them to a restau-

---

10. *Haoshou* 好手, skillful hands, is a pun on *haoshou* 好守, chastity of a widow.

rant,[11] but you would have none of it, you jackass. You insisted on cooking for them yourself! If you knew how to cook for company, then it would have been fine. All you had to do was to scoop out a few large bowls of our finest white flour, roll the dough out nice and thin, cut them into wide noodles, and then season the noodles with aged vinegar. But you hadn't made a meal in five hundred lives, you jackass—you can only talk. Instead, you purposely took half a bushel of black flour,[12] poured half a bucket of water into it, and cut that cowhide of a dough into finger-sized noodles. The noodles crackled when you put them in the pot! When they were scooped into bowls, the pointed ends of the noodles were sharp enough to pierce one's hands and feet! I asked my dear friends to help themselves—they took one look and didn't know what to do with them. They finally bit into the middle part of your noodles and then fled our house and spat them out all over the yard. I was so mad when I came back into the house. But there you were, having a jolly good time of it.

WIFE: I was having a jolly good time?

ZHANG SAN: As soon as my friends fled and the house was empty, you cut yourself several huge pieces of cooked meat and washed them down with seven—no, ten—big gulps of wine. When you saw me, you moved that stuffed mouth of yours a few times but said nothing about stealing the food.

WIFE: (*Begins to sing.*) Ah—ee—

ZHANG SAN: No fear! I fear not the wife today—I've got my Bravery Charm!

WIFE: (*Sings.*)

A dog licks at an oil lamp when it's within reach,
I steal food because my tummy was empty.
If you had fed me nine times a day,
See if I would ever steal food again?

ZHANG SAN: Listen to her! Just listen to her! This rotten bitch wants to eat nine meals a day! No wonder I'm poor. Hey—this woman is too expensive to keep. Let me take out my Bravery Charm and divorce her. Here, take a look at your nine meals! (*Gives her the charm.*)

WIFE: He wants me to look at what nine meals?

ZHANG SAN: Here are your nine meals, take them and eat them.

WIFE: Ah, goodness gracious! There are even chicken scratches[13] on it! Oh

---

11. Restaurants in the villages are very scantily stocked and do not seem to mind if customers bring foods not available there.

12. Unrefined, whole wheat flour.

13. Literally, *jiaomu shouyin* 脚木手印 foot traces and hand imprints. This is one of the ways illiterates referred to writing.

no, my dearest, darling Zhang San, this wouldn't be a divorce paper, would it?

ZHANG SAN: This is called a "husband's relief."

WIFE: Ah! My darling Zhang San!

ZHANG SAN: Don't you "darling" me!

WIFE: (*Sings.*)

> My tears poured before I could speak,
> Opening my mouth, I address my darling Zhang San:
> Divorce me this morning and marry a witch tomorrow afternoon.
> If the new wife is all right, you might thrive.
> But if you marry a terror, you might not live!

ZHANG SAN: (*Sings.*)

> My dear mother without a child,
> I, Zhang San, am drenched in regretful tears,
> Quickly, I kneel down and kowtow.
> If you don't beat me up this very day,
> What need is there to divorce you away?

WIFE: Stand up.

ZHANG SAN: Thank you for this imperial favor.

WIFE: 'Tis only out of marital love.

ZHANG SAN: Ah! How great marital love is! (*Sings.*)

> I implore you, dear audience, not to laugh.
> Not to laugh that I, Zhang San, am not unafraid of my better half!

WIFE: (*Continues the tune.*)

> Henpecked husbands come in groups and hordes,
> Officials are even more afraid of their wives.

ZHANG SAN and WIFE: (*Sing.*)

> Henpecked husbands come in groups and hordes,
> Officials are even more afraid of their wives.
> Beating is intimacy, scolding shows love.
> The more beating, the more intimate and hotter it gets.

WIFE: (*Tugs at Zhang.*) Let's go. The play is almost finished. Let's go home.

ZHANG SAN: Why such a hurry?

WIFE: Let's go home to warm our quilts.

ZHANG SAN: My wife is the one who loves me the most. The play is done, go home and warm your quilts everyone.

The End

8: *Rotten-Kid Dong Sells His Ma.* Shadow figures are from Yang Fei's 陽飛 collection. Photo: Huo Zhanping 霍展平.

Rotten-Kid Dong Sells His Ma
董爛子賣媽

Introduction

Rotten-kid Dong Sells His Ma was collected by the Folk Theatre of Shaanxi Province (*Shaanxisheng minjian yishu juyuan* 陝西省民間藝術劇院). Transmitted in written form, this skit has probably been revised many times and is of a much higher caliber than those skits which have been transmitted only orally. Rotten-kid's desire to wear leather shoes, foreign socks, and gold-rimmed glasses suggests that the skit was first conceived during the early twentieth century.

Replete with irony and wit, *Rotten-kid Dong Sells His Ma* is a hilarious skit which is unethical, even immoral, from a Confucian point of view. A gambler, Rotten-kid Dong successfully spins a web of lies in order to pay his debts by selling his mother. It was and is even now inconceivable for the elite class to countenance such subjects or humor, but for less fastidious, lower-class peasant audiences, such skits have always been immensely entertaining. Whatever the situation at home, the audience could always feel superior to the characters in playlets like this. Rarely would anyone have as a good-for-nothing son as Rotten-kid Dong.

Rotten-kid Dong, who plays the clown role, not only sings, which the clown role doesn't do in formal theater, but he is also the protagonist. The young male role, Dong's uncle, would ordinarily be a dashing scholar in a regular play, but in *Rotten-kid Dong Sells His Ma* he is the dumb fool duped by the devious Rotten-kid Dong. The ultimate salesman with an uncanny ability to switch successfully from sweet talk to threats depending on the situation, Rotten-kid Dong is comical but not really evil. The outrageous lies he spins always sound convincing, and his greed and real intentions are always masked by the grandiose sentiments he expresses until he reveals his true sentiments himself. Despite his chicanery, he is neither castigated nor punished. In fact, his wit and wiles are affirmed, and no one seems devastatingly hurt. The play is a comedy that remains one by keeping the mother out of the final scene.

The lessons, if any, seem to be these: beware of gamblers; he who uses his wits wins; and the gullible deserves to be cheated. Issues of morality and chastity are totally ignored. Peasants don't seem overly concerned with such niceties. One might worry about being laughed at, but survival is of weightier significance. Also, it's important to note that at the same time common people appear to accept widow remarriage, a dowry is not expected of the remarrying bride. The widow usually agrees to remarriage in order to survive, and the family of the deceased usually marry her off in order to obtain a bride price.

Cast

FATHER: *father of Rotten-kid Dong; a* lao 老, *old man.*
MOTHER: *mother of Rotten-kid Dong; a* dan 旦, *female protagonist.*
ROTTEN-KID DONG: *a* zhou 丑, *clown.*
UNCLE: *uncle of Rotten-kid Dong*; *his mother's brother-in-law*; *a* sheng
生, *young scholar/man.*

Scene 1

ROTTEN-KID: (*Recites.*)
A turtle I am,[1]
A loser I am,
Capable I was even of selling the fir trees of my ancestral cemetery.
Carried away by carts,
Transported by boats,
The dug-out holes are still there, not yet filled in.
(*Speaks.*) Little old me, I'm surnamed Dong and called Rotten-kid. I earned this nickname on account of my fondness for gambling those horrible coins. I've been very unlucky these days—lost thirty strings of cash[2] at one go! But I don't even have a penny to pay my debts. Every day the creditors come after me. I'm going to die from grief and worrying. What can I do? What am I to do? (*He gestures that he's thinking.*) Oh, yes! I have it! I'll go home and tell my old lady who gave birth to me that my old man has died while he's been gone. I'll get her to re-marry and sell her for thirty or fifty taels of silver to pay for my gambling debts. Isn't this a grand idea! (*Sings.*)
Full of gimmicks, I, Rotten-kid Dong, can be quite devious;
I plan to trick my own ma into remarrying and do a change of household.
Spinning a web of lies, I will persuade her with a load of clever words,
If I can't sell you today, my dear ma, consider this son of yours useless. (*Exits.*)
UNCLE: (*Recites.*)
It has been exactly half a year since my old wife died,

---

1. A turtle is a derogatory appellation similar to a rogue or bastard.
2. Each string of cash normally contained a thousand copper coins and was equivalent to one ounce or tael of silver.

Being a widower, life for old me has been very bad.

(*Speaks.*) My surname is Zheng 鄭, my name is Bai 白, and my style is Duyi 獨一. My wife had died and there's no one to look after our son and daughter. So when I heard about this widow at Dongzhuang Village 東庄村, I thought I'd find out about her. Let me go to my nephew Rotten-kid's place and ask him about her.

ROTTEN-KID: (*Recites.*)

> Desiring to make life easier for everyone,
> I conjure up tricks and set up traps each day.

UNCLE: Ai! Speak of the devil, isn't this Rotten-kid right here?

ROTTEN-KID: Hei! So it's my uncle here! Your nephew was just thinking about you and here you are! Let your nephew greet you with a bow.

UNCLE: There's no need.

ROTTEN-KID: Then your nephew will kowtow to you.

UNCLE: There's no need.

ROTTEN-KID: If you say there's no need, then there's no need—saves me from all that bending over. Uncle, what did you want to see me for?

UNCLE: Rotten-kid, I heard that there's a widow at your village. Uncle has a mind to marry her, but I don't know what she's like. I came here especially to find out about her.

ROTTEN-KID: (*Turns aside.*) Aiya! Isn't this a case of being better on time than being early—talk about good timing. There's always a buyer when there's a seller! Let me talk to him. (*Turns back.*) My dear uncle, that widow's no good.

UNCLE: Why is she no good?

ROTTEN-KID: She's got big feet—destined for hardship. And she's got a tiger's temper. You can't afford to provoke her!

UNCLE: If I can't afford to provoke her, then I won't marry her.

ROTTEN-KID: But, dear uncle, your nephew has found you someone else.

UNCLE: Who would that be?

ROTTEN-KID: Listen to me, uncle. (*Sings.*)

> If I should mention it, this person is someone you are quite familiar with,
> Daughter of the Ma family and wife of the Dong family, she's someone you know.

UNCLE: Daughter of the Ma family and wife of the Dong family—isn't it, isn't it your—mom?

ROTTEN-KID: So it is!

UNCLE: Ai! Aren't you full of baloney? Your dad is still alive, how can I marry your mom?

ROTTEN-KID: My dear uncle, what you don't know! Remember the plague that went through Sichuan a few years ago? That plague killed off my old dad!

UNCLE: How come I didn't hear about it? Did your dad really die in Sichuan?

ROTTEN-KID: Aren't you a funny one? Wouldn't I know about my own dad's death? Would I make up something like this? Now, it would be perfect for you to marry my mom—see, you are already related.

UNCLE: Actually . . .

ROTTEN-KID: (*Recites.*)

> I know well you have feelings for my ma—
> It's only natural for a son to sell his ma.

If you marry someone unrelated, then those little cousins of mine would have to suffer the wrath of an evil hag. But if you marry my ma, then the little cousins would be held by their aunt, just like their own ma. There'll be nothing like it.

UNCLE: If you say I can marry her, then I'll marry her.

ROTTEN-KID: Yes, yes, of course you can marry her.

UNCLE: Then I'll marry her as you say. But how much silver do you want?

ROTTEN-KID: What are you talking about? You are my own uncle! It's my ma who wants to remarry herself, it's not me who wants to sell her. Besides, she's going to my own uncle's household. How dare I argue with the price? I'm willing to give you twenty to thirty percent off.

UNCLE: If that is the case, then listen to me. (*Sings.*)

> I will give you an ingot of silver fifty ounces in weight,

ROTTEN-KID: (*Interrupts.*) Don't forget the meeting gift, the marriage gift, the mother-son separation fee, the leaving-the-house fee. . . . You can add and add to that amount—I won't refuse.

UNCLE: (*Continues singing.*)

> Plus ten ounces of loose silver in a small packet.
> Go home and discuss it with your mom,
> I will send over a matchmaker shortly after I return home.

ROTTEN-KID: (*Turns away from his uncle.*) Stupid old man! Rotten-kid is selling his ma in secret—how can we make a public display of it? (*Turns back.*) Ah, ah! My dear uncle, dear uncle—what need do we have for a matchmaker? Let's save the expenses. Just give me the money we agreed on and I'll send my ma to your gate.

UNCLE: We'll do it this way then.

ROTTEN-KID: Yes, yes, yes. We'll do it right away—and work on it without delay. (*They exit.*)

Scene 2

MOTHER: (*Sings.*)

> My husband left home more than ten years ago,

To this date, he is away, he has not yet returned.

ROTTEN-KID: I've faked a letter to trick my mom.

MOTHER: My son, Rotten-kid, you've come home.

ROTTEN-KID: Ai ai! My dear mother, my old mom! (*Weeps.*) Your son was strolling downtown today. There was a messenger from Sichuan eating at a restaurant and he gave this letter to me. Since your son can't read a single word, I went to the school and asked the master there to read it to me. When he read the letter, I was so shocked that I broke out in a cold sweat.

MOTHER: What was it?

ROTTEN-KID: It's finished.

MOTHER: What did the master say? You haven't finished.

ROTTEN-KID: My dad was finished in Sichuan.

MOTHER: (*Sings.*)

Hearing this my liver and intestines burst from the pain,

My dear husband can never come home again to be united.

ROTTEN-KID: Mama, don't feel so bad. Please return your tears![3] There's also happy news.

MOTHER: There's so much grief, how can I feel happy?

ROTTEN-KID: I say, please listen to me, my dear mother. (*Sings.*)

It has been exactly half a year since my aunt died,

Uncle had to be both mom and dad, it has been hard.

My two poor little cousins have no one to care for them,

Uncle wants to marry you so that their aunt can be mom.

MOTHER: (*Hits him.*) Your father just died and you want your mom to remarry. Don't you worry about people laughing and cursing at me, you rogue?

ROTTEN-KID: Hei! If you're worried, then you go right ahead and continue to live this poor life of yours. I'll be gambling and having fun myself. I'll leave, I'll fly away for three years, five years, may be eight, ten years and never come back again. So, do you want to go?

MOTHER: What a hard life!

ROTTEN-KID: Your hardship is yet to come.

MOTHER: Oh, Rotten-kid my son!

ROTTEN-KID: This old dame is so full of it. So what is it now?

MOTHER: I have no choice. I'll do as you suggested—go find me a matchmaker.

ROTTEN-KID: This is a remarriage—what do we need a matchmaker for? Why not be simple about it? No one can interfere with a widow remarriage. Let's go. Go with me right now.

---

3. The expression sounds as ridiculous in Chinese.

MOTHER: What a hard life!

ROTTEN-KID: Your hard life is ending, the good life is about to begin. Hurry up and follow closely. Watch the way carefully. As we talk, we've arrived at uncle's gate. Uncle, open the door!

UNCLE: I'm having a meal at home and suddenly I hear someone calling for me outside. It must be Rotten-kid Dong bringing his ma. Let me lock the dog in the backyard and throw the spade into the pigsty. I open the door and take a look. Ah, Rotten-kid Dong, you've arrived! Please come in, come in!

ROTTEN-KID: Not so loud, I've brought my ma here.

UNCLE: Very good, very good. Bring her into the living room.

MOTHER: (*Enters.*) I'm so embarrassed.

ROTTEN-KID: Ai, ai! There was never enough to eat and drink at our home. How can you be embarrassed about marrying into a rich household. Your muscles must have been formed by poverty!

UNCLE: What an efficient kid you are! You've brought your ma over before I had a chance to send the silver over. Do sit here while I go fetch your silver.

ROTTEN-KID: (*Takes his uncle to one side and whispers.*) Uncle ah, my dear uncle! You get what you pay for. Now that I've brought her over, please make sure that you give me enough silver of good quality.

UNCLE: (*Turns away from Rotten-kid.*) The bastard is so proficient when it comes to money. He knows about everything. (*He goes behind a curtain.*) Accountant, weigh enough top-quality silver. (*Off stage: It's all prepared. Here you are, sir.*) Good, good. (*Hands the silver over to Rotten-kid.*) My dear Rotten-kid, this is the bride price for your mom. Take it, but make sure that you don't squander it. You can only sell your own ma once. Don't loaf around in the gambling houses any more.

ROTTEN-KID: Good advice, good advice! Rotten-kid will remember every word of it, remember every word of it! Just remember what we talked about concerning my mom. Don't believe in any rumors or gossip others might have. Bye!

UNCLE: You go right ahead. I should tend to your ma now. (*Exits.*)

ROTTEN-KID: (*Sees his uncle exit.*) Ah! That stupid uncle of mine has left. Let me check the quality of this silver. (*He bites the silver; looks to the left and the right.*) This is truly good silver, good silver. See how smoothly I conducted this business? Although I lost thirty strings of cash, in the twinkle of an eye and a twist of my mind, I've made sixty taels of silver, solid and heavy right in the hand. What a good deal! Well, never mind that. Let me go to the city of Xi'an 西安 first. I'll buy a pair of leather shoes, a pair of foreign socks, a pair of gold-rimmed glasses, and a wallet. I'll get all spruced up and look rich for a change. (*Exits.*)

Scene 3

FATHER: (*Recites.*)

>Having left home for twelve years, I now return home;
>Silver and cash I've earned, the family can reunite to celebrate.

(*Speaks.*) I am none other than Dong Cheng 董成. I've come to my own house. Let me yell for someone to open the door for me. Rotten-kid, open the door!

ROTTEN-KID: I was in the middle of a good daydream, but someone is at the door. Who is it? What do you want?

FATHER: Rotten-kid, my son, open the door!

ROTTEN-KID: Who's this stranger? Let me go take a look. (*Retorts.*)

>From where have you come
>To the gate of my house?
>My ma has remarried,
>And I don't owe you from gambling.

FATHER: (*Beats Rotten-kid.*) Ho!

ROTTEN-KID: Ho! This old man is awfully brave—how dares he hit a son of the Dongs! (*Tries to hit back with his fist.*)

FATHER: I've been gone for twelve years—don't you recognize your own father?

ROTTEN-KID: Ai, ai! Ah, my dear dad! See, you left so early, I was so young. I wasn't looking closely. Allow me to welcome you back. (*Kneels.*)

FATHER: Get up and go fetch your mother!

ROTTEN-KID: (*Aside.*) Aiya! Goodness gracious! This request of the old man has truly shocked me stiff. (*He gestures that he's thinking.*) I've got it! (*Turns to his father.*) Daddy, don't be so anxious. My uncle, ma's brother's home is putting on a shadow show. They took her there to watch shadow plays. (*Aside.*) Let me fool around with him first.

FATHER: Bring her back!

ROTTEN-KID: Oh, oh! Let your child go fetch her. Why don't you go rest in the back room? (*Father exits.*) Aiya my daddy! Aiya my mommy! Rotten-kid lives in this rotten hovel all by myself. Now I've become a tutelary god which dropped into a well and got stuck real deep.[4] I invented that story only to make a few bucks. Who could have known that within less than three days after I sold my ma, my old man would crop up from the middle of nowhere. Oh, oh, oh. . . . (*He gestures that he's thinking.*) What can I do? What am I to do? (*He gestures that he's gotten an idea; sings.*)

---

4. The implication is that even a deity won't be able to get out of this situation.

Rotten-kid is full of ideas—thousands and thousands of them.
Why be worried by something so insignificant and so small?
I have arrived at the gate of my uncle's house,
I'll think of a way to move my mother back home.
(*Speaks.*) Uncle, please open the door!

UNCLE: I was just sleeping with my kids' aunt when I heard someone at the gate. Who can this untimely caller be? (*Opens the door.*) So it's you, Rotten-kid.

ROTTEN-KID: Close the door quickly!

UNCLE: Why are you so anxious?

ROTTEN-KID: I'm not anxious, I'm just in a big hurry.

UNCLE: Take your time and tell me all about it.

ROTTEN-KID: Well, it was all because of the silver you gave your nephew the other day. When I went home with it, all the neighbors who got along with me and those who didn't fight with me found this nephew of yours a wife. With the marriage proposal, fetching of the bride, and all that, I was wondering who might keep watch over my house for me? Your nephew has a mind to fetch my ma home to help me manage the household for a few days, but I don't know whether, dear uncle, you'd let her go or not?

UNCLE: This is a happy occasion. How can she not go? (*Yells towards the inside.*) Hey, wife,[5] get up!

MOTHER: What are you talking about, husband?[6]

UNCLE: Rotten-kid is getting married. I'm going to let you go help him out for a few days. I'll ask the servant to get a horse ready for you. You two go on ahead, I'll be there too as soon as I'm done with a few things here.

ROTTEN-KID: Since the horse is ready anyway, my ma and I will go on ahead. You go busy yourself with your own affairs. And don't bother to go to my place either. I won't presume the honor of your presence, and I don't want to get stuck.

UNCLE: How is that?

ROTTEN-KID: Well, look, you've only given your nephew a few dozen taels of silver. I have to spend it carefully. I'm getting married, but I'm not entertaining any guests. You'd better not come, better not come.

UNCLE: When I'm done with my business, I'll come for sure. I'll come for sure.

ROTTEN-KID: (*Turns away.*) The old man is so thick! "I'll go for sure, I'll go for sure!" Well, I'll just have to rewrite my play script, rewrite my

---

5. He calls her *wulide* 屋裡的, literally, the one inside the house, or the one in charge of the house.
6. She addresses him as *laoye* 老爺, literally, "my lord" which indicates formality and respect.

play script. (*He gestures that he's holding the reins of a horse.*) Ma—
let's hurry. (*The mother mounts the horse.*) Here we've made some
turns, turned some circles, went down some slopes and up some hills—
I've got another idea. My dear ma, get off the horse, get off.

MOTHER: We still have a ways to go—why get off the horse?

ROTTEN-KID: You've become stupid from old age. As the adage goes: a
man may be poor in cash but never in spirit. We went there using our
two legs, and we can go back using the two legs. How can you act like
a toad who's gone up to Heaven after remarrying for less than three
days?[7] How can you insist on riding on a horse? Aren't you worried
that people will laugh at you?

MOTHER: If that's the case, then I'll dismount. You can take the horse
back. (*She dismounts.*) Take it back right away.

ROTTEN-KID: I'll take the horse back. You go on ahead home.

MOTHER: All right. Ma will go home first. Be sure to come back quickly.

ROTTEN-KID: The old lady has got to leave. If you don't go, how can
Rotten-kid continue the play? (*He watches her leave.*) I, Rotten-kid
Dong, sold my ma and got myself into a big mess. I gave my ma to my
uncle, but then my dad cropped up out of nowhere. What a jumble it
has become—who will forgive Rotten-kid? Of the thirty-six military
tactics, running away is the top tactic. Now that I've got money around
my belt and the reins of a horse in my hand, I'll run away to Xinjiang
新疆 and Ili 伊犁.[8] (*Sings.*)

Rotten-kid Dong was born with a good brain,
He cheated his uncle and tricked his ma.
Now that he's gotten both silver and a horse,
He'll run afar, fly high, and slip to the ends of the earth.

It is truly a case of: With money in hand, I'll go to Xinjiang riding on
this horse. Who cares about those two old men fighting over a woman?
I'm slipping away! (*Exits.*)

Scene 4

UNCLE: I huffed and puffed and ran all the way. Let me see if Rotten-kid
is here. Hum—this kid is getting married today, but why is his gate so
tightly shut? (*Knocks.*) Rotten-kid, open the door!

FATHER: I've been home for half a day without seeing a soul. Someone is
finally at the door—it must be that mother of Rotten-kid Dong. (*He

7. He is suggesting that she shouldn't parade herself as a rich man's wife by returning to the
village on horseback.
8. Wilderness territories in the northwest.

opens the door.) You cheap slut[9]—(*The men see each other; both gesture being shocked.*)

UNCLE: How can sixty taels' worth be a cheap thing? How can she be a cheap thing?

FATHER: Hi! So it's my brother-in-law who has arrived. Please come in, please come in!

UNCLE: (*Moves back.*) A ghost! A ghost!

FATHER: I'm alive and well—how can I be a ghost?

UNCLE: Your kid said that you were de, de . . .

FATHER: I was what?

UNCLE: It's been so long, you aged a lot, and you even got a beard.

FATHER: One ages without being hastened by the sun and the moon.

UNCLE: (*Turns aside.*) Your son has sold your wife already, and here you are still reciting poetry! (*Turns back.*) My dear brother-in-law, let me treat you to dinner to welcome you back.

FATHER: We are close relatives. There's really no need for such formalities. There's really no need for it.

UNCLE: Is Rotten-kid's mom home?

FATHER: She went to her brother's home to watch shadow plays.

UNCLE: Where's Rotten-kid?

FATHER: He went to fetch his mom.

UNCLE: (*Turns aside.*) Rotten-kid, ah Rotten-kid! Oh you good-for-nothing cheater. You got your mom to take care of old me—here I thought that I got myself a woman to warm my feet with for sixty taels of silver. But now the woman has disappeared, and the two brothers-in-law meet again. No, I won't take it. I'm going to sue him at the county court! (*Off stage: This affair was shoddily done. You didn't even have a matchmaker. Who's going to testify for you? Who's going to verify your claim? You were simply too careless.*) I was too careless. I've lost money and embarrassed myself.

FATHER: Brother-in-law, what were you talking about?

UNCLE: I, I, I was saying, "Three old ones can't outwit a ne'er-do-well."

FATHER: It's been a long time, but I see you're still into writing plays. Tell me, what play did you write today?

UNCLE: I wrote, *Rotten-kid Dong Sells His Ma.*

FATHER: Ah, ah!

UNCLE: Ah, ah!

The End

---

9. The term, *jianren* 賤人, is a common appellation used by husbands to address their wives in such after-midnight plays. It denotes informality just as the wives as a rule call their husbands in similar situations, *qiangdao* 強盜, robber.

9: *The Jade Swallow Hairpin.* Shadow figures are from Yang Fei's collection. Photo: Huo Zhanping.

The Jade Swallow Hairpin
玉燕釵

Introduction

The Jade Swallow Hairpin is a *wanwanqiang* masterpiece from Shaanxi by the *juren* scholar Li Fanggui (died 1810), one of the most famous shadow theatre playwrights.[1] Shadow plays with known authors are very rare.[2] *The Jade Swallow Hairpin* (*yuyancai*) is not only one of the ten plays[3] written by a high-ranking scholar, but it is also one of the most popular *wanwanqiang* still being performed. It is also by far the most literary of all the plays translated in this book.[4]

In Shaanxi on two different occasions I watched the episode in which Zou Liniang 鄒麗娘 murders the drunken pirate boatman Ye Xing 乜性 by stabbing him with a knife that she holds in her mouth at one point. Her face is fitted with a movable piece of parchment so that it can become streaked with blood instantly. Liniang weeps and hugs her maid after the murder, thereby covering the maid's face with blood as well. Unlike the anonymous

---

1. See Huan Zhi 驩之, "Huabu taidou – weida de xiqujia Li Fanggui" 花部泰斗 – 偉大的戲曲家李芳桂. Weinan Shizhuan xuebao 1992: 2: 92; quoted in Jiang 2000, "Section 3" for Li Fanggui's biography.
2. In Leting, a licentiate (*xiucai* 秀才) by the name of Gao Shuyao 高述堯 wrote six famous plays during the Daoguang 道光 reign (1821-1851), and a juren, Gao Keting 高可亭 wrote a dozen plays starting in the Guangxu 光緒 reign (1875-1908). Others like Liu Huanting 劉煥亭 and Li Dazhao 李大釗 also wrote during this century (Wei 1990, 17-21).
3. Li Fanggui is believed to have written seven full-scale (*daben* 大本) plays and three one-scene (*zhezi* 折子) plays. See the Introduction for further information on Li Fanggui and on *wanwanqiang*.
4. I would like to thank Prof. Zhao Jianxin 趙建新 of Lanzhou University 蘭州大學 in Gansu for finding some of the references for me. I would also like to thank Mr. Zhang Qi 張琪 of the Record Bureau 檔案館 of the County of Huaxian 華縣, Shaanxi, for presenting me with a beautifully copied play script of *The Jade Swallow Hairpin* in his own elegant calligraphy.

play *The Coral Pagoda*, the jade swallow hairpin of the title not only appears in the tale, but also links the entire plot together. All the young women in the play recognize each other through seeing the hairpin, which also serves the vital function of saving the hero's life. Mistaken identities, irony, and humor interweave with the promulgation of moral rectitude, as viewers can see in the character of Zou Liniang. The speech of each character is appropriate to his or her background, personality, and intellectual level, and ranges from refined and literary to coarse and forthright. Characters like the innkeeper, Miao Run 苗潤, are appropriately coarse in nature and language, and readily express ideas like, "Now that it's our own court, even killing a few people won't matter" when a relative is imprisoned for murder.

Coincidences abound, but they are pieced together so carefully that they seem credible. The parts of the tale fit snugly. All the characters serve important roles; their paths crisscross and influence each other in ways that complicate the plot but ultimately benefit the hero. The hero, Yue Jun 岳俊, is a quintessential figurehead. Neither commonsensical nor physically strong, he is nevertheless the possessor of title and potential power. A magistrate, he is an emperor in the world of the common people. As such, he is adored, chased after, and protected by an array of women without whom he would perish and by a servant whose ingenuity serves simultaneously to save the hero and entertain the audience.

Cast

BOATMAN A
BOATMAN B
JAILER
JIA CHONG 賈充 (CATFISH IN THE MUD; Niliqiu 泥裡鰍): *a pirate boatman; Ye Xing's brother-in-law.*
LI HANJIAO 李漢蛟: *a warrior.*
LINIANG 麗娘 (ZOU LINIANG 鄒麗娘): *wife to Yue Jun.*
LIU QIANJIN 劉千金: *a bandit leader.*
MIAO RUN 苗潤: *an innkeeper; father of Meiniang.*
MIAOYING 妙英: *wife of Shanjing; maid to Liniang.*
MEINIANG 媚娘 (ZOU MEINIANG 鄒媚娘): *adopted daughter of Miao Run.*
OLD WOMAN
QIANQIAN 倩倩 (LI QIAN QIAN 李倩倩): *a female warrior; sister of Li Hanjiao.*
SHANJING 山精: *servant of Yue Jun.*
SHOPKEEPER
SOLDIER
YAMEN RUNNER A
YAMEN RUNNER B
YE XING 乜性 (SNAKE IN THE WATER; Shuilishe 水裡蛇): *a pirate boatman.*
YE MING 乜明: *son of Ye Xing.*
YUE JUN 岳俊: *a young scholar.*
ZHU YONG 朱永 (FUNINGHOU 撫寧侯): *the Earl of Funing.*

Scene 1

YUE JUN: (*Enters and recites.*)
As soon as I see the three-tiered waves in front of Yu's 禹 door,[5]
I plant flowers over the entire county of Heyang 河陽.
If only I could obtain Wang Qiao's 王喬 shoes of paired ducks,[6]

---

5. Alleged founder of the Xia dynasty, Yu (supposedly reigned 2205–2197 b.c.) is known for taming a flood which raged through the central plains of China. The exact significance of this reference is not clear.

I'd fly over Changsha 長沙 in a twinkle of the eye.

(*Speaks.*) I, Yue Jun, styled Xiufeng 秀峰, am a native of Tongbo 桐柏 County. I just passed the palace examination and was awarded the post of magistrate for Shishou 石首 in Huguang 湖廣. I have a wife by the name of Zou Liniang who is both clever and wise. We harmonize like a lute and a zither in perfect tune. I have to proceed to my post right away. Shanjing, go get your mistress.

LINIANG: (*Enters and recites.*)

> Grooming myself this morning, I face the lotus-blossom mirror attentively,
>
> A few hairpins of filigree gold, I fasten onto my crow-black coiffure.

(*Speaks.*) Greetings, my lord. I have finished packing and am ready. When will we depart?

YUE JUN: We'll leave soon. The only problem is that we have only Shanjing as attendant—doesn't this look inappropriate for an official?

LINIANG: My lord, an extra attendant will cost more money. The less we spend, the more we will save for the people—wouldn't that be better? According to the opinion of your humble wife, let's make do until we arrive at your post.

SHANJING: The mistress is quite right. My lord, you see, you've got me to look after all the affairs outside, and my wife will attend to the mistress. We'll stay close the whole trip. I guarantee you a safe trip, that's what counts. Quality rather than quantity: a good man is worth ten mediocre ones.

YUE JUN: If so, get the carriage and horses ready and we'll depart tomorrow.

SHANJING: Yes, sir. I wonder how corrupt he'll be when he becomes an official. The mistress at least has integrity.

YUE JUN: The advice my wife just gave is the best medicine for officialdom. (*Sings.*)

> My wife's advice arouses great admiration in me,
> You are my best secretary and advisor.

LINIANG: Oh, you are joking! (*Sings.*)

> I only hope that when you assume the post, you will be upright,
> And will not carry yourself with unsightly pomp.
> An official must care for the people. (*They exit.*)

---

6. Wang Qiao was a magician who used to visit Emperor Ming (r. 58–76) during the full and new moon. His mode of transportation was eventually discovered to have been a pair of birds which turned into shoes upon being caught.

Scene 2

MIAO RUN: (*Enters and recites.*)
> When the meal is good, one's taste is improved.
> When the wine is fine, its golden fragrance sparkles right.

(*Speaks.*) I, old man Miao Run, am the owner of this inn at Bright Port Station (*minggangyi* 明港驛). My daughter asked me to wait outside the inn this evening. She said that an official on the way to his post will be coming here. I asked her how she knew and she said that she dreamt it last night. Ai, when a daughter grows up, even her dreams become strange. Hey, here comes a carriage. There might be something to her dream after all!

YUE JUN: (*Enters with Shanjing, Liniang, and Miaoying.*) Shanjing, speed up the horse and carriage. (*Sings.*)
> Half hidden, the sun at dusk descends the western mountains,
> Nonstop, the evening crows caw in the woods.

LINIANG: (*Sings.*)
> I see afar a few houses with dark blue curtains,
> I wonder at which inn we will stay?

YUE JUN: (*Sings.*)
> Outside the inn we dismount from our horse and carriage.

MIAO RUN: Ha ha ha! He has indeed come! Are you Yue Jun, the official on his way to his post?

SHANJING: You old fool! Is my lord's name to be used by the likes of you?

YUE JUN: Don't scold him. Old man, how did you know of me?

MIAO RUN: My daughter dreamt of you last night.

YUE JUN: Rubbish. How ridiculous!

SHANJING: I am afraid there's something fishy about this inn.

LINIANG: Old man, what is your name?

MIAO RUN: My surname is Miao, first name is Run. Please come in and sit down. (*They enter the inn and take their seats.*)

LINIANG: Please ask your daughter to come here. I would like to ask her something.

MIAO RUN: My child, her ladyship summons you!

MEINIANG: Coming.

MIAO RUN: I was afraid you had the dream wrong.

MEINIANG: (*Sings.*)
> Last night, I saw my father in a dream,
> He repeated the same message two, three times.

Who would have thought that it would really come to pass?
But what's really on my mind, I'm too embarrassed to tell.
Leaving my room, I cast a quick glance at my future benefactor.[7]
(*Speaks.*) Greetings to my lady. (*Curtsies.*)

LINIANG: I return the greetings. (*Curtsies.*) Who would have expected old Miao to have such a pretty daughter?

MIAO RUN: Actually, I'm just an old man she'd adopted.

LINIANG: Tell us in detail how you knew that we would be here.

MEINIANG: Allow me to tell you, my lady. (*Sings.*)
My father was also a magistrate,
When he passed away, there was nothing but clear breeze in his sleeves.
Leaving me, a headless goose, floating like duckweed.
(*Speaks.*) Therefore, I came to this old uncle and became his adopted daughter.

LINIANG: So you were a young lady of a prominent family.

MEINIANG: (*Sings.*)
Last night, my father came to me in a dream,
He said that a Lord Yue, with the style of Xiufeng,
Would pass here on the way to his post and that I must wait for him.
By this evening he would surely arrive at this inn.

MIAO RUN: The dream turned out true after all. My dear child, there's more to your dream; tell the lady all about it.

MEINIANG: He also said that my marriage is at stake and that I should make sure not to miss this favorite student of his.

YUE JUN: My lady, according to her words, her father would be Zou Yunxian 鄒雲軒, who served at Changge 長葛 as magistrate.

MIAO RUN: That was him. That was him.

YUE JUN: Ah, teacher Zou! (*Sings.*)
Thinking back, it was because of you that I got lucky,
Now that I've become an official, I was just going to repay your kindness.
Who would have expected you to die while attending the jade pavilion,[8]
Leaving behind your sole daughter, alone and in dire straits?
How can one not feel grieved?

LINIANG: Since she is your teacher's daughter, you should take care of her.

---

7. The word *tanlang* 檀郎, which is used to refer to Yue Jun may be related to *tanyue* 檀越, the benefactor of a convent.
8. *Yulou* 玉樓, a coveted official post.

YUE JUN: Certainly. We'll send her some silver once I assume office.

LINIANG: A thousand taels of silver won't do her as much good as a marriage. It would be much better if I adopt her as a sister and the two of us will serve my lord together.

YUE JUN: My lady is teasing me?

LINIANG: Not at all. The common saying goes, "How can there be waves without the work of a fisherman?" In our case, even this title of Seventh Grade Ladyship I possess I owe to your teacher.[9] How can one forget such a great favor from him? Miss, what is your name?

MEINIANG: My name is Zou Meiniang.

LINIANG: Amazing, just amazing! You and I share the same family name. I am called Liniang and you are called Meiniang. We are like two real sisters. How would you like to serve the lord with me, like Ying 英 and Huang 皇 of the past?[10]

MEINIANG: I would be deeply grateful to my lady.

LINIANG: My dear little sister, at first I thought that we should go to the official post together. But now I think that not only is the carriage situation inconvenient, but also one shouldn't be so rushed and careless with your marriage. It would be better for us to go ahead without you right now and within at the most a month we will dispatch a sedan-chair here to fetch you.

MEINIANG: In that case, I have a family treasure which I would like to present to his lordship as a token. I had an ancestor who went to Korea as an ambassador and traveled to Angel[11] Island (*anqidao* 安期島) with their king. This island was inhabited by immortals. There an old man gave my ancestor a piece of black jade. Later the ancestor had a jade carver fashion it into a hairpin, modeled after a piece left behind by a goddess at the Spirit Summoning Platform (*zhaolingtai* 招靈臺) during the Han dynasty. This hairpin is called the jade swallow hairpin. The person who possesses it will not be burned in fire nor drown in water. It is a priceless treasure. Please guard it carefully.

YUE JUN: Uncle Miao, you won't have to keep this inn any longer.

MIAO RUN: I'm now a relative of an official! What would I need to keep an inn for?

YUE JUN: Shanjing, go and fetch thirty taels of silver for them. (*Shanjing exits and re-enters.*)

SHANJING: Ahem. How could I have done this?

---

9. Without the help of Meiniang's father, Yue Jun would not have attained his position and Liniang similarly would not have become a lady.

10. Ying (Nüying 女英) and Huang (E'huang 娥皇) were daughters of the legendary sage king Yao 堯. They were both married to the legendary sage king Shun 舜.

11. *Anqi* 安琪.

YUE JUN: Oh, what's the matter?

SHANJING: Hm. Your servant just opened up our luggage and found out that we didn't bring the silver presented by the Earl of Funing.

YUE JUN: What have you done, you knave?

SHANJING: I forgot about it. There's no need to say another word. Your servant will go home and fetch it.

YUE JUN: I am due to arrive at my post soon. Am I to wait for you here?

SHANJING: My lord, you go ahead. I'll travel day and night and catch up with you in five or six days.

MIAO RUN: Don't worry. I'll go with the lord and take care of him until he gets to a boat. Then the boatman will take care of them.

SHANJING: That's good. I'll leave tonight. This is just like turning a door knob, one turn in the wrong direction and I need to turn back. (*He exits.*)

MIAO RUN: My child, you keep her ladyship company while I find another room for his lordship. Let's all go to the back.

MEINIANG: Elder sister, please go ahead. (*Recites.*)

Hundred-year-long conjugal ties were fated three generations ago,

LINIANG: (*Continues.*)

Thousand-mile-distant[12] marital destinies are connected by a single thread. (*Liniang and Meiniang exit.*)

YUE JUN: (*Recites.*)

Before I reach Heyang, flowers are already in bloom.[13]

MIAO RUN: Not counting the money for the food and wine tonight, I even donated fodder for the animals to this son-in-law. Tut, this is bad business! (*They exit.*)

Scene 3

YE XING: (*Enters with Jia Chong.*) Hm, hm. (*Recites.*)

We sold a piece of gold to buy a thing that would float.

Anyone who comes aboard will have a plague to hoard.

(*Speaks.*) I am Snake in the Water. My name is Ye Xing.

JIA CHONG: I am Catfish in the Mud. My name is Jia Chong. Us brothers-in-law have been ferrying the boat for quite a while now. Although we've had quite a few profitable hits, we haven't been able to get rich. What can we do?

YE XING: It's easy. If you want to get rich, you have to become an official.

---

12. Literally, *li* 里, which is 360 paces or 1,890 feet.
13. This seems to refer to his good luck in getting another wife.

JIA CHONG: Speaking of becoming an official, I have something funny to tell you. When we were on land a few days ago, I met a fortune-teller who said, "Aiya! You'll be an official for a couple of days!"

YE XING: Idiot! He was just after your money!

JIA CHONG: As if I didn't know! Hey, look at that nephew of mine! He's drunk again. Look at him tottering his way back here.

YE MING: (*Enters.*) That was one hell of a drink! (*Sings.*)
> I'll let people laugh at me, curse me, and spit at me,
> As long as I can enjoy myself.
> I don't fear incurring Heaven-shocking calamities,
> I'm always ready when it comes to doing evil deeds.
> Should any hapless soul dare to provoke me,
> I'll fight him to death, that's for sure.

YE XING: Ai, look at this fine son of mine!

YE MING: Who's talking there? Oh you stink!

YE XING: Ye Ming, don't you even recognize your old man?

YE MING: Of course I recognize you. I was only wondering if you also had a son who's not fine. I'm almost thirty and want a not-so-fine son. Am I supposed to dredge one out from this river?

JIA CHONG: Brother-in-law, the kid is asking you for a daughter-in-law!

YE MING: No, no! Don't you think I'm fated to have one? Your boat is a pirate boat anyway. Whether I become a pirate or a highwayman, I'd still be no different from a bandit. I've decided to make it big: Liu Qianjin has started a rebellion at Nanzhang 南漳 and I'm going to join him. I'll kidnap a couple of women and who'll worry about not having wives then? So long, old man!

YE XING: Hey, the kid's really got over his head!

YE XING: (*Sings.*)
> I am going to Nanzhang to join the gang,
> It'll beat your life of murder and arson anyway.
> Villages will be mine to loot,
> Women by the scores will be mine to plunder.
> I will pick and choose among them for my wives,
> From now on, you mind your business and I'll mind mine. (*He exits.*)

YE XING: I'm so mad.

JIA CHONG: You can't really blame him. When you get the chance, find him a wife and he'll be fine.

MIAO RUN: (*Enters with Yue Jun, Liniang, and Miaoying; recites.*)
> The travelers' road is beyond the blue mountains,
> A ferryboat is moored by the green water.

(*Speaks.*) Boatman, where are you?

YE XING: Here I am, what do you want?

MIAO RUN: We are looking for a boat to hire.

YE XING: Where do you want to go?

MIAO RUN: My lord here is going to assume his post as a magistrate at Shishou County. Take good care of him and you'll be well paid.

YE XING: If this is the case, bring up the luggage and ask the lord to get into the boat.

MIAO RUN: My lord, if you please.

YUE JUN: (*Recites.*)
>When traveling the scenery is particularly appealing,
>Even clouds and such appear fresh and novel.

LINIANG: (*Continues.*)
>Unable to bear the hardship of carriage and dust,
>Clear waves are the most appealing.

MIAO RUN: Hold on to the railing. (*Yue Jun, Liniang, and Miaoying embark.*) Farewell, my lord! Excuse me for not accompanying you further.

YUE JUN: Thank you for the help. Boatman, let's go.

YE XING: Ho! Here she goes!

YUE JUN: (*Sings.*)
>The heavenly gate disappears, River Chu (*chujiang* 楚江) widens,
>The emerald water flows east and then turns to the north.
>Azure mountains across the banks emerge in pairs,
>Beside the sun emerges this one lonely sail.
>Dreamily, I feel as if we have floated beyond the edge of Heaven.

YE XING and JIA CHONG: Mumble, mumble . . .[14] (*They exit.*)

Scene 4

LIU QIANJIN: (*Enters a military tent and recites.*)
>A treasured sword hangs from my waist, the barbarian frost is cold.
>A carved bow wrapped around my arm, the moon of Chu is lonely.
>Dominating this territory and shaking the mountains,
>I pronounce nonchalantly that Huang Chao 黄剿 was no real hero.[15]

(*Speaks.*) I am Liu Qianjin. People call me Liu Qianjin[16] because I am able to lift a thousand pounds. Since I am not willing to submit to the

---

14. They chat in a low voice.
15. Huang Chao was a rebel of the Tang dynasty who forced the Xizong Emperor (r. 874–889) to flee to the southwest but was finally defeated.
16. Literally, Liu One Thousand Pounds.

Ming dynasty, I have paired up with the priest Yun Tianfeng 允天峰 and raised a rebellion. At the end of the Shuntian reign (1464), I declared myself an emperor in Nanzhang. Yesterday a scout reported that Zhu Yong, the Earl of Funing, is leading an army towards us. I have to get prepared to meet the enemy.

SOLDIER: (*Enters.*) I report to the great king. A man is here to enlist.

LIU QIANJIN: Bring him in.

YE MING: (*Enters and recites.*)
> If one wants to get wealthy,
> One must strive to death.

(*Speaks.*) This enlisting man kowtows to you.

LIU QIANJIN: What kind of martial talents do you have that you dare to come join us?

YE MING: I know something about military strategy, that's why I've come to serve the new emperor.

LIU QIANJIN: Announce your name.

YE MING: Your servant's name is Ye Ming.

LIU QIANJIN: Ah! I was just going to seize the realm of the great Ming dynasty and your name happens to be Ye Ming.[17] You must be my god-sent fine general. I'll make you general of the Middle Army in command of ten thousand soldiers. You can set up another camp and form an anchor to my army.

YE MING: Thank you for your magnanimity, Your Majesty.

LIU QIANJIN: There's something else: Zhu Yong is leading an army against us, and I need to know the particulars concerning his formation. Go find out for me, incognito, as soon as you finish setting up camp.

YE MING: I obey the imperial will. (*Recites.*)
> On the platform, the frost threatens the grass and trees,
> In the garrison, the mood to kill accompanies the banners. (*He exits.*)

LIU QIANJIN: Dispatch the order: "Officers of the four camps should hold a drill in preparation for battle against the imperial army." (*Recites.*)
> In the past, among wind and dust, I wielded a three-foot sword,
> This very day, attired in military uniform, I aspire to own the state.
> (*All exit.*)

Scene 5

YE XING: (*Enters with Jia Chong.*) Hm. (*Recites.*)

---

17. The name is homophonous with "also Ming," *yeming* 也明.

If you want to make lots of dough,

JIA CHONG: (*Continues.*)

You have to play it rough.

YE XING: Brother-in-law, let's do it now.

JIA CHONG: Brother-in-law, since that nephew of mine doesn't have a wife yet, we can give the woman to him. That way you won't have to put up with his aggravating behavior any more. You can even have that maid too, but I want the luggage.

YE XING: Just as you say. But how should we do it?

JIA CHONG: Tonight is the Autumn Festival.[18] Invite him to the bow to watch the moon. Let me whisper the rest—

YE XING: Wonderful, wonderful! My Lord Yue, please come out to the bow to watch the moon.

YUE JUN: (*Enters and recites.*)

The ground in the courtyard gleams white, crows perch in the trees,

The cold dew noiselessly dampens the cassia flowers.

Tonight the bright moon is admired by everyone,

But who knows which ones are laden by autumnal thoughts?[19]

YE XING: My lord, see how bright the moon is. The couplet you wrote for me in the cabin can be seen so clearly out here.

YUE JUN: It truly is a bright moon.

YE XING: You've never seen the moonlight by the riverbank—it's even brighter there.

YUE JUN: Really? Why don't we take a look from there?

YE XING: Look at the moonlight and how it merges with its reflection in the water. And you can also look for the King of Hell tonight! (*He pushes Yue Jun into the water.*) He's gone far, far away.

JIA CHONG: Can't see him any more. Aiya! Help! Help!

MIAOYING: (*Enters.*) What happened?

YE XING: The lord has fallen into the river!

MIAOYING: Oh no! (*She exits and re-enters with Liniang who promptly faints.*)

JIA CHONG: Brother-in-law, goodbye! I won't be back. (*He takes the luggage and exits.*)

YE XING: Just a minute, let's talk about it some more. (*He runs after Jia Chong and exits.*)

LINIANG: (*Sings.*)

Hearing the news, my soul flew to the Nine Heavens,

---

18. The moon is supposed to be brightest on the night of this twenty-fifth day of the eighth lunar month.

19. Thoughts which are sad.

Heavy and dizzy, I fell at the front of the boat.
For a long while, I failed to hear the hustle and bustle around me;
Already, my fragrant soul has entered the land of water and clouds.
(*Speaks.*) Aiya, My lord! (*Sings.*)
You were just about to assume your post,
Who would have expected a calamity half way there?
I had hoped that together we would enjoy wealth and glory,
Who would have thought that it would end like this?
Hurriedly, I run to the bow to take a look,
But see nothing but the boundless water of Changjiang 長江.[20]
The bright moon shines like daylight upon the churning waves,
But I don't see where my lord might be.
In the sky the moon is round, cassia flowers bloom in full;
Among mortals a sad tune is sung, the mirror is broken.[21]
Ai, Miaoying ah! I only ask, what are we going to do?
Half way there, who will now make the decisions?
Adding my tears to the river, the autumnal waves rise,
Weeping so hard, Zou Liniang almost dies from crying.
Mistress and maid hug each other and wail loudly.

YE XING: (*Enters.*) He took the luggage after all. So be it. My lady, don't cry any more. Crying won't help anyway.

MIAOYING: Grandpa, what do you think we should do in light of this great tragedy?

YE XING: Actually, I have an idea. My son is serving in Liu Qianjin's army right now. He'll become a great official for sure. My lady, marrying him won't be an indignity to you.

LINIANG: Aiya, Miaoying, listen to this. His lordship was obviously murdered by this man. Oh villain! (*Sings.*)
We have just endured this great calamity,
And you dare to say this right away?
I see right through the event today,
The murder of his lordship is obviously the handiwork of these
    brigands!
I wish I could chop off your bandit head immediately.

YE XING: He fell into the water by accident. How can you say that we murdered him? Well, so be it. If you want to call it a murder, then it's a murder. You can't fly away anyway!

LINIANG: Ah, Miaoying, ah! (*Sings.*)
I thought as a lady I was fated to be lucky,

---

20. The Long River 長江 or Yangzi (Yangtse) River 揚子江.
21. A broken mirror signifies a broken marriage.

Who would have thought that I was going to end like this?
Until death, mandarin ducks refuse to be separated,
I am willing to follow him to death, like Xiang 湘 and E 娥.[22]
If destined to die early, one cannot escape one's fate;
To meet King Yama in Hades tonight must have been in my stars.
Do wait for me, my dear lord,
We will meet yet in the crystal palace.[23]
(*Speaks.*) So be it. My fragrant soul will flow away with the limpid water. (*She tries to jump but is held back by Miaoying.*)

MIAOYING: Grandpa, go buy some funerary money to perform a sacrifice to his lordship. I'll persuade her ladyship for you in the meantime.

YE XING: That's good. That's good. I'll go right now. (*He exits; Liniang beats Miaoying.*)

LINIANG: Fine help you are! Now you are on the bandit's side!

MIAOYING: Pay attention, muddle-headed madam! All you can think of is dying. It may be easy for you to die today, but who'll avenge his lordship's death tomorrow? The way I see it, the bandit's son is still in Nanzhang so he can't get back for a while yet. Why don't we settle down in this boat for the time being? My husband did say that he would catch up with us in six to seven days. When he arrives, we'll go sue them at an official's court and avenge his lordship's death. Wouldn't that be better?

YE XING: (*Enters.*) Little lady, I've already burned a hundred pieces of funerary money at the bow.

MIAOYING: I've persuaded the lady to go along with you. We only want to know how his lordship died. You can tell us the truth now.

YE XING: Ah, now that we are all one happy family, why should I lie to you? He really did slip accidentally. Do I look like a murderer to you?

MIAOYING: My lady, it does seem that we may have blamed him wrongly.

YE XING: This is not good. Lots of people know me here. What if someone should see through this? Oh, I know. Miaoying, we are boat people without a permanent place for a home. Things are too expensive here, but Shishou County downstream is really nice. Let's go there.

MIAOYING: Whatever you say, grandpa.

YE XING: Yes, let's leave. (*Recites.*)

---

22. Xiang and E are Xiangfei 湘妃 and Jiang'e 江娥, variant names for E'huang 娥皇 and Nüying 女英, wives of the legendary sage king Shun 舜. They were supposed to have drowned themselves upon hearing of the death of their husband and subsequently became goddesses of River Xiang.

23. The palace of the dragon king at the bottom of the sea. The bottom of the river is being referred to here.

Today, she'll be taken for a ride around the five lakes.[24]
LINIANG: (*Recites.*)
Not until all is clear will I be able to avenge myself.
Lying on sticks and tasting bile, when will it all end?[25]
(*Speaks.*) Ah, my lord! (*They exit.*)

Scene 6

LI HANJIAO: (*Enters with Li Qianqian; recites.*)
When the lotus quivers, the fish must be near.
QIANQIAN: (*Recites.*)
When the fishing line draws out, the water must be deep.
LI HANJIAO: (*Recites.*)
River Pan 磻溪 finally enters the dream of the flying bear.[26]
QIANQIAN: (*Recites.*)
We won't imitate Ziling 子陵 and hide in Mt. Fuchun 富春.[27]
LI HANJIAO: I hail from the Shishou County. My family name is Li, and I'm called Hanjiao. Because I use an iron pole for my boat, people call me Iron Pole Li Hanjiao. My younger sister, Qianqian, is a hero among women. It's unfortunate that we are now wanderers. My sister, I've been thinking—when will we two ever amount to anything if we stay on this fishing boat? Now that Liu Qianjin has rebelled, the Earl of Funing is leading a military expedition against him. Why don't we round up some of our brave friends and go support our emperor? Wouldn't achieving merit this way be better than being fishermen?
QIANQIAN: My brother, I've learnt the art of physiognomy recently. You have the chin of a swallow's beak and the forehead of a tiger—just like

---

24. Xishi, known as one of the most beautiful women in Chinese history, was sent by the duke of Yue 越王 during the Spring and Autumn period (722–484 b.c.) to ruin his archenemy, the duke of Wu 吳王 by distracting him from attending to state affairs. Tradition has it that after the fall of the State of Wu, Xishi rejoined her lover, Fan Li, the emissary who accompanied her to the State of Wu; and the two spent the rest of their lives traveling around the five most famous lakes of China.
25. The duke of Yue slept on sticks and licked daily at the bile of an animal to harden his resolve to avenge himself when he was imprisoned by the duke of Wu.
26. River Pan was supposed to have been the river by which Jiang Taigong 姜太公 was fishing before he was discovered by the future King Wu 武王 of the Zhou dynasty. The arrival of this brilliant advisor to the Zhou camp was forecasted in a dream in which Jiang Taigong was symbolized by what became known as the flying bear. Here Li Hanjiao and his sister are insinuating their imminent discovery by a worthy master.
27. Ziling, whose formal name is Yan Guang 嚴光, went to school with Emperor Guangwu 光武 (r. 25–58) founder of the Later Han dynasty. When the emperor assumed the throne, Ziling rejected the offer to join the court and preferred instead to live as a hermit on Mt. Fuchun.

Ban Chao 班超[28] in the past. You'll be enfiefed with a title in the future for sure.

LI HANJIAO: Look at your own physiognomy and see if you will become a lady with a title too?

QIANQIAN: Mine is almost as good as yours.

LI HANJIAO: That's good. Guard the boat well. I'll go ashore and look for some brave men to join the army with me.

QIANQIAN: There's an ominous aura on your face, my brother. Although you'll rise to great heights in the future, you are due for some misfortune in the near term. It would be better for you not to go.

LI HANJIAO: Don't mind me. If I go right now, I may not be able to secure your title, but my title is almost a sure thing. (*Sings.*)

> Riding winds and breaking waves are for real men,
> Why should I bother to guard one small boat forever?
> Little sister, you need not dissuade me any longer,
> Just wait and watch me enfiefed for ten thousand miles—
> Why would I then envy Lord Ban of the past? (*He exits.*)

QIANQIAN: (*Sings.*)

> He went ashore ever so confidently,
> I'm afraid for him that it won't go smoothly.
> Sitting sorrowfully at the bow, I watch the scenery,
> What desire do I have for casting my fishing line now?
> Oh! A man floats down from upstream,
> Like the Great Monad (*taiyi* 太乙)[29] riding on a red lotus.
> Flowing on the current, rapid as a shooting arrow,
> In the blink of an eye, he's already next to my boat.
> Let me save him immediately without any delay.

(*Yue Jun takes the end of a pole and sits down backward.*)

YUE JUN: Aiya! Oh, how hateful!

QIANQIAN: Whom do you hate? Do go inside the boat first and get changed. (*Yue Jun exits and re-enters.*)

YUE JUN: Elder sister, please accept my greetings. May I ask for elder sister's name? Why are you on the boat alone?

QIANQIAN: My family name is Li, my personal name is Qianqian. My elder brother, Li Hanjiao has gone ashore.

YUE JUN: I'll remember you and will be sure to repay your favor in the future. Let me go ashore now.

QIANQIAN: Just a minute. What official post do you hold? Why were you in the water? You should at least explain this much.

---

28. A famous general during the reign of Emperor Ming (r. 58–76) of the Later Han dynasty, known for subduing numerous countries in Central Asia.
29. The Great Monad is that from which all things sprang.

YUE JUN: Elder sister, how do you know that I am an official?

QIANQIAN: I see an imperial angular bulge around your temples and a pearly glow on your forehead.[30] You are obviously a man of high status.

YUE JUN: You do know your physiognomy. (*Sings.*)

This humble person's name is Yue Jun.

I am a native of Tongbo in Nanyang.

I was on my way to assume office at Shishou.

On a pirate boat I met misfortune and was pushed into the river.

I thought that my life was fated to end this very day,

Fortunately, the all-embracing Goddess of Mercy came my way.

Elder sister, your great favor I shall never be able to repay.

(*Speaks.*) I should leave now.

QIANQIAN: Just a moment. You were floating effortlessly on the water. Do you know how to swim?

YUE JUN: Actually, it was quite strange. It must have been the treasure I carry on me. Listen to this, elder sister, (*Sings.*)

Entering the water but not drowning is really miraculous,

It's all because of the jade swallow hairpin I carry with me.

This treasure originated far away beyond the ocean,

It came from the immortal island of the Angels.

Neither fire nor water can harm the person who carries it.

(*Speaks.*) Let me go now.

QIANQIAN: Slow down. Why are you in such a hurry? If you go now, what am I going to do?

YUE JUN: I don't understand.

QIANQIAN: There is no third party on this boat today. I'm still a maiden, yet I saved your life without worrying about damaging implications. Should anyone find out about this, how can I bear to continue living in this world? I've actually harmed myself by saving your life.

YUE JUN: Oh, now I understand. If you don't mind lowering yourself, we can become engaged to be joined in matrimony. Here is the jade swallow hairpin Zou Meiniang gave me, I will present it to you in turn. Please see me off right away.

QIANQIAN: I told you not to be in such a hurry because I see a dark aura on your face. You'll encounter yet another disaster soon and would be better off to stay here and avoid it.

YUE JUN: Could there possibly be another pirate boat?

---

30. *Rijiao yueyan* 日角月偃 refers to the physiognomy of kings and emperors.

QIANQIAN: The roads are not safe because of Liu Qianjin's uprising. If you must go, take my brother's treasured broadsword along for protection.

YUE JUN: Fine. Bring it quickly. (*Qianqian exits and re-enters.*) Farewell, elder sister, I'm leaving now. (*Sings.*)

> Even before I can repay her for the favor of saving my life,
> She has further presented me with a treasured sword before departure.
> After I assume my post and my fortune turns for the better,
> I'd be happy to harbor Ajiao 阿嬌 [31] in a house of gold. (*He exits.*)

QIANQIAN: Very well! (*Sings.*)

> The fishing boat has become a path to Heaven,
> The fishing rod is better than a flute in attracting phoenix.
> Dear brother, don't you laugh at your younger sister from now on.
> My title as a lady has already been set—
> The way Heaven predestines marriages is truly amazing. (*She exits.*)

Scene 7

SHANJING: (*Enters and recites.*)

> I was set on turning back the time,
> But who would have known that three inches of good fortune could crush a person?
> Upon reaching home, I was taken ill for half a month,
> It dragged on and on, until this very day.

(*Speaks.*) It's Shanjing here. A while ago, half way to our destination, I told the others that I'd catch up with his lordship in five or six days. Who could have known that I'd contract a weird disease when I got home? Was I ever miserable until now! His lordship must have assumed office for several days by now. I'll head for Shishou County directly. I'm already at the gate of the yamen and am simply exhausted. Let me take a break at the wine shop here. Shopkeeper!

SHOPKEEPER: Coming. Sir wants some wine?

SHANJING: Yes. Shopkeeper, what is the surname of your magistrate?

SHOPKEEPER: Liu.

SHANJING: Who's Liu?

SHOPKEEPER: The last magistrate was Liu, the new one is Yue.

---

31. When Emperor Wu (r. 140–86 b.c.) of the Former Han dynasty was a child and asked whether he would like to marry his cousin, Ajiao, he answered that if he could marry Ajiao he would harbor her in a house made of gold.

SHANJING: Where is he from and what's his name?

SHOPKEEPER: I don't know. A person came yesterday, his name is whatever—

SHANJING: Is he a court official?

SHOPKEEPER: Yes, yes. A court official. The new magistrate's name is—

SHANJING: His name is Yue Jun. He's a native of Tongbo in Henan province.

SHOPKEEPER: That's right, that's right. But, how did you know?

SHANJING: I'm his housekeeper. How could I not know?

SHOPKEEPER: Ah, so we have a junior lord here! What is your honorable surname, sir?

SHANJING: My surname is Shan 山 but I prefer doubling the character and use Chu 出 instead.[32]

SHOPKEEPER: My junior lord has quite a sense of humor. The lord magistrate has just arrived today, so the yamen runners have gone to welcome him.

SHANJING: How come he only just arrived today? He must have been delayed on the way. (*The sound of yelling is heard offstage.*)

SHOPKEEPER: The new magistrate is here. Let me go and have a look.

SHANJING: I'll go too. He's probably more imposing than at home. (*A crowd appears.*) How come that's not him at all? This is awfully strange, unless his lordship had undergone a metamorphosis? I've got it. I still have two sets of his lordship's robes in my luggage, I'll wear his clothes and claim that I'm a teacher of criminal law recommended by the Earl of Funing for him. Let me change my outfit and meet him. (*He exits and re-enters.*) Hm, shopkeeper!

SHOPKEEPER: Coming! Sir, you're all decked up like a dressed-up monkey. Guess you must be heading for the yamen.

SHANJING: Aren't we full of stings! Drop by tomorrow for the wine money.

SHOPKEEPER: No problem, sir. Go right ahead. (*He exits.*)

SHANJING: This is awfully strange. (*Sings.*)

> The surname and personal name are exactly the same,
> But how could he be that loser there?
> Methinks something smells foul here,
> Somebody is impersonating his lordship.
> To get the facts, I have to formulate a scheme.
> Pretending to be a gentleman, I have to put a sway in my gait.
> Who could then tell what my real background is? (*He exits.*)

---

32. The character *chu*, is formed by writing two characters for *shan*, one on top of the other.

Scene 8

JIA CHONG: (*Enters with a yamen runner; sits down and recites.*)
  To become an official is easy,
  You just need to kill somebody.
  Although I wear a gauze hat on my head,
  I have no learning at all in my belly.
  (*Speaks.*) I, your humble official, am named, named, named Yue! Actually, I'm Catfish in the Mud, Jia Chong. After we murdered Yue Jun the other day, I got his luggage and found the official documents for his post. I bribed the superiors, assumed Yue's name, and have now arrived at Shishou County to be its magistrate. Ha ha! I guess I must have saved up a lot of good karma when I left the corpses of the dozens of people I murdered on my boat intact. That's why I got to become an official today. No wonder the fortuneteller said that I'm destined to become an official. There is only one problem: I can't read a single word. How am I going to get around this?
YAMEN RUNNER: I report to my lord. A teacher of criminal justice, recommended by the great general of the southern expedition, is here to see you.
JIA CHONG: Excellent! Ask him to come in right away, hurry!
YAMEN RUNNER: If you please, teacher.
SHANJING: (*Enters.*) Hm. If you want real information, you must first become a fake teacher.
JIA CHONG: Are you the teacher who has been recommended to me?
SHANJING: So I am.
JIA CHONG: Greetings. May I ask the teacher what your name is?
SHANJING: My family name is Chu.
JIA CHONG: Aiya! I haven't heard of a Chu in the hundred surnames.
SHANJING: Shush, since my surname is Chu, which means "out," of course my surname would be outside of the hundred surnames—the so-called neglected surnames. Such is precisely that which this refers to.
JIA CHONG: Yes, yes, yes. Do you have the letter of recommendation?
SHANJING: Naturally I do. But I inadvertently left it at the inn. You may dispatch someone to fetch it.
JIA CHONG: There's no need for that. I'll be honest with you, my teacher. I don't read much and can't understand it well anyway.
SHANJING: You are simply being modest among the most modest. The Earl of Funing mentioned that you have even tutored at his own home.
JIA CHONG: Hm.
SHANJING: And that you passed the palace examinations this year.
JIA CHONG: Hm, passed the palace examinations.
SHANJING: How could you say that you cannot read then?

JIA CHONG: This—

SHANJING: Funing told me that when the southern expedition ends, he will be sure to come here to meet us. He has a quick temper, you know. When he found out about an impostor soldier the other day, he pulled out his broadsword and, whoosh, cut the guy in half right across the waist!

JIA CHONG: Attendants, you may all leave. (*They exit*.) My dear teacher, sir! (*He kneels*.)

SHANJING: Ai, what's with this behavior?

JIA CHONG: I will be honest with you, my dear teacher. I am not really Yue Jun. What can I do when the earl comes here? Please think of something for me quickly.

SHANJING: Don't worry. Get up first. Tell me, where is Yue Jun, the person you pretend to be?

JIA CHONG: He fell into the river by accident.

SHANJING: Oh, so he drowned.

JIA CHONG: Yes.

SHANJING: He must have had his family with him. Where did they go?

JIA CHONG: When I left, I asked my brother-in-law to take care of them. I don't know where they went after that.

SHANJING: As long as Yue Jun's dead, your official position will be safe. Even if the Earl of Funing should find out, we can take care of it with silver ingots. Just leave it to me.

JIA CHONG: What a wonderful teacher! If I make a thousand taels of silver a year, you'll get five hundred; if I make ten thousand taels, you, sir, will get five thousand. And I'll listen to your instructions in dealing with all the court cases. Let me go to the kitchen personally and have a complete banquet set up for my dear teacher. (*He exits*.)

SHANJING: Ahem, son of a rascal turtle! (*Sings*.)
> Jia Chong became an official through "falseness"[33]
> I curse you, false impostor turtle bastard!
> Now that you have hired a fine teacher,
> I'll guarantee that your end will be near.

(*Speaks*.) Oh, my lord! I am pained to death by what's happened to you. Shanjing truly wants to assist you in your court, but who would have thought that you would take office at the crystal palace?[34] You had an official post but didn't make it. Now even her ladyship has disappeared without a trace. I can only grope around at the yamen for

---

33. *Jia* is homophonous with *jia* 假 falsehood, and *chong* means "to assume the identity of."
34. The dragon king's palace underwater.

now, and then slowly will send people to investigate. Flustered and grieved, I shed buckets of tears. (*He exits.*)

Scene 9

LINIANG: (*Enters.*) Miaoying, Miaoying! How can you sleep so well! (*Sings.*)
> I cry and ask my lord, where are you?
> Day and night tears flow incessantly down my cheeks.
> Standing on the pirate boat, there is nothing I can do,
> I'm also worried that the bandit's son will return soon.
> This was all from the bad karma in my previous life.
> And I have no idea as to what will happen to me next?
> Days pass as slowly as years, I feel so weary and shiftless,
> Accompanied by a lone lamp, this bitterness is hard to endure.
> The sound of waves from the flowing river clamors outside my window,
> The night gibbon howls for me in sorrow.

(*Speaks rapidly.*) As soon as his lordship died, Jia Chong robbed us of our luggage. Judging from the circumstances, the two of them jointly plotted the murder of his lordship. I don't know when I'd be able to avenge this grievance. Ah, Shanjing, Shanjing! What a heartless serf you are! (*Sings.*)
> I have been waiting for you for so long,
> And why did you leave and not return?
> How could you have known that his lordship would be murdered,
> And that no one takes care of the women in this roaming boat?
> As if sitting on a carpet of needles, I can hardly bear it,
> When will Heaven finally open its eyes?

YE XING: (*Enters in a drunken state.*) That was some wine! (*Sings.*)
> Good news arrived from afar today,
> My son has become a general at Nanzhang.
> Drinking with close friends, my delight was boundless,
> I return at night in a drunken daze.
> I embark on my boat, feeling so dizzy.

(*Speaks.*) Aiya! I'm drunk. Daughter-in-law, I've just received some good news! Someone came from Nanzhang today and told me that my son has become general of the Central Army under Liu Qianjin. I guess when Liu Qianjin ascends the throne, my son will become prime minister to the new dynasty, and you will be the prime minister's wife. Ha, ha! It's all due to the fact that I pushed Yue Jun into the river that night.

LINIANG: Murderer!

YE XING: You would have been wife to a mere magistrate—so much lower than being wife of a prime minister. Aiya! I'm drunk, I'm drunk. (*He falls down and sleeps.*)

LINIANG: Murderer! (*Sings.*)
> Suddenly hearing him telling the truth,
> Unwittingly, black blood rushes and fills my entire chest.
> The suspicions I harbored for so many days are now confirmed,
> This is truly a case of confession without any slashing.
> Crunch, crunch, my teeth can't stop grinding,
> Vengeance for the grievances will be done this very night.

(*She exits and re-enters with a knife; speaks.*) Ah! My dear lord! (*Sings.*)
> I will avenge your death this very night,
> Help me with your spirit so that I might succeed.
> For the murderer, the time for your death has arrived,
> Even if you have wings, you won't be able to take flight.

YE XING: Daughter-in-law, get me some cold water.

LINIANG: Ah! (*Sings.*)
> There he still calls me daughter-in-law,
> It makes me boil with anger and become even more infuriated.
> In the blink of an eye, I'll have you gushing with blood!

(*She kills him, sits and calls.*) Miaoying, come here right away! Aiya, Miaoying!

MIAOYING: (*Enters.*) Why is my lady calling for me in the middle of the night? My lady, you seem awfully tense.

LINIANG: Shut up. Miaoying ah, Miaoying! Just now the bandit told the truth in his drunkenness. Our lordship was indeed murdered by him.

MIAOYING: Oh, so it was him! The rascal murderer!

LINIANG: Now that I have avenged myself, I am going to jump into the river. You'll have to fend for yourself, I can't worry about you any-more.

MIAOYING: How silly of you, my lady. Don't you remember that his lord-ship wore that treasure, the jade swallow hairpin, which would protect him against both fire and water? His lordship may not be dead after all. If you should drown yourself right now, when he returns he'll call for you but there won't be an answer. Wouldn't he die of grief then?

LINIANG: So, what is your suggestion?

MIAOYING: The way your maid sees it, there's a small boat tied to ours— why don't we cut the rope and escape in it. We might find help and stay somewhere temporarily, or we might run into Shanjing, that hus-band of mine. We can then search for his lordship's whereabouts.

LINIANG: Your idea is good. Let's get away quickly.

MIAOYING: Just a minute. We can't leave like this. There is a brush and an inkwell in the cabin. You should leave a few words on the cabin door.

LINIANG: Bring them here quickly.

MIAOYING: Yes. (*She exits and re-enters.*) Here are the brush and ink-well.

LINIANG: (*Writes while speaking.*) In the middle of the night, someone murdered the father-in-law and then forced the daughter-in-law to drown herself. If anyone should report this to an official, I would be grateful in the realm of the dead. Ah, let's go quickly. Heaven, oh Heaven, please protect us if my husband is still alive; but if my husband is already dead, let this little boat capsize. (*Sings.*)

>We hurry onto the small boat and untie the rope,
>Churning and boiling, the waves roll.
>Flowing along with the current, we are as fast as an arrow,
>Maid and mistress entrust our lives to Heaven.
>The bright morning stars approach the northern bank,
>The light boat has already passed ten thousand folds of mountains.
>I wonder where we would be able to stand up again? (*They exit.*)

QIANQIAN: (*Enters and recites.*)

>When the tide is low, the banks are far apart.
>When the wind is direct, the sail stretches taut.

(*Speaks.*) Oh, I see two women approaching in a small boat. Ah, why are they splattered in blood? There must be a reason for it. Let me draw their boat in and find out. (*She exits and re-enters with Liniang and Miaoying.*) You've killed someone and yet you are afraid of getting into my boat?

MIAOYING: Well then, we will get into her boat.

QIANQIAN: Let me ask you—

MIAOYING: Don't ask us anything. Let me ask you a question first. There was an official by the name of Yue Jun. He was on his way to his post. Have you seen him?

LINIANG: Miaoying, why are you asking her?

MIAOYING: My lady, look at the jade swallow hairpin in her hair.

LINIANG: Ah! Elder sister here, so you did see him.

QIANQIAN: Lord Yue was saved by me. Who are you two?

MIAOYING: This is his lordship's wife.

QIANQIAN: Ah, so elder sister has arrived! Why did you come here in a lone boat with blood all over you?

LINIANG: I killed the pirate who murdered his lordship.

QIANQIAN: Elder sister, lower your voice and tell me about it in the cabin.

LINIANG: Yes.

QIANQIAN: (*Recites.*)

Meeting relatives where one least expects to meet relatives,
Encountering another from a thousand miles away, it turns out that
we all come from the same family.

LINIANG: (*Continues.*)
When mountains cease and rivers end and I assumed there's no
more road,
Seeing dense willows and bright flowers, there comes yet another
village. (*They exit.*)

Scene 10

YUE JUN: (*Enters and sings.*)
Filled with hatred, my anger gushes up to the Milky Way,
How many times have I scratched my head and inquired of
Heaven?
The three officials I could not meet—I've traveled back and forth
in vain.
I don't know when I'll be able to avenge my grievance.

(*Speaks.*) I, Yue Jun, went to see the officials in charge, but they've all
gone to the main army camp. I thought that I should go see the Earl of
Funing, but then my wife is still on the pirate boat with no news at all.
Why don't I find out about her before reporting my grievance at the
army camp? (*Recites.*)
I'll first seek news of my wife,
And then return to avenge my grievance.

(*He exits, re-enters and sings.*)
Walking along I raise my head,
How come the pirate boat is here?

(*Speaks.*) There's a couplet on the cabin door, let me have a look at it.
(*Sings.*)
The sun and moon take turns rowing one thousand miles,
Intersecting the wind and clouds is one lone boat.

(*Speaks.*) Ah! This was the couplet I wrote on the pirate boat during the
Autumn Festival. My wife must still be in it. Let me go and take a look.
Oh no! (*Two boatmen enter and block his exit.*)

BOATMAN A: Where do you think you're going? Hey partner, this guy
just came off old Ye's boat. Let's take a look there.

BOATMAN B: Sure. (*They exit and re-enter.*) Oh no! He's killed Old Ye!

YUE JUN: Ah, Heavens! I wonder which brave soul has avenged me. Oh,
fellows, where did the two women go?

BOATMAN A: What a creep—still after someone else's daughter-in-law!
You forced her to jump into the river. What's more to ask?

BOATMAN B: Say no more! Take his broad sword and then take him to the court.

YUE JUN: Ah, my dear wife!

BOATMAN A: Look at him—who are you calling wife? Go! (*They exit.*)

JIA CHONG: (*Enters with a yamen runner and recites.*)
>   I force myself to preside over the court,
>   And feel awkward all over.
>   Who would have thought that at a place like this,
>   Being a fake is so tough?

(*Speaks.*) I, the official, am named, named, named Yue. Although I started out from the Department of Water, my belly is full of mud.[35] Ever since I assumed this office, I have never dared to preside over the court. Today my teacher is here to steer the helm, that's why I feel brave enough to preside over the court.

YAMEN RUNNER: I report to my lord. There are two boatmen to see you.

JIA CHONG: This is familiar territory for me. It should be easy. Order them to come in.

BOATMEN: (*Enter.*) We boatmen kowtow to our lord. A man killed Old Ye. We caught him and here's the murder weapon.

JIA CHONG: Did he die?

BOATMAN A: He was stabbed eight to ten times right in the heart. You don't think he would die?

JIA CHONG: That would be quite tricky. What happened to the two women?

BOATMAN B: They drowned themselves in the river that night.

JIA CHONG: What a pity! Have the coroner examine the corpse.

BOATMAN A: What an all-knowing magistrate! He knew that there were two women on board without being told. Ah, just as if he'd seen it all. (*They exit.*)

JIA CHONG: Bring the criminal in.

YUE JUN: (*Enters with a yamen runner and recites.*)
>   Disaster struck out from nowhere,
>   I wish I could make snow fall in mid-summer.[36]

(*Speaks.*) How come it's him! Ah, murderer!

YAMEN RUNNER: Shush!

JIA CHONG: Hey, hey, hey—you are the murderer and you're calling me a murderer! Quick, put him in jail!

YUE JUN: Ah, murderer! (*He is pulled away.*)

---

35. Instead of being filled with learning. This is also a pun on his nickname, Catfish in the Mud.
36. In the Yuan drama, *Dou'e yuan* 竇娥冤 by Guan Hanqing 關漢卿, Dou'e's innocence is made apparent by the fact that snow fell during the sixth month when she was executed.

JIA CHONG: Close the door! Come here quickly, my teacher.

SHANJING: Hm. How now such haste and whence that broadsword?

JIA CHONG: Ah, teacher. Please no literary babble. I'm in deep trouble.

SHANJING: What's the problem?

JIA CHONG: That Yue Jun didn't die!

SHANJING: Did you ask him why he murdered him?

JIA CHONG: He started yelling at me as soon as he entered the court. How could I get to ask anything?

SHANJING: He didn't murder the person. It is obviously and simply thus.

JIA CHONG: How did you know that it wasn't him?

SHANJING: You really can't read, can you? Look at the engraving on the sword. It says, "Li Hanjiao—man with the iron boat-pole." Obviously he is the murderer. Send someone to capture him right away!

JIA CHONG: Come in, yamen runner!

YAMEN RUNNER: At your service.

JIA CHONG: Go catch Li Hanjiao right away. Don't let him get away.

YAMEN RUNNER: Yes, sir.

JIA CHONG: My teacher, what are we going to do with Li Hanjiao when he is caught?

SHANJING: Have him executed.

JIA CHONG: What are we going to do with that Yue Jun?

SHANJING: Release him.

JIA CHONG: This won't do, this won't do. What happens to me if he gets out? It'd be better to drug him and dump him in the river. This way he won't have to suffer the pain of being knifed.

SHANJING: Excellent, excellent! A kind Buddha's heart such as yours is indeed rare! Go fetch the drug.

JIA CHONG: Let me go fetch the drug. (*He exits and re-enters.*) I will count on you, my teacher. (*He exits.*)

SHANJING: Who needs any reminders from you? Ahem, you son of a turtle! (*Sings.*)

> Upon hearing of his lordship's whereabouts,
> My heart is filled with irrepressible joy.
> Rascal, your end is clearly inescapable,
> Yet you still wish to play one more trick.
> You, as an official, are a forgery,
> I, as a teacher, have no more authenticity.
> Controlling the situation from both within and without,
> I will guarantee that the turtle in the vat will be caught.
> Just watch to see if I've got enough tricks up my sleeves.
> (*He exits.*)

LI HANJIAO: (*Enters and recites.*)

> Heaven has direly trapped this hero of a man,

Buried in the rivers and lakes, unknown for twenty years.
When will the great roc get to span his wings,
And fly ten thousand miles up the Nine Heavens?
YAMEN RUNNER: Take him. (*Li hits the yamen runner who falls.*) Hey, hey, hey. My nose is bleeding. You murdered someone and you are still so vicious!
LI HANJIAO: Nonsense! Whom are you calling a murderer?
YAMEN RUNNER: We've got a broad sword here with your name "Li Hanjiao" on it. How dare you dispute this?
LI HANJIAO: I haven't been back to my boat for a few days and was just going to ask where you got the broadsword from. Since the sword is mine, take me with you.
YAMEN RUNNER: What a brave man!
LI HANJIAO: (*Recites.*)
Knowing that I didn't commit the crime,
Why worry about being trapped into bondage? (*They exit.*)
JIA CHONG: (*Enters with a yamen runner and recites.*)
With a boatman judging a boatman's case,
One only fears that mud will stick to water and make a mess.
(*Speaks.*) I, the official, will again preside over the court under the name of Yue. I've ordered Li Hanjiao arrested. How come they are not here yet?
YAMEN RUNNER: I've brought Li Hanjiao.
JIA CHONG: Bring him here. Are you Li Hanjiao?
LI HANJIAO: Yes, my lord.
JIA CHONG: Is this broadsword yours?
LI HANJIAO: Yes, it is mine.
JIA CHONG: Why did you commit the murder?
LI HANJIAO: I didn't commit any murder, my lord.
JIA CHONG: So, you're a stubborn one!
LI HANJIAO: My lord, this broadsword couldn't have flown into the court on its own. Someone must have brought it here. You can question him about it.
JIA CHONG: Ah, this would create a big problem. If I summon him here, he'll be sure to curse and yell at me to no end. I'll have to be tough about this. There's no need to verify any further, Li Hanjiao. This sword is yours; therefore, you must have been the murderer. There's no need to say anything else. Drag him away!
LI HANJIAO: You dog official, you! (*He is dragged away.*)
JIA CHONG: Close the door! (*He exits in a hurry.*)

Scene 11

LINIANG: (*Enters with Qianqian and sings.*)
> Wind gushes, the sky is high, gibbons cry in sorrow.
> Banks are clear, the sand is white, birds fly in circles.
> The leaves in this boundless forest fall gloomily and desolately,
> The endless Long River approaches, turning and churning.
> I wonder where my lord is at this very moment.

QIANQIAN: Don't worry, elder sister. When I saw his lordship the other day, the aura around him showed that he was finally due for an improvement of luck.

OLD WOMAN: (*Enters.*) Qianqian, there is a problem.

QIANQIAN: What happened?

OLD WOMAN: Your brother killed someone and has been taken to the county yamen.

QIANQIAN: Why did he kill the person?

OLD WOMAN: I don't know.

QIANQIAN: Who is the present magistrate?

OLD WOMAN: I don't know that either.

QIANQIAN: What kind of a fool are you?

OLD WOMAN: Hey, I didn't come here to be abused! (*She exits.*)

QIANQIAN: Elder sister, could you guard the boat while I go to the yamen to find out more. (*Sings.*)
> When I saw the ominous aura around him,
> I knew he was due for an ill star today. (*She exits.*)

LINIANG: Ah! (*Sings.*)
> I am doomed by ill fate these days,
> My presence seems to upset the peace everywhere.
> When will I be able to attain tranquility again? (*She exits.*)

MEINIANG: (*Enters with Miao Run; sings.*)
> Father and daughter arrive at Shishou County,
> For my marriage, we traveled many roads.
> Unaccustomed to such hardship,
> The delicate flower is battered by wild winds.
> This is a case of demeaning oneself in search for another,
> One can't quite call it "bound by a string for one thousand miles."
> I can't stop lowering my head and sigh softly.

MIAO RUN: Rest for a while, my child. Excuse me, buddy, how far are we from Shishou County? (*Offstage: It's not far—about three miles.*[37]) What's the name of your magistrate? (*Offstage: His surname is Yue.*) Oh good, we're not far from the county seat, and he is the official there.

---

37. The original says ten *li* 里.

MEINIANG: Daddy, (*Sings.*)
> He said that he would send for me as soon as he reached office,
> Why then was there such a long delay?
> One can't trust the words he gave,
> The rich and wealthy have always been heartless.
> I'm afraid that he may have broken the marital mirror of mine,
> Such that father and daughter have traveled all in vain.

MIAO RUN: My child! (*Sings.*)
> Even if he refuses to own up to you and me,
> We can still go back, what's wrong with that?
> My child, you are not a piece of used ware,
> So don't worry about not finding a mate.
> You won't have trouble anywhere.

MEINIANG: Ai!

QIANQIAN: (*Enters.*) Ah, my brother! (*Sings.*)
> I knew that you'd encounter a calamity today,
> Ever since antiquity heroes have had to endure more.
> Ah, whose daughter is this sitting on the roadside?
> Her pretty face is so full of auspiciousness,
> The aura of ladyship about her is as brilliant as mine.

(*Speaks.*) Hello, elder sister there, where are you from?

MEINIANG: Ah! Look papa, isn't that my jade swallow hairpin she's wearing?

MIAO RUN: So it is. Go ask her about it, my child.

MEINIANG: Elder sister, you must know Magistrate Yue of the Shishou County.

QIANQIAN: How did you know that?

MEINIANG: I know because you are wearing the jade swallow hairpin I gave him.

QIANQIAN: Then you must be elder sister Zou Meiniang. Am I right?

MEINIANG: Absolutely.

QIANQIAN: No wonder you are full of the aura of a lady.

MIAO RUN: She seems to know something about fortune telling.

MEINIANG: So who are you?

QIANQIAN: My name is Qianqian. The magistrate got on a pirate boat by mistake and was pushed into the river. It was I who saved his life. Our eldest sister[38] eventually avenged him by killing Ye Xing. She also escaped to my boat.

---

38. Zou Liniang is referred to as the eldest sister by the other wives since she ranks the highest as the first wife.

MIAO RUN: Quite a lot of danger he got himself into. No wonder he didn't have us fetched.

MEINIANG: Where are you going now, my sister?

QIANQIAN: My brother killed someone. I'm going to the county seat to ask about it.

MEINIANG: Since his lordship has already assumed office, I don't think that should be a problem.

MIAO RUN: Now that it's our own court, even killing a few people won't matter.

YE MING: (*Enters and recites.*)

> Having spied on the enemy's military intelligence,
> I am now reporting back to my liege.[39]

(*Speaks.*) I, Ye Ming, have just returned from spying on the enemy. I spot two pretty girls here. They must be the bandit queens Heaven is bestowing upon me. Soldiers, grab these girls and bring them across the river. (*They kidnap the girls.*)

MIAO RUN: Oh no! Bandits have kidnapped my daughter! Let me find out more details so that I'll be able to ask Magistrate Yue for help. You bandit punks, see what I'll dole out to you! (*He exits.*)

YE MING: (*Recites.*)

> Having arrived from a thousand miles away,
> I plucked two beautiful flowers.

(*Speaks.*) Soldiers, bring me those two girls.

QIANQIAN: (*Kneels.*) Please spare our lives, great king!

YE MING: Ha, ha, ha! Of course I'm not going to kill you. Get up! Attendants, you may leave.

SOLDIERS: Yes, sir. (*They exit.*)

YE MING: I am the general of the Central Army of Liu Qianjin from Nanzhang. Becoming my queens won't demean you.

MEINIANG: Oh, you bandit! (*Sings.*)

> Rebelling against the imperial court, you are courting disaster.
> Yet you still dare to plunder and kidnap among the common folks.
> The law of Heaven is clear, your behavior won't be tolerated,
> We'll see how you'll eventually fare.

(*Speaks.*) Oh, miserable me! (*Sings.*)

> I thought I was going to be a lady and was fortunate in fate,
> Who would have guessed that I would be trapped in a bandit's snare?
> Enough! Let history remember my good name,

---

39. He refers to Liu Qianjin as *qiansui* 千歲, "one thousand years," rather than *wansui* 萬歲, "ten thousand years" which is reserved solely for the emperor of China. This indicates a prejudice on the part of the playwright.

Let the bandit chop off my head.
Bring the knife and kill me right away!
QIANQIAN: My sister, when one stands under low eaves, how can one dare not to lower one's head? It would be better to go along with him.
MEINIANG: Ah, my dear Yue! Ah, dear Yue! You have given the jade swallow hairpin to the wrong person! (*Sings.*)
In life only a good name and chastity are of utmost importance
Who fears having the body hacked into ten thousand pieces?
Who would have thought that you are just a cheap whore,
Willing to become a bandit's old lady?
The words "modesty" and "shame" you have completely tossed out,
You are really no different from the birds and the beasts,
Unafraid of being cursed by thousands and spat on by ten thousands.
QIANQIAN: What a bitch! I was nice to you. How can you be so rude? General, give me your broadsword and let me kill this slut!
YE MING: Here's the sword. Just scare her.
QIANQIAN: Here rascal, don't you escape! (*She kills Ye Ming.*) Elder sister, how did you like my trick with the bandit?
MEINIANG: You almost scared me to death! What shall we do now?
QIANQIAN: There are some soldier's uniforms here. Let's put them on and make our escape. (*They exit and re-enter changed.*) Let me set the place on fire. (*She sets fire.*)
SOLDIERS: (*Enters.*) What happened?
QIANQIAN: The general has given an order. The Central Army camp is on fire. Go put out the fire right away! (*The soldiers exit.*) Let me carry you on my back. (*They exit hurriedly and re-enter.*) Here we are at the riverbank. There's a boat here. Let's take it.
MEINIANG: (*Sings.*)
The waves surge up to the sky as my soul sinks,
In the blink of an eye, we have already crossed the Yangzi River.
Thank goodness for the scheme devised by this female Jing Ke 荆軻.[40]
I could have died from the nasty scare!
MIAO RUN: (*Enters and recites.*)
Searching but finding not a trace,
An auspicious event has come to naught.
MEINIANG: Daddy!
MIAO RUN: How come you're here and dressed like this?

---

40. A famous assassin of the Warring States period (403–221 b.c.).

QIANQIAN: Don't ask now. You two go to the yamen first. I'll go see my brother in the jail and join you shortly. (*They exit from different sides.*)

Scene 12

YUE JUN: (*Enters and sings.*)
> Someone else did the killing, but I am to take the blame.
> Escaping justice, Catfish in the Mud assumes my name and office.
> Truth and falsehood are so topsy-turvy,
> Furiously angry, I wish to question Heaven.

LI HANJIAO: (*Enters.*) What a joke! (*Sings.*)
> Based on words on a broadsword, a murder case is adjudicated.
> I don't even know who it is that implicated me?
> The most ridiculous person around is that muddle-headed magistrate,
> Who, for no reason and without questioning, puts me in jail.
> It forces my anger to surge up to the Milky Way!

YUE JUN: May I ask you, young hero, what crime you have committed?

LI HANJIAO: I don't even know where to start. Someone killed Ye Xing, but because the broadsword used has my name on it, I was put in jail without any trial.

YUE JUN: You must be Li Hanjiao then?

LI HANJIAO: Yes, precisely.

YUE JUN: It was I who got you into this trouble.

LI HANJIAO: How's that?

YUE JUN: Please listen to me, Brother Li. (*Sings.*)
> I was a magistrate en route to my official post,
> But who would have expected to board a pirate boat half way?
> The night of the Autumn Festival I was thrown into the river but floated on it,
> Thanks to your sister I was saved from the dragon pool.
> She presented me with your broadsword, for my own protection,
> But who would have thought that it would inadvertently implicate me?

LI HANJIAO: Did you kill that Ye Xing?

YUE JUN: No. (*Sings.*)
> That day, tracing my route, I was looking for my family,
> But because of the corpse on that pirate boat, I encountered more injustice.

LI HANJIAO: May I ask for your honorable name?

YUE JUN: (*Sings.*)
> I am the new magistrate of Shishou County,

My name is Yue Jun, my style is Xiufeng, renowned during the last two examinations.

LI HANJIAO: That's strange. Who is the present magistrate then?

YUE JUN: He's the rascal who tried to murder me. (*Sings.*)
It is tragic that the jade and stone are no longer distinguished,
The real official is in jail, while a bandit has become the official.
This kind of event is truly rare.

LI HANJIAO: Hearing the story my angry hair stands on end. Let me break out of jail and kill that rascal!

YUE JUN: Don't be rash. I don't think that he will be able to get away with it.

LI HANJIAO: He has a few extra days to live then. My lord, there's one more thing I want to ask you. My little sister is skilled at physiognomy, and she said of herself that she has the look of a lady. I beg my lord to grant her wish.

YUE JUN: I've already presented her with my jade swallow hairpin. I just haven't had a chance to inform you, brother-in-law.

LI HANJIAO: It is a great honor.

SHANJING: (*Enters and recites.*)
The world recognizes the false rather than the real,
Everyone takes turnips as ginseng.

JAILER: The honorable teacher has arrived. Please come in.

SHANJING: Guard the place carefully.

JAILER: Yes, sir.

SHANJING: There's my lord.

YUE JUN: Shanjing, how come you just got here?

SHANJING: I got here early. I've assumed office before my lord got to office.

YUE JUN: What office did you assume?

SHANJING: Listen to me, my lord. (*Sings.*)
After I returned home, I took ill.
After that I rushed right to your office.
I had heard that my lord had assumed office,
Who would have thought that the one in office was Jia Chong?
Since I had no way of getting news of my lord,
I also falsely assumed the position of a teacher.

YUE JUN: What teacher?

SHANJING: (*Sings.*)
A letter from the Earl of Funing made my recommendation,
The rascal entered the snare and was tricked.
So highly respected by the rascal I am,
That he told me the truth about what had happened.
He said that my lord had drowned in the river,

News of my lady, I've had no way of finding.
Seeing my lord this very day,
Is all due to my lord's involvement in the murder.
This is truly a great fortune in the midst of misfortune.
LI HANJIAO: So, this honorable teacher is actually your housekeeper!
SHANJING: Who is this exposing my background?
YUE JUN: I owe him. His name is Li Hanjiao.
SHANJING: Aiya, I tied the wrong string! When I saw the engraving on the broadsword, I told the rascal official that the murderer was Li Hanjiao and that he should be arrested immediately.
LI HANJIAO: Thanks a lot!
SHANJING: The bandit gave me a packet of sleeping power. He wanted me to drug my lord and throw you back into the river.
LI HANJIAO: I'm so mad. Let me finish off that rascal soon!
SHANJING: Wait. Let me get the seal in the yamen first. Then we can kill the bandit and welcome his lordship to his office.
LI HANJIAO: Go quickly then.
SHANJING: (*Recites.*)
    In order to help the real magistrate,
    The false teacher runs around like mad. (*He exits.*)
QIANQIAN: (*Enters and recites.*)
    Happy though I am that my husband has become a magistrate,
    Yet I grieve that my flesh and blood is in a field of thorns.
JAILER: What are you doing here?
QIANQIAN: There's a Li Hanjiao in the jail. He's my elder brother. I've come to see him.
JAILER: Oh, so it's Miss Li! Please come in.
QIANQIAN: Aiya! Goodness heavens! (*Sings.*)
    Entering the jail, I took a look and got a big fright,
    How is it that Magistrate Yue is also in the jail?
    Who is the official at the yamen with the same name and surname?
    And why is Magistrate Yue put in chains?
    All this makes me confused and skeptical.
LI HANJIAO: My sister, you've come!
QIANQIAN: Why did you kill someone, my brother?
LI HANJIAO: You're asking me? You sent me here!
QIANQIAN: How's that?
LI HANJIAO: Let me ask you a question first. To whom did you give my broadsword?
QIANQIAN: Ah, I gave it to—
LI HANJIAO: No, you don't need to tell me. I already know about the details. I'm happy for you that you are indeed blessed with good fortune. Come see Magistrate Yue.

YUE JUN: My benefactor is here.

QIANQIAN: My lord has been wronged. May I ask why you are here and who the present magistrate of Shishou County is?

YUE JUN: There were two villains who tried to murder me. The one, called Jia Chong, took my document and assumed my post. The other, called Ye Xing, was killed by someone. I was searching for my wife when I got involved in this murder case.

QIANQIAN: Do you two know who killed Ye Xing?

YUE JUN: Who was it?

QIANQIAN: It was none other than your wife, Zou Liniang. She killed the villain to avenge your wrong and then she escaped to my boat as well.

YUE JUN: Ha, ha, ha! This is so amazing! (*Sings.*)
>Hearing her words, my city of grief is conquered,
>My wife is truly a pillar-circling Jing Ke.[41]
>Able to take care of herself and escape disaster,
>Such an event truly fills me with such delight,
>Who cares that I should be sitting in jail today?

LI HANJIAO: Ai, I could die from frustration!

YUE JUN: You should be thrilled by this incident. What's this talk about frustration?

LI HANJIAO: Look at us. We men have bodies seven feet tall, yet all the earth-shaking affairs were accomplished by women. Why shouldn't I be upset?

QIANQIAN: The fact that our elder sister killed Ye Xing is not that amazing when compared with the woman who went amongst an army of a hundred thousand in Nanzhang and chopped off the head of a bandit as easily as taking something out of a bag.

LI HANJIAO: Who did that?

QIANQIAN: It was little old me.

LI HANJIAO: Tell me right away how you killed that bandit!

QIANQIAN: Listen, elder brother. (*Sings.*)
>That day because elder brother had encountered great disaster,
>Your sister traveled to the county seat to find out about it.
>Half way en route, I met a father and daughter duo,
>She saw my jade swallow hairpin and tears ran down her cheeks.

YUE JUN: Who was she?

QIANQIAN: She was none other than sister Meiniang.

LI HANJIAO: My lord, please don't interrupt. Let my sister tell how she killed the bandit.

---

41. When Jing Ke tried to assassinate the founder of the Qin dynasty before the king became the first emperor of China, he circled around a pillar in the palace when the king tried to strike him with a sword.

QIANQIAN: Listen, elder brother. (*Sings.*)

> That day the bandit from Nanzhang passed by,
> He had both your sister and Meiniang kidnapped.
> Fortunately, your sister has always been brave and clever,
> Using the scheme of borrowing a knife, I managed to trick the bandit.
> Chopping off his head was as easy as grabbing something out of a bag.
> Before leaving, I set fire to the tents of their Central Army.
> Taking their mandate arrow,[42] we left the camp entrance and made our escape that night.
> A strategist among women, such is precisely what I am.

LI HANJIAO: Ha, ha, ha! My lord, so both of your wives are executioners!

YUE JUN: You're joking. May I ask elder sister where the father and daughter are now?

QIANQIAN: They thought my lord has assumed office and have gone to the yamen.

LI HANJIAO: Oh no! They'll be trapped in the bandit's snare.

YUE JUN: With Shanjing there, there shouldn't be any problems.

QIANQIAN: Let me fight my way into the yamen.

LI HANJIAO: My sister, please allow your brother to have this honor. Why don't you go back to the boat and bring her ladyship to the yamen? Jailer, let her out.

JAILER: Yes.

LI HANJIAO: (*Recites.*)

> Last night my precious sword sang in its case,
> Only because injustice in this world has been done.

YUE JUN: (*Continues.*)

> But today Heaven has opened its eyes,

QIANQIAN: (*Continues.*)

> We'll now see clouds clear away and the evil star fall. (*They exit.*)

Scene 13

JIA CHONG: (*Enters with yamen runners and recites.*)

> A boatman has become a magistrate,
> Nothing is clear or understood.
> Casting the anchor is not up to me,

---

42. The *lingjian* 令箭 is an arrow with a triangular flag attached. They are given by commanders to represent conferred authority.

Handling the rudder, I also leave to the teacher.

(*Speaks.*) I am Jia Chong. Since Yue Jun didn't die, I told the teacher to finish him off in jail. I am sitting alone in the hall waiting for his news. How come he hasn't returned yet?

YAMEN RUNNER: Ho! Where do you think you are going?

MIAO RUN: (*Enters with Meiniang.*) I'm going inside. You asked me where I was going? Well, I'm your Senior Lord Miao, the magistrate's father-in-law. Go report our arrival at once.

YAMEN RUNNER: I don't know you.

MIAO RUN: Damn you, son of a bitch!⁴³ Why haven't you rushed in to report our arrival yet?

YAMEN RUNNER: Yes, sir. Yes, sir. I report to my lord. The Senior Lord Miao and my lord's wife have arrived.

JIA CHONG: This is my lucky day. This is a profitable business which comes to me on its own. It's obviously intended for the other guy but has ended up with me. Needless to say, the chicken which arrives on its own needs no capturing. What are we waiting for? Ask them to come in.

YAMEN RUNNER: Please come in, Senior Lord Miao.

MIAO RUN: (*Recites.*)

> After so many scares and frights,
> Finally there is peace and quiet.

(*Jia Chong looks at Meiniang who turns away from him; Miao speaks.*) Damned servant, this is the magistrate's wife! What do you think you're gawking at? I'll tell the magistrate and have your bones crushed!

JIA CHONG: Old Miao, I'm the magistrate you are looking for.

MIAO RUN: Damned son of a bitch, now you're pretending to be the magistrate! Let me ask you what your name is?

JIA CHONG: My surname is Yue, my personal name is Jun, and my style is Xiufeng.

MIAO RUN: Go, go, go! Yue Jun is my son-in-law. Do you think I don't know him? How can the likes of you pretend⁴⁴ to be him?

JIA CHONG: How does this old guy know that I'm called Jia Chong?

YAMEN RUNNER: This is the magistrate. How come you don't recognize him?

JIA CHONG: Ah, now I know. The Yue Jun you're looking for is already dead. I'm also called Yue Jun. I took his place.

MIAO RUN: Oh no, my child! We've paid our respects to the wrong grave!

---

43. Literally, "You, turtle egg, who ought to die!"
44. The word used here is *jiachong* 假充 which means to be an imposter of.

MEINIANG: How strange! (*Sings.*)
>We've verified along the way quite clearly,
>So how did things change so suddenly?
>Two people bearing confusingly the same surname and name,
>One a coolie, the other a scholar, they differ as sheep from tiger.
>How did the real Yue vanish without a trace?
>Something strange must have transpired behind all this.
>(*Speaks.*) Daddy, let's leave the yamen and find out more.

MIAO RUN: Let's go!

JIA CHONG: Wait a minute. This is an imperial yamen. You think you can come and go at will? If you want to leave, you'd better leave my wife behind. Let me tell you, once a woman enters an official establishment, nine oxen can't drag her away.

MEINIANG: Oh, you rascal! (*Sings.*)
>Even officials have to follow laws and regulations,
>Infringing upon women by force is no mean crime.
>Luofu 羅敷[45] has a husband, it was preordained three lives ago,
>Changing a plan or switching a musical string, is out of the question.
>Don't count on the heavy weight of your officialdom,
>How can it be tolerated by the mighty Heaven?
>The imperial court has appointed a bandit by mistake,
>How could such a fool look after the people?
>Ah, daddy! It was all because of my ill-fated beauty,
>That disaster follows one upon the other.
>Still shaken from the incident at Nanzhang,
>Who would have expected that I'd fall into a thief's snare again?
>How can one endure the bandit official making trouble left and right,[46]
>I vow to wreck vengeance until the hall is splattered red!
>Ah, if only I had come with elder sister Qianqian,
>We would be sure to slay that highwayman.

JIA CHONG: If she had come with you, then I'd have a pair of beauties locked up in my Bronze Bird Pavilion.[47]

---

45. During the Warring States period, the duke of Zhao 趙王 saw the beautiful Luofu picking mulberry leaves and wished to possess her. She composed a song about the accomplishments of her husband and noted that while the duke had a wife, Luofu herself also had a husband. Meiniang is comparing herself to Luofu here.

46. The word used here, *sheying* 射影, refers to the spurting of sand by an imaginary demon at the shadows of men, causing them to die.

47. The two beauties, *erjiao* 二嬌, refer to the two beautiful Qiao sisters, *Er Qiao* 二喬 whom Cao Cao 曹操 (ruler of the Kingdom of Wei; r. 220–227) of the Three Kingdoms Period supposedly coveted. Cao Cao supposedly had a Bronze Bird Pavilion (*tongquetai*) built in order to

MIAO RUN: You gassy windbag!

JIA CHONG: Father-in-law of mine, what kind of talk is that?

MIAO RUN: (*Sings.*)

> Who has ever seen an official like this?
> His mouth and face do not look at all human.
> Dreaming of lust under a locust tree,
> He is surely cooking other schemes.
> Ho! I'd give up this old life of mine today,
> Who's afraid of you, turtle bastard son of a bitch.

JIA CHONG: You are getting rude, father-in-law.

MIAO RUN: (*Sings.*)

> You dare to make any more farts—
> Bastard son of a turtle is your father-in-law!
> We'll deal with this ugly mess today!

(*Speaks.*) My child, we'll see if he dares to do anything to you.

JIA CHONG: How nasty!

SHANJING: Hm, hm. (*Sings.*)

> Having met his lordship in the jail,
> We'll work from within and without to set up a trap.
> When the real boss re-appears soon,
> I will be the Number One meritorious statesman.
> Oh no, another twist and turn lies ahead of the bend,
> What are these two, father and daughter, doing here?
> Say no more! I'll sing with the tune once there.

JIA CHONG: My teacher, you've come back.

MIAO RUN: Isn't this Shanjing?

SHANJING: Of course I'm *xianshing*,[48] the teacher. Don't be mouthy. I'll talk for you.

JIA CHONG: Come here, my teacher. How did that affair go?

SHANJING: Absolutely perfectly. After drugging him, I threw him into the river myself. I saw to it that he returned to the road he came from.

JIA CHONG: In that case, I can safely accept the wife that old guy brought for him.

SHANJING: But of course.

JIA CHONG: What if that woman refuses to go along with it?

SHANJING: That's not hard at all. Please leave the room, my lord. Let me talk to her, and I'll guarantee that you'll be married after a few words from me.

JIA CHONG: I will rely on the teacher then. (*He exits.*)

---

keep the sisters, but he was unable to defeat Sun Ce 孫策 (ruler of the Kingdom of Wu; r. 222–252) and Zhou Yu 周瑜 (chief military advisor of Sun Ce), the husbands of the beauties.

48. Teacher, *xiansheng* 先生, is pronounced as *xianshing* in Shaanxi dialect.

SHANJING: Goodness gracious! What are you two doing here?

MEINIANG: Let me just ask you where the magistrate is?

SHANJING: He's in jail.

MEINIANG: How did he end up assuming his office in jail?

SHANJING: Let's skip the details for now. Go along with the scoundrel right now. With me here, nothing can go wrong. Once we have the seal in our hands, his lordship can assume the office.

JIA CHONG: (*Enters.*) How did your speech go?

SHANJING: She accepted as soon as I talked to her.

JIA CHONG: My good teacher is even good at matchmaking!

SHANJING: There's only one thing. She's concerned that you may have a wife already.

JIA CHONG: I don't have a family, as my teacher knows.

SHANJING: That's what I said too, but she wouldn't believe me. She said if you want her to go along, you'll have to let her keep the official seal.

JIA CHONG: My teacher, do you think I should?

SHANJING: Why not? Is there any official whose seal is not guarded by his wife?

JIA CHONG: If I should, then I'll fetch it right now. (*He exits and re-enters.*) Here is the seal. Just give it to her. It's getting late, you can accompany my father-in-law to the study.

SHANJING: Ah, let me bring you some wine first. I will see my lord drink the wedding wine before I go. . . . Oh no! I've got myself into a sticky situation here! (*Sings.*)

> Whenever one is in too much of a hurry, problems arise,
> I have no time to think right now.
> When one is too busy, one simply will have to make do,
> I will learn to fly if I need to.
> The sleeping drug he gave me the other day,
> Ha ha, it's perfectly handy right this way.
> Slipping a handful into the wine pot,
> We'll see if you get to live or die this very night.
> This is a calamity you've brought upon yourself.

(*Speaks.*) Hm. My lord, you must drink three rounds of wedding wine tonight. You will have two, the bride will have two, and then you'll drink one exchanged round together.

JIA CHONG: Thank you very much, my teacher. (*Sings.*)

> Thanks to the teacher for his amazing schemes,
> The darling beauty, I'm delighted, will enter my dragon cell.
> Remembering the past and thinking ahead, I laugh secretly,
> It must have been on account of my accumulated virtue,
> I can't help but turn up my face and laugh heartily.

SHANJING: Let me serve the wine. My lord, if you please.

MEINIANG: Ai, daddy, look at Shanjing. I think he's up to no good. (*Sings.*)

> People can't be fathomed even after repeated scrutiny,
> The carp was caused to be hooked by crook.
> Ah villain, his lordship treated you kind and fair,
> Why would you toil like horse and ox[49] for others?
> Heaven will not protect unrighteous villains.

SHANJING: Listen, the bride says that the lord has been so kind to me. I don't think serving my lord wine can be considered as toiling like horse and ox for you.

JIA CHONG: The honor is entirely mine.

SHANJING: Now that my lord has drunk, let me persuade the bride to drink a cup as well. Brides tend to be shy, she probably won't drink.

MIAO RUN: (*Smashes the cup to the ground.*) Shanjing, you heartless serf. I'll . . .

SHANJING: Yes. (*Jia Chong falls.*)

MIAO RUN: You slave of a slave, I'm going to . . .

SHANJING: Hey, the scolding is getting better.

MEINIANG: Daddy, how come that rascal has toppled over?

SHANJING: Keep on scolding! Your scolding has already toppled over your new son-in-law.

MIAO RUN: I'm so confused. Shanjing, what's going on?

SHANJING: Don't rush me. I need to catch my breath first.

MEINIANG: Shanjing, how did that rascal get this way?

SHANJING: He got drugged.

MEINIANG: But where did the drug come from?

SHANJING: Well, it's a long story. You'll know all about it later. Let's get our lord to assume office first. Come, come, come. Let's tie this scoundrel up and put him aside. I'll inform the attendants outside to get the court ready for the magistrate. (*He exits.*)

MIAO RUN: I'm still somewhat suspicious.

MEINIANG: Let's see who will preside over the court. (*They exit.*)

YAMEN RUNNER A: (*Enters with Yamen Runner B.*) Partner, isn't this the strangest thing on earth—the magistrate we had was actually a pirate!

YAMEN RUNNER B: Now the real magistrate will preside over the court. Get ready, everyone.

SHANJING: (*Enters and recites.*)

> Having caught the fake official, we now swap him with the real,
> Let's watch the new official cross examine the old.

---

49. Beasts of burden, in other words, slave.

(*Speaks.*) Yamen runners, bring up the rascal.

JIA CHONG: (*Enters under the custody of yamen runners.*) Is that Teacher Chu?

SHANJING: My name is not Chu any more, it's only half of the Chu character. You were a pretender official, Jia Chong, so I became an impostor teacher to match. Now the real magistrate will preside over the court, you can act some more at the court.

JIA CHONG: Oh no! I am sunk!

SHANJING: What are you afraid of? The magistrate is coming into the court. Announce his magistrate's presence!

YUE JUN: (*Enters and recites.*)
Clouds have dispersed and mists dissipated,
Only now can one see the real face of Mount Lu (*lushan* 盧山).[50]
The swallow stone[51] ultimately cannot pass for jade,
How can a fish eyeball get palmed off as a pearl?
Once the distinction has been analyzed and made,
The fiery sheen of the authentic is clearly distinguished.
(*Speaks.*) Bring in Catfish in the Mud!

YAMEN RUNNER: Ho! Kneel towards the front!

YUE JUN: I ask you only how many people you have killed on the boat?

JIA CHONG: There were so many, I can't remember them all. But I did let all the corpses remain whole.

YUE JUN: Ha, ha, ha! What a nasty pirate! (*Sings.*)
Hearing him, my anger cannot but gush up to the Milky Way,
How dare a boatman kill so many, his crime billows up to Heaven.
On this account alone you should be hacked into ten thousand pieces,
Furthermore you dared to use my name and pose as an official.
Pull him down from the docket, and give him forty lashes first.
(*He is dragged down.*)

YAMEN RUNNER: (*Enters.*) We've finished the lashing.

YUE JUN: Sigh!

YAMEN RUNNER: (*Enters.*) I report to my lord. My lord's three wives have arrived.

YUE JUN: Ask them to come in. (*The three wives enter and exit.*)

YAMEN RUNNER: I report to my lord. The general of the southern expedition has sent a messenger with a letter.

YUE JUN: Ask him to come in.

SOLDIER: (*Enters and recites.*)

---

50. A famous mountain in Jiangxi province.
51. A man in the state of Song during the Spring and Autumn period was derided for valuing a *yanshi* 燕石, "swallow stone" as a treasure.

Straddling the saddle, his manly sword sings,
Holding a brush, his winged letters soar.
(*Speaks.*) Your humble messenger kowtows to my lord.
YUE JUN: How is the rebel situation at Nanzhang?
SOLDIER: Please read this, my lord.
YUE JUN: Hand me the letter and wait down there.
SOLDIER: Yes sir. (*He exits.*)
YUE JUN: The Earl of Funing has sent me a letter. Let me take a look. Aiya! This is terrible. Ask Master Li to come here.
SHANJING: Master Li, please come in.
LI HANJIAO: (*Enters backwards and recites.*)
Leaning on the railing, I test out my blue-bladed sword,
Its ten thousand shimmers pierce through the nine Heavens.
(*Speaks.*) My lord has summoned me. What is your command?
YUE JUN: The rebels in Nanzhang are a real scourge. The Earl of Funing has dispatched a letter for me to raise an army to assist the emperor. You can lead the army and stamp out the bandits.
LI HANJIAO: I accept the command. (*He exits.*)
YUE JUN: Send Catfish in the Mud to the drill area and have him executed.
(*A yamen runner responds; recites.*)
Like Chao 超, I throw away my brush to begin a military career,[52]
Riding on dust and smoke, I will achieve extraordinary merit.
To avenge the remaining shame suffered by the Han people,[53]
I will repay the favor bestowed by my sagacious emperor. (*He exits.*)

Scene 14

EARL OF FUNING: (*Enters and recites.*)
Hearing the news, the six prefectures show their bravery,
Within days, the five barbarians will be pacified.[54]

---

52. Ban Chao 班超 was a famous general who served under Emperor Ming (r. 58–76) during the Later Han. He was known for dramatically tossing away his writing brushes to show his determination to pursue a military career.
53. In shadow plays, the Han people as well as China itself, refer to the realm under the control of the central government. Bandits, rebels, and borderland peoples are all grouped together as non-Han barbarians. Hence, although Liu Qianjin and his followers are all ethnically of the Han race, they are represented by shadow figures of barbarians.
54. The "five barbarians" is a common term which refers to all barbarians, but here the number five is used to match the number six in the line above. Only one group of rebels is in fact involved.

(*Speaks.*) I am Zhu Yong, the Earl of Funing. The soldiers have reported that the bandits have come in swarms. Let me go forward and fight them. (*He fights and is routed.*)

YUE JUN: (*Enters with Li Hanjiao.*) The imperial army is losing ground. Brave friends, let's advance and help them. (*Li Hanjiao fights and the rebels get routed. The earl enters.*) Your humble servant came late and caused my lord to suffer a fright.

EARL OF FUNING: If it weren't for my wise younger brother, I would have died. Who is this here?

YUE JUN: His name is Li Hanjiao.

EARL OF FUNING: What an exceptional warrior—just admirable! Return to Shishou County for the time being. I'm going to the capital to present the prisoners first. (*Recites.*)

> The great general, having received imperial favor, defeats barbarians from afar,
>
> The victory report, I will memorialize first to the imperial court.

YUE JUN: (*Recites.*)

> The Son of Heaven[55] has opened the Qilin[56] Pavilion (*qilinge* 麒麟閣),

LI HANJIAO: (*Continues.*)

> Because the general has just defeated Nanzhang. (*They exit.*)

Scene 15

LINIANG: (*Enters with Meiniang, Qianqian, and Miaoying; recites.*)

> Orioles sing in the deep green woods,

MEINIANG: (*Continues.*)

> Swallows chirp encircling carved beams.

MIAOYING: (*Continues.*)

> They all announce good news,

QIANQIAN: (*Continues.*)

> After the stars have fallen, they vie to rise early.[57]

---

55. The emperor.

56. An auspicious, mythical lion-like animal with antlers.

57. The meaning of this line is not clear. It may be related to the fact that prominent people such as rebels and ministers were believed to be represented by their own individual stars in the sky. When they die, their stars fall. Qianqian, as a fortuneteller, may be voicing her observation that because the stars of the rebel generals have fallen, the birds are now chirping bright and early.

SHANJING: (*Enters.*) I report to my ladies. His lordship's support troop to the imperial army scored victory after one battle. The troop will return to the yamen today.

LADIES: What happy news!

YUE JUN: (*Enters with Li Hanjiao; recites*)
>The expanding *qi* from my chest reached right to the rainbow,

LI HANJIAO: (*Continues.*)
>A brave army of one million was within the palm of my hand.

LINIANG: We congratulate his lordship for achieving merit in battle.

YUE JUN: Thanks to Elder Brother Li here. I don't deserve any merit.

QIANQIAN: Elder brother and my lord, the spaces between your eyebrows are broad and open; you will surely be promoted soon.

LI HANJIAO: Here goes your physiognomy again!

SHANJING: (*Enters.*) I report to my lord. An imperial edict has arrived.

YUE JUN: Ladies, please withdraw. Set up the incense table for the reception. (*They kowtow to the earl.*) Please announce the edict my lord.

EARL OF FUNING: The imperial edict proclaims, "According to the memorial presented by the Earl of Funing, Yue Jun, the magistrate of Shishou County, and Li Hanjiao, a local brave, have achieved merit in defeating the rebels. We promote Yue Jun to be governor of Jingxiang 荊襄. We bestow upon Li Hanjiao the title of the barbarian-conquering general (*pingrong jiangjun* 平戎將軍). The Earl of Funing will bring you for an audience immediately." End of the edict.

YUE JUN and LI HANJIAO: Long live the emperor!

EARL OF FUNING: Congratulations to you two!

YUE JUN and LI HANJIAO: We are deeply grateful for your recommendations.

LI HANJIAO: There is one more thing, my lord. My sister, Qianqian, and Zou Meiniang are both engaged to Magistrate Yue, but they are not yet married. I was wondering if my lord would condescend to formalize the marriages as their matchmaker?

EARL OF FUNING: Of course, I would be delighted. Today is an auspicious day. I will have them perform the wedding rituals right away.

YUE JUN: Shanjing, be the master of ceremony.

SHANJING: Yes, sir. (*Recites.*)
>Bow once, bow twice, bow a third time.[58]
>One from an inn, the other from a dinghy;
>How many things conspired,
>Before the marriage transpired.

(*The newlyweds perform the ritual bowing in the hall.*[59])

---

58. Bride and groom bow to each other three times during the wedding ceremony.

EARL OF FUNING: My wise younger brother[60] will head for his new post soon. I will leave for the capital to report on the delivery of the edict.

YUE JUN: Prepare the wedding banquet to bid farewell to his lordship. Please come to the banquet, my lord.

EVERYONE: Yes, please go ahead. (*They exit.*)

The End

---

59. *Baitang* 拜堂, the ritual bowing in the main hall of a residence with all the attendant cere-monies and personages (parents, ancestors in the form of ancestral plaques, the matchmaker, etc.) constitutes one of the most significant formalities of the traditional marriage.
60. This shows the intimacy between the earl and Yue. They are not in fact related.

10: *White Jade Hairpin.* Shadow figures are from Yang Fei's collection. Photo: Huo Zhanping.

The White Jade Hairpin
白玉鈿

Introduction

The White Jade Hairpin is probably one of the most intellectual shadow plays ever written. The plot is tightly knit, and it is also full of humor, idealism, wishful desires, and romanticism. The playwright Li Fanggui, not only uses abundant literary references as he does in his other plays, but he displays amply his knowledge of Buddhism through a debate between a Confucian scholar and a Buddhist monk. As a Confucian scholar very much in the tradition of Han Yu 韓愈 (768–824)—the Tang dynasty Confucian scholar famous for his denunciation of Buddhism—Li Fanggui attacks Buddhism with vehemence, sarcasm, and relish. Although impressive and convincing, his knowledge of Buddhism reflects a Confucian bias. His understanding of Buddhism remains at a mundane rather than philosophical level, and his depiction of the foreign priest is indicative of traditional Confucian pride, insecurity, and distrust of influential Buddhist priests.

The White Jade Hairpin is also very Confucian in its depiction of the romance between the protagonists. Young lovers always meet illicitly and betroth themselves to each other in Chinese operas. But *The White Jade Hairpin* follows a specific trope in Chinese literature which allows the girl to preserve her chastity and integrity, by either meeting with their beloved through a dream or by leaving their corporal bodies. The souls, rather than the bodies, rendezvous and promise themselves to each other.[1] In the case of

---

1. The most famous story of this trope depicts the elopement of the soul of a girl with her beloved who does not realize it until the soul finally merges back into the ailing body. See Chen Xuanyou's 陳玄祐 (Tang dynasty figure) "Lihunji" 離魂記, Zheng Guangzu's 鄭光祖 (Yuan dynasty figure) *Miqingsuo Qiannü lihun* 迷青瑣倩女離魂, and Wang Jide's 王驥德 (Ming dynasty figure) *Lihunji* (Wang 1975, 342).

The White Jade Hairpin, the hero's soul enters the heroine's dream where they vow to marry each other. Despite a certain emphasis on propriety, however, the play is basically a romantic *caizi jiaren* story in which a suspension of disbelief is taken for granted, and the beauty eventually marries the talented after many tribulations. Love transcends mundane reality. The power of love is recognized and the succumbing to love of the protagonists is affirmed. Only an unethical fool would doubt the authenticity of dream meetings.

Compared to human actors' *caizi jiaren* operas, *The White Jade Hairpin* is immensely comical. Dong Yin 董寅, the *chou* 丑 or clown role plays such a large part that he is almost as important as the hero. Narrow-minded and crafty as he is, he is ultimately more of a joker and a rogue than a villain. Sensible but too practical for his own good, Dong provides comic relief with a frequency not found in human actors operas. Indeed, although the playwright enjoys using literary and historical references to show off his erudition and is greatly influenced by *chuanqi* and *zaju* 雜劇 opera, he does add elements to his shadow plays which indicate an awareness of the preferences of a plebeian audience. The preponderance of comic characters like Dong Yin and the impertinent, spoilt Cui Shuanglin 崔雙林—a funny but unlikely young lady of an elite family—are examples in *The White Jade Hairpin*. The playwright provides a sense of satisfaction in having the evils of Dong and the foreign monk exposed and punished. But since Dong is more of a fool than a villain, his punishment is muted. He suffers a beating rather than death. Only the "barbarian" monk, who is portrayed as lecherous, hypocritical, and evil, is executed. But even his demise is summarily carried out. There is definitely a lack of bloodthirstiness in Li Fanggui's plays when compared with the two anonymous plays by semi-literate playwrights that follow this translation.

Cast

BOATMAN: *a boatman fording Dong Yin and Li Qingyan (Scene 4); a later one for Lü Sicheng (Scene 6).*
BUTLER: *housekeeper at Cui's residence.*
CROWD: *officials at Jiangnan* 江南.
CUI SHUANGLIN 崔雙林: *a comic maiden; daughter of Madam Cui.*
DONG YIN 董寅: *a clown.*
INNKEEPER: *innkeeper of the inn where Lü Sicheng, Shang Feiqiong and Li Qingyan stay.*
JIALINZHEN 迦璘真: *Monk's disciple*
LI QINGYAN 李清彥 (LI YAOTIAN 李堯天): *a young scholar; main male protagonist.*
LÜ SICHENG 呂思成: *a bearded official with the rank of Censor; friend of deceased Censor Cui and foster father of Shang Feiqiong.*
MADAM CUI: *an old dame; wife of Censor Cui, mother of Cui Shuanglin.*
MAID: *Shang Feiqiong's maid.*
MATCHMAKER: *a woman hired by Shang Zhi to look for Li Qingyan.*
MONK (NIANZHENCHILA 辇真吃喇): *an evil character with the title of Great Imperial Priest.*
OFFICER: *military officer sent by Monk to arrest and escort Li Qingyan to the capital.*
SERVANT: *Su Tianjue's servant; delivers a letter toil Qingyan.*
SHANG FEIQIONG 尚飛瓊: *a young maiden; main female protagonist.*
SHANG ZHI 尚志 (SHANG LETIAN 尚樂天): *an old scholar; Shang Feiqiong's father.*
SOLDIER: *an underling of Monk (Scene 2 and 5); an underling forLü Sicheng (Scene 7); and an underling for Li Qingyan (Scene 10).*
SU TIANJUE 蘇天爵: *a young Hanlin scholar; Cui Shuanglin's cousin and Li Qingyan's sworn brother.*
YAMEN RUNNER: *a minor civil officer under Su Tianjue.*

Scene 1: Departure for the capital

LI QINGYAN: (*Enters and recites.*)
The aura of a sword has nothing to do with the moon.
The fragrance of a book is not from the flowers.

(*Sings.*)
Alone, I embrace profound learning,
A night-illuminating pearl buried in the dark.
Not selected as a *jinshi* at the Southern Palace,
In vain I possess enough talent to have composed the rhymed
prose on the Western Capital.[2]
(*Speaks.*) I am a native of Jurong 句容 County in Jiangning 江寧. My
surname is Li, the name is Qingyan, and the style is Yaotian. I am a
student twenty years of age. My parents died early. I am not yet engaged—there is no need to mention such things. Very shortly the
Yuanshun 元順 Emperor[3] will be holding an examination to select officials. I would like to go to the capital for the examination, but I am
short of funds for traveling. Fortunately, I have a schoolmate, Dong
Yin, who is the son of an official's family. He has invited me to travel
with him. He will be responsible for all the expenses, provided that I
help upgrade his examination paper somewhat.[4] It's getting late, but I
don't see him yet.

DONG YIN: (*Enters and chants.*)
On the outside, I am one who simply loathes trickery,
In my belly, however, there really ain't nothing.
If you'd like to see the grandeur of a licentiate,
Just look at me stumbling each time I take a few steps.

LI QINGYAN: Elder Brother Dong, you have come.

DONG YIN: Old Li, I greet you with a bow.

LI QINGYAN: I return your courtesy. Please sit down.

DONG YIN: Thank you.

LI QINGYAN: Elder Brother Dong, we are about to leave. Is the luggage
packed and ready?

DONG YIN: Old Li, the luggage has been packed ages ago, but my skills
are not packed at all. So I'd like to clarify our arrangement once
again—the expenses along the way are all on me, the essays in the
exam are all on you.

LI QINGYAN: That is not to be denied. Your younger brother's learning
is scarce and his talent is quite shallow—I only worry that I might
impede elder brother's chances at gaining merit and fame.

---

2. He is comparing himself to the famous rhyme-prose poet, Zhang Heng 張衡 (78–139) of the
Han dynasty.
3. This is a fictional emperor.
4. Li Qingyan has agreed to cheat and go over Dong Yin's examination paper for him.

DONG YIN: You are being modest again! You know that I can hardly hold a brush. Am I to hand in a blank sheet and impede my chances that way?

LI QINGYAN: Oh, you jest.

DONG YIN: Old Li, I heard that a living Buddha from among the western barbarians has just arrived. Let's go welcome him tomorrow.

LI QINGYAN: Elder brother, please go ahead as you wish, but I won't be going.

DONG YIN: Old Li, even the emperor and all the officials will go welcome him. Why not us mere licentiates?

LI QINGYAN: If elder brother is afraid, please go right ahead and don't mind me.

DONG YIN: I'll bid you farewell then.

LI QINGYAN: I'll see you off.

DONG YIN: No need to. Ah, Old Li, Old Li, your learning may be great, but you have no skill in mundane affairs. (*He exits.*)

LI QINGYAN: Ha, ha, ha! This is truly ridiculous! (*Sings.*)

It's lamentable that the entire imperial court has no sense.

Why does it listen to apostasy and favor strange heretics?

All the officials welcome him with absolutely no sense of shame.

I must uphold the religion of light and not disgrace the Apricot Altar,[5]

Even at the risk of having my head chopped off by the baldy.[6]

(*He exits.*)

Scene 2: Scolding the Monk

MONK: (*Led to the stage by an official; sings.*)

The courtyard of the Purple Forbidden City has become my temple,

Jade belt with dragon embroidery[7] exchanged for the monk's robe.

How do I contain this breast full of poisonous dragons?

I count on my glib tongue to enjoy this heavenly luxury.

---

5. Confucianism is known as the religion of light, and Apricot Altar is the place where Confucius established his school.

6. This is a snide reference to the monk's bald head.

7. The Purple Forbidden City refers to the emperor's palace; the jade belt and robe embroidered with dragons refer to the emperor's outfit.

(*Speaks.*) I am a western barbarian monk by the name of Nianzhenchila.[8] Ever since my arrival to China, I have been blessed that the reigning emperor, Yuanshun, is a devout worshipper of the Buddha. The prime minister, Hama 哈麻, recommended me as the Great Imperial Priest. Every day I perform magic with my disciple, Jialinzhen, at the palace. I have petitioned to the Son of Heaven to build a high platform to perform rituals for his immortality. I will select a group of "jade maidens" to hold the banners below the platform. Ha, ha! Emperor Yuan, you may not attain immortality, but I will have the joy of long nights. We have arrived at the Jiangnan region. Guards, get the men and horses ready. (*Sings.*)

> The guards in brocade uniform[9] shout,
> Mountains hum and valleys echo,
> Better than the beating of drums and chiming of bells at temple halls.

CROWD: We, officials of the entire province, greet the Great Imperial Priest.

MONK: No need to be so formal. (*Sings.*)

> Every official, great and small, burns incense to welcome me.
> All the commoners kneel by the roads, chanting Buddhist sutras in unison.
> Underlings, holding staffs, call out before me and crowd behind me.
> Truly, my power shakes mountains and moves the earth.

SOLDIER: I report to the Great Imperial Priest. The students of Jiangnan have set up a Buddhist temple here for Your Reverence.

MONK: Play Buddhist music. (*Music is played; he exits, re-enters, and chants.*)

> Along the river my Buddhist palace sits,
> The mountains glow emerald, the waters clear.
> How many famed flowers[10] will be here
> To set a screen of flesh[11] in front of the altar platform?

---

8. This name sounds foreign and has no meaning. Later changed to Nianzhenhalasi 輦真哈喇斯 in the playscript, it is obviously a concocted non-Chinese name which was even confusing to the playwright/copier.

9. The brocade uniform is worn only by imperial guards.

10. Beautiful girls.

11. Unofficial history has it that the notorious Yang Guozhong 楊國忠 of the Tang dynasty (618–907) was known to have had beautiful women form a screen around him during the winter, which he called a screen of flesh. Yang eventually became a prime minister. He was a paternal cousin of the famous beauty, Yang Guifei 楊貴妃, the beloved consort of Emperor Xuanzong 玄宗 (Minghuang 明皇; r. 713–756).

SOLDIER: (*Enters.*) I report to the Great Imperial Priest. All the students of Jurong County have come to greet you; here is a list of their names.

MONK: Bring forward the list.

SOLDIER: Yes.

MONK: Let me take a look. I heard that there is a licentiate of great talent in Jurong County by the name of Li Qingyan. I must get to know him and use him as an assistant. Why did he purposely not come here today? Attendants, ask one of the Jurong County licentiates to come in, I want to talk to him.

SOLDIER: Come in here—any licentiate of Jurong County. The Imperial Priest wants to ask some questions. (*Off stage: I don't dare go. I don't dare go.*)

DONG YIN: (*Enters.*) I dare go. I dare go. I am licentiate Dong Yin. Greetings to the Imperial Priest.

MONK: Do you know Li Qingyan?

DONG YIN: He is my schoolmate. Of course I know him.

MONK: Why didn't he come to welcome me?

DONG YIN: I did remind him to come, but he said, "You go if you wish, but I am not going." He obviously doesn't care to have the good fortune to see a living Buddha and help with diverting disasters.

MONK: Ha, ha! You are a good fellow. Stand aside, I'll need you later.

DONG YIN: Yes, yes, yes. I am sucking up to the top this time.

MONK: Take this gold placard[12] and subpoena Li Qingyan immediately for questioning.

SOLDIER: Yes, Your Reverence.

DONG YIN: Oh no! If you want to execute him, wait till the exams are over. Otherwise, what am I to do?

JIALINZHEN: Your disciple is here.

MONK: Take ten brocade-robed guards to the Jiangnan area. Look for beautiful girls and bring them here.

JIALINZHEN: Yes, Your Reverence.

SOLDIER: I have brought Li Qingyan here.

MONK: Bring him in. (*Li Qingyan enters.*)

SOLDIER: Kneel!

LI QINGYAN: No.

DONG YIN: Just kneel, Old Li.

LI QINGYAN: Stop it. You are a Buddhist disciple, I am a Confucian scholar. We don't need go through ritual greetings with each other.

---

12. The golden placard bestows upon the bearer imperial authority.

MONK: How rude! Are you implying that Buddhism is inferior to Confucianism'?

LI QINGYAN: It's not necessarily not true. (*Sings.*)

> Succeeding Yao 堯 and Shun 舜,[13] the way of Confucius has ruled continuously,
> His career truly ranks as one with Heaven and earth.
> Your Buddhism is full of exaggerated absurdities,
> No more than heresy to confuse and create havoc in the Central Plain.

MONK: Rubbish! How would a youngster like you know that the Three Thousand Great Thousand World Realms,[14] and all births, deaths, disasters, and fortunes are ordained by the Buddha? If you don't believe in the Buddha, you will die. How can you attain the way of longevity then?

LI QINGYAN: Say no more. In the past, Shennong 神農[15] lived for a hundred and ten years; Zhuantian 顓頊[16] lived until he was ninety-eight years of age; Shaohao 少昊[17] lived for a hundred years; Emperor Shun lived for a hundred and fifteen years; both Yu 禹[18] of the Xia dynasty and Tang 湯[19] of the Shang dynasty lived to a hundred. King Wen 文王 lived until ninety-seven, King Wu 武王[20] lived until ninety-three. I have never heard that these kings and emperors had ever kept a vegetarian diet or invoked the Buddha. Why did they become Sons of Heaven, possess everything within the Four Seas, and live to such advanced age? Tell me.

MONK: As for this . . .

DONG YIN: Aha, he is caught by Old Li!

LI QINGYAN: (*Sings.*)

---

13. The original says Tang Yu 唐虞, which refers to Yao's name, Tao Tang 陶唐; and Shun's name, You Yu 有虞. Yao (r. 2356–2255 b.c.) and Shun (r. 2255–2205 b.c.) were legendary sage kings of high antiquity.

14. A system of three thousand million worlds. My original hand-copied script says, *santian dajie* 三天大界, the Great World of Three Heavens. I thank my friend, A. W. (Anthony) Barber of the Department of Religion at the University of Calgary, for providing me with all the translations for the Indian names in this section. According to Dr. Barber, this should in fact read *sanqian dajie* 三千大界, Three Thousand Great Realms, short for *sanqian daqian shijie* 三千大千世界, Three Thousand Great Thousand World Realms. The Sanskrit words for it is: *trisahasra mahasahasra lokadhatu.*

15. A legendary emperor ca. 2838 b.c., he is also the purported founder of agriculture.

16. A legendary ruler of ca. 2513–2435 b.c.

17. A legendary ruler of ca. 2597–2513 b.c.

18. Founder of the Xia dynasty, Yu was supposed to have ruled from ca. 2205–2197 b.c.

19. Founder of the Shang dynasty, Tang was supposed to have ruled from ca. 1766–1753 b.c.

20. Kings of the Zhou dynasty. King Wen was the reputed founder, but his son, King Wu, was the real usurper and ruler (r. 1122–1115 b.c.).

As the histories of the Five Emperors and Three Kings amply illustrate,
Every one of them enjoyed the throne for no less than a hundred years.
At that time, they did not recite the incantations nor mind the sutras.
How come all under Heaven was prosperous, and people lived in peace?

MONK: Did you know that it was all on account of the protective powers of the Buddha?

LI QINGYAN: You are a follower of the Buddha, do you know when the Buddha's date of birth was?

MONK: That is nonsense. How could the Buddha have a date of birth?

LI QINGYAN: Wait a minute. You are a disciple of the Buddha, yet you don't even even know his date of birth? When Maya,[21] the queen of King Brahma[22] in India, dreamt of a golden person descending from heaven, she became pregnant and gave birth to Siddhartha,[23] the Crown Prince. This took place on the eighth day of the fourth month in the twenty-fourth year of King Zhao 昭王's reign[24] during the Zhou dynasty. This was referred to as Time of Bathing the Buddha.[25] It was not until the third year of King Mu 穆王,[26] when a bright star appeared, that he became Buddha. This King Zhao was the great grandson of King Wu, and King Mu was a great-great grandson of King Wu. How could the Buddha have existed before the three sages[27]? Isn't it total nonsense?

DONG YIN: He managed to dredge it to the bottom this time!

LI QINGYAN: (Sings.)
On the eighth day of the fourth month of King Zhao's reign, Buddha was born.
During King Mu's reign, he became Buddha and preached the sutras in India.
How could his golden body appear before the time of the three sages?
Since you don't know, how dare you babble all this nonsense?

---

21. *Moye* 摩耶 in the Chinese original.
22. This *jingfanwang* 淨梵王 (King Jingfan) is in fact God Brahma, the Creator God of Hinduism.
23. *Xidaduo* 西達多 in the original Chinese.
24. King Zhao ruled from 1052–1001 b.c.
25. The "Time of Bathing the Buddha," *yufuozhiqi* 浴佛之期, refers to the Buddha's birthday.
26. King Mu ruled from 1001–946 b.c.
27. The most famous three legendary rulers, the Yellow Emperor, Yao, and Shun are usually referred to as the three sages.

MONK: What an arrogant pedant! Even after the three sage kings, many imperial families have supported monks and revered the Buddha. Are they all inferior to you?

LI QINGYAN: Not necessarily. For what purpose did they support the monks and revere the Buddha?

MONK: To pray for good fortune and longevity.

LI QINGYAN: Tut, well said! During the Han dynasty, Emperor Ming had dispatched people to India to copy twelve volumes of sutras. He also brought the Indian monk Matanga Dharmaraksha[28] and built the Temple of White Horse outside the western gate of Loyang 洛陽. He is considered a very pious Buddhist. Why, then, did he lose his throne to the constant turmoil and upheavals in his kingdom? Later, Emperor Wu[29] of the Liang dynasty took the tonsure three times; he was eventually forced out by Hou Jing 侯景 and died of starvation at Taicheng 臺城. Where was Buddha then? And, pray tell, why didn't Buddha help?

MONK: As for this . . .

DONG YIN: Got him again!

LI QINGYAN: Listen, Baldy. (*Sings.*)

> Emperor Ming of the Han built the White Horse Temple, yet his throne didn't last.
>
> Emperor Wu of the Liang took the tonsure three times, yet he starved to death at Taicheng.
>
> One might say that the Buddha was not only unable to save others' lives,
>
> He couldn't even prolong his own.

MONK: You are really talking nonsense now. Do you think the Buddha is dead?

DONG YIN: That's correct. The Buddha should be immortal.

LI QINGYAN: Hold it. In the past, the Buddha suffered abscesses on his back. He slept on his side underneath the sala tree[30]—this was the origin for the Sleeping Buddha. He died of this disease later. His disciple Kashyapa[31] came to the tree and wept aloud. His other disciples missed him so much that they carved a wooden statue of him and made offerings to it. Was this death or not? Tell me.

---

28. *Motengzhufalan* 摩騰竺法蘭 in the Chinese original. A. W. Barber provided me with the correct version, *tianzhu motengfalan* 天竺摩騰法蘭, which means "the Indian *motengfalan*," Matanga Dharmasksha. He was a famous monk-translator from Central Asia.

29. He reigned from 502–550.

30. The original calls it a *shuanglinshu* 雙林樹, which should really be *suoluolin* 娑羅林, sala grove or *suoluoshu* 娑羅樹, sala tree.

31. *Jiaye* 迦葉 in the Chinese original.

MONK: This . . .

DONG YIN: Only "this" or could it be "that"?

LI QINGYAN: Let me ask you again. During the first year of the Zhen-guan reign of the Tang dynasty,[32] the Son of Heaven sent his entire court of civil and military officials to welcome the arrival of Buddha's bones outside of the western gate of the capital. Was this true?

MONK: That was the Tang emperor's reverence for Buddhism. How could it not be true?

LI QINGYAN: If Buddha wasn't dead, where did his bones come from? Tell me.

MONK: This . . .

DONG YIN: Oh, yet another "this"!

MONK: Who in this world doesn't die? The important thing is to convert people to do good deeds—this is the compassion of us devotees.

LI QINGYAN: Speaking of compassion, the Buddha might have had it, but baldies like you have hardly any.

MONK: That's utter nonsense! Why would we devotees have no compassion?

LI QINGYAN: Listen. (*Sings.*)

 From the beginning of creation until now, human relationships
  have been of utmost importance.
 How can you bear to sever your flesh and blood, abandon your
  relatives for the tonsure?
 Your own father and mother are completely uncared for,
 Instead, you turn around to preach sutras and dharmas to others.

DONG YIN: This time Old Li has cut him right to the bone.

MONK: Oh, we devotees are beyond the Three Worlds and the Five Forms. What do we care about human relationships?

LI QINGYAN: What—an existence beyond the Three Worlds and the Five Forms? If so, shouldn't you practice self-cultivation in some remote mountain instead of mingling with the imperial court? Neither priestly nor worldly[33]—what the heck are you?

DONG YIN: He is a gourd.

MONK: Oh. . . .

LI QINGYAN: (*Sings.*)

 To practice self-cultivation, you should be in an old temple deep
  in the mountains.

---

32. 627 a.d.

33. The playwright plays a pun here. The words for priestly and worldly, "*seng* 僧 and *su* 俗" resemble the words, "*sheng* 生 and *shu* 熟" which mean "cooked versus raw (food)."

Why dress in crimson and purple robes, and lust after vain luxuries?

You even dare to abuse imperial edicts to tyrannize all under Heaven.

Such transgressions and crimes from you are as countless as the hair on one's head.

MONK: This is outrageous! Do you know that your death is imminent?

DONG YIN: Oh no, Old Li, you are going to die!

LI QINGYAN: Of course, I know. Buddhist temples are veritable killing fields, and monks are the executioners. No wonder the emperor values you.

MONK: So why does he value me?

LI QINGYAN: Because you are good at killing people.

MONK: What a sharp tongue! Kick him out!

LI QINGYAN: There is no need to chase me out. You can't keep me here even if you beg me. (*Sings.*)

    To talk any more with this baldy here,

    Would disgrace the walls and doors of Confucius and Mencius.

    Keeping my head high, I brush past the bright moon curtain.

MONK: (*Sighs.*)

DONG YIN: Your student begs to take my leave.

MONK: Get out! You talk too much.

DONG YIN: Yes, yes, yes. I was just wondering what Your Reverence might want of me. So it's only that I talk too much. Phew!

MONK: What am I going to do? This guy talked like a flowing river. His questions got me completely tongue-tied; he was impossible to rebuke. It's very upsetting! How can I avenge this terrible grief? Yes, let me write a letter to the Prime Minister Bo Yan 伯顏, and ask him to halt the examinations. When Li Qingyan is stuck, he will surely come to me for help. Li Qingyan, ah Li Qingyan, even with your eight pecks of awe-inspiring talent, I'll make you into a Ruan Ji 阮籍[34] and let you weep at the end of your rope. (*Exits.*)

Scene 3: Encounter in the Garden

SHANG ZHI: (*Enters with Shang Feiqiong and maid; recites.*)

    Reading poems and books in a famous Mountain, this is truly the land of happiness.

---

34. One of the most famous scholars of his time, Ruan Ji (210–263) refused to serve the imperial government initially, but was eventually forced to agree most unhappily.

For long, I have considered official carriages and titles as mud for plastering.

SHANG FEIQIONG: (*Continues.*)
> Most heartless are those birds on the branches,
> They purposely fly in pairs towards those in sorrow.

SHANG ZHI: I am a native of Zhenjiang 鎮江. My surname is Shang, the name is Zhi and the style, Letian. I have studied all my life but do not look for fame and glory. My wife had died, leaving one daughter, Feiqiong. Although she is but female, she is quite literary. I would like to find a good husband for her but do not have anyone suitable yet. What can I do?

SHANG FEIQIONG: Daddy, I know not why but for days I have felt restless and would like to go to the garden to cheer up. I wonder if daddy would permit me to go?

SHANG ZHI: Go with the maid but come back soon.

SHANG FEIQIONG: Your child will honor your wish.

SHANG ZHI: It is improper for a girl to leave her boudoir, but I will be lenient because of her youth.

SHANG FEIQIONG: Maid, follow me to the garden for a stroll. (*Sings.*)
> After having traced the pattern for mandarin ducks, I feel no wish
> to embroider it.
> Endless melancholy knits my brows.
> I wish I could confide to the fallen flowers,
> But am afraid that more grief would be added to the sorrowful,
> And I would end up a loser even more. (*They exit.*)

LI QINGYAN: (*Enters with Dong Yin; sings.*)
> The other day, I scolded the evil monk on the riverbank,
> And relieved somewhat the anger in my chest.

DONG YIN: (*Sings.*)
> From now on I must take lessons from superior brains,
> Lest I should appear incompetent in front of others.

(*Speaks.*) Old Li, that monk the other day was awesome, but you snared and then released him seven times.[35] Your questions made that baldy into a gourd without a mouth! Now that we are on our way to the capital and have nothing better to do on the boat, how about teaching me what you said so that I, too, can show off in front of others?

LI QINGYAN: Elder Brother Dong, to know the affairs about the past and present, you will need to read five cartloads of books.

---

35. This is a reference to Zhuge Liang 諸葛亮, the most famous strategist in popular culture. He was the military advisor of the Shu 蜀 kingdom during the Three Kingdoms period (221–220).

DONG YIN: Forget it, forget it then! If I could only read half a cartload of books, I wouldn't need to pay your way!

LI QINGYAN: Oh, you are joking again. Elder Brother Dong, look at how green the mountain is, and how beautiful the river is along the bank! Let's disembark and engage our muses for a while.

DONG YIN: You go ahead and engage your muses, I have nothing to engage. I'll stay on board and engage a couple of chicken eggs. Out of the way, loafers, engaged muses are coming through. (*He exits.*)

LI QINGYAN: He's a funny one. (*Sings.*)
> So coarse, so vulgar, yet so very funny.
> How could he understand my strong desire to seek beauty?
> The lone cloud unintentionally draws the bluebird,
> The flowing river, like a belt, wraps around the waist of the mountain.
> Wine taverns, along the bank, are lined with blue curtains.
> Falling flowers, fluttering in the wind, a shower of red color.
> Singing from fishing boats, the startled birds fly,
> Riding on ox-back, a cowherd crosses the bridge.
> How would that vulgar thing understand the wonder of all this?
> (*He exits.*)

SHANG FEIQIONG: (*Enters with her maid; sings.*)
> One flower blossoms but another falls,
> Auntie Wind mindlessly whirls the fallen petals.
> Withered red adorns the perfumed steps below,
> My golden lotuses[36] move lightly, not bearing to tread on them.
> Ah! My jade hairpin got stuck on the trellis of the climbing rose.

MAID: Miss, please sit down here and take a rest.

SHANG FEIQIONG: (*Sings.*)
> I sit on a garden rock to groom my hair.

LI QINGYAN: (*Enters.*) Whose lovely garden is this? (*Sings.*)
> Exotic flowers and wondrous plants, such varied scenery,
> Variegated shadows from the bamboo adorn the painted walls.
> Cold is the water flowing through the rock,
> Fragrant is the breeze blown from the flowers.
> (*Speaks.*) Wonderful, wonderful, just wonderful! The gate is not closed yet. Let me go in and have a look. (*He enters the garden.*)

MAID: Miss, look at that handsome fellow.

LI QINGYAN: Good gracious! (*Sings.*)
> To which household belongs this gorgeous maiden?
> To what purpose is she strolling in the garden?

---

36. Golden lotuses refer to women's small, bound feet.

Her pear-blossom face is lightly dusted with powder,
The corners of her dark eyebrows resemble distant mountains.
From under the luan-birds on her red sleeves emerge jade bam-
boo shoots,[37]
From the embroidered mandarin ducks on her verdant skirt peek
out golden lotuses.
Surely she is the Goddess of Mercy at her Water Moon Temple,
Surely she is the Goddess of the Moon emerging from her Palace
of Pervading Coldness.
Constantly, her eyes gaze at me,
From time to time she lowers her head and lets cloud-like hairdo
droop to one side.
Such a damsel is truly a rare sight to behold!

SHANG FEIQIONG: Oh, what a handsome man! (*Sings.*)
I espy the face of an immortal in the garden,
It's truly a reincarnation of the handsome Pan An 潘安.[38]
How I would like to ask him his name.

MAID: Miss, what's the matter?

SHANG FEIQIONG: (*Sings.*)
Between us stands only this obstructing maid.
Maidenly shyness touches my pear-blossom face,
Let me lower my head and gently adjust my silk skirt.

MAID: Miss, let's go back.

SHANG FEIQIONG: Fine. (*Sings.*)
Before leaving, I glance his way,[39]
Just like a broken lotus, its silken fibers are yet connected.[40]
(*They exit.*)

LI QINGYAN: Ah, what is this here? It's a white jade hairpin. She must
have dropped it. (*Sings.*)
In an instant, the immortal fairy has returned to Heaven,
In a rush, I hide the hairpin in my sleeve.
Although I can no longer hear the twinkling of her bracelets,
The fragrance of orchid and musk still lingers in the air.
Before leaving, her glimmering eyes glanced my way,
As if she wanted to confide her heart's desires to me.

---

37. Her fingers.
38. Pan An (short for Pan Anren 潘安仁; also known as Pan Yue 潘岳; 247–300) was so handsome that women used to surround him and toss fruits at him.
39. Literally, she sends "autumnal ripples" with her eyes.
40. When a lotus root is broken into halves, silk-like fluid-fibers are produced which continue
to link the two parts. The character for silk, *si* 絲, is homophonous with the word *si* 思, meaning "thoughts and longing."

This love debt from five hundred years ago,
Makes it hard to rein in my galloping will.
Returning to the lakes and mountains, I grieve in vain. (*Exits.*)

Scene 4: Dream Connection

DONG YIN: (*Enters.*) It's getting late. How come Old Li still hasn't come back yet?

LI QINGYAN: (*Enters backwards and sings.*)
> Clearly she dropped a jade hairpin,
> Otherwise, I could have met an immortal in my dream.
> Could it be I entered the Nanchang Garden 南吕院[41] by mistake?
> Or else was I in the Peach Orchard after escaping from the Qin?[42]
> I will have to re-examine carefully the road whence I came,
> So that I can make a trip there to visit once again.

DONG YIN: Ha, ha, ha! Old Li, you are so clever, you can even walk backwards. Watch that you don't fall into the river!

LI QINGYAN: Oh, I am at the boat already.

DONG YIN: Old Li, where did you go? And what's that in your hand?

LI QINGYAN: This is a white jade hairpin dropped by a lady.

DONG YIN: Old Li, where is the lady?

LI QINGYAN: I went up the bank, walked into a garden. There, I saw a lady of such beauty that fish would sink and geese would fall, that the moon would hide in shame and flowers would close![43] She spoke to me with her eyes and would have talked to me. But her maid was there, so she had to leave reluctantly.

DONG YIN: She left herself. The reluctant part was something you imagined. The other day a friend told me about the meaning of lovesickness—it made a lot of sense. He said that during lovesickness, the man lusts after the woman's beauty and the woman adores the man's brain. Because they have no means of meeting, they long for each other and, hence, they contract this lovesickness. You and the girl don't even know each other. The girl has probably tossed out any

---

41. This reference is not clear, it could imply a high-class brothel.
42. According to a famous piece of prose written by Tao Yuanming 陶淵明 (365–372 or 376–427), the protagonist of the tale went to a utopia full of peach orchards inhabited by refugees of the Qin empire. After returning home, however, the protagonist was unable to find this utopia again.
43. She is so beautiful that these animals, plants, and objects hide because her beauty would outshine them. This is a literary cliché.

thought of you beyond the Ninth Heaven already, leaving unlucky you to suffer lovesickness by yourself!

LI QINGYAN: Oh no, where did I lose my purple gold fish?

DONG YIN: See? Luck is as thin as a piece of paper. As soon as you find one thing, you've lost something else. And just now, you were rambling about having gained something extra! I suggest that it's best for you to go to bed, instead of thinking about such absurd things.

LI QINGYAN: But how can I sleep tonight?

DONG YIN: In that case, I'll excuse myself. (*He exits.*)

LI QINGYAN: Where did I lose my purple gold fish? If only it fell in her garden and she found it, then Heaven would be granting our wishes. I should go to bed and look for it tomorrow. (*Recites.*)

> I await the sound of midnight drums from the watch tower,
> So that Duke Xiang 襄王[44] may enter the land of dreams.

(*He sleeps and his soul emerges from the body.*) Elder Brother Dong is fast asleep. Let me take advantage of the bright moonlight and make a visit to the beauty. (*Sings.*)

> On the three mountains the icy wheel[45] surges the midnight tide, the night is still.
>
> I see the dews chilled white and the Dipper tilting its stars,
> And still remember the to-and-fro pathway from yesterday.

Let me take advantage of this bright moonlit night to express my passion. (*He exits.*)

SHANG FEIQIONG: (*Enters with her maid; sings.*)

> My kingfisher-green blanket grows cold on embroidered cushions.
>
> I am in no mood to perfume them with orchid and musk,
> All because of that person's bewitchment,
> All day long I think of love and feel forever dizzy.

(*Speaks.*) Maid, I dropped a jade hairpin in the garden and told you to look for it. Have you found it?

MAID: Miss, I couldn't find the jade hairpin, but I did pick up a purple gold fish by the gate. Please take a look.

SHANG FEIQIONG: What an exquisite piece! I wonder who lost this and who picked up my jade hairpin?

---

44. This seems to be a reference to Song Yu 宋玉's (Warring States period; 403–221 b.c.) poems, "Gaotangfu 高唐賦" and "Shennüfu 神女賦" in which the protagonist meets an alluring goddess at a certain Witch Mountain and enjoys an amorous relationship with her. Song Yu served under Duke Xiang of the state of Chu 楚. These poems may have described shamanic experiences of the king, but have come to represent love affairs with beautiful women.
45. The moon.

MAID: No one else came to the garden today. That person must have picked it up, and he must have been the one who lost the purple gold fish.

SHANG FEIQIONG: If that person had picked it up, that would further add to my worry.

MAID: Miss, let's go to sleep.

SHANG FEIQIONG: I really cannot sleep tonight.

MAID: You can't sleep? Well, I can sleep. Even as I speak, my upper eyelids are begging to join the lower eyelids. (*She exits.*)

SHANG FEIQIONG: My brocade robe hangs loose—for whom have I become thin? Don't know if his heart is the same as mine. (*She sleeps.*)

LI QINGYAN'S SOUL: (*Enters and sings.*)
 Twisting and turning through the fragrant path,
 Around the curving verandahs I arrive at the oriole court.
 Aiya! The lady must have intended to wait for me,
 Inside the small window a dim lamp is lit.
(*Off stage: That man in the garden was so handsome.*)

LI QINGYAN'S SOUL: (*Sings.*)
 The lady is sincere after all,
 Behind my back, she speaks of me two or three times.
 Let me go and rap the double-ringed doorknockers.

SHANG FEIQIONG: (*Her soul emerges from her body.*) Ah! (*Sings.*)
 I rush from my perfumed boudoir to take a peek outside,
 Who is rapping on the double-ring doorknockers at midnight?
(*She opens the door; Li Qingyan's soul enters the room. She sings.*)
 So embarrassed that I don't know where to hide.
 Pray thee, good sir, why have you come hither?

LI QINGYAN: I bow to greet you.

SHANG FEIQIONG: My curtsy to wish you, good sir, ten thousand fortunes.

LI QINGYAN: Deeply moved by your favorable glance in the garden, I have allowed myself to transgress propriety and hope that my lady will not turn her back on my sincerity.

SHANG FEIQIONG: Judging from your appearance, good sir, you must be a man of scholarship. Are you not aware that it is improper for a man and a woman to be in the same room without decreed consent from their parents and the promise of marital arrangement? I am truly ashamed of this situation.

LI QINGYAN: I am not here to seek for anything improper. I beg only for my lady's golden promise. As for marriage, we will need to wait until I attain fame, and then I will arrange for a matchmaker to come with the marriage proposal.

SHANG FEIQIONG: If the good sir has the heart, how could I not share the same feeling? Our vow tonight I will abide by for the rest of my life. Do not let me live till my hair is white to regret this.

LI QINGYAN: I am not the unfaithful type either. My lady can rest assured.

SHANG FEIQIONG: My maid found a purple gold fish by the garden gate. Was it dropped by you, good sir?

LI QINGYAN: So, my lady picked it up after all. I will use this object as my token to you. My lady's white jade hairpin is here with me.

SHANG FEIQIONG: They certainly seem like a heavenly made pair. I will also present this hairpin to you, and we will use them as vouchers when we meet again. Pray thee, good sir, where are you from and what is your name?

LI QINGYAN: I am a licentiate on my way to the capital. I am a native of Jurong County in Jiangning. My surname is Li, my name is . . .

(*Off stage: Miss, who are you talking with?*)

SHANG FEIQIONG: Leave quickly.

LI QINGYAN: Yes. (*Exits.*)

MAID: I was sleeping soundly when I heard Miss chatting away with someone. Hey, there is no one here! Miss, who were you talking with?

SHANG FEIQIONG: Hai! Blasted serf, how dare you make fun of me? (*She hits the maid.*)

MAID: Ouch! Well hit! Well hit! What I just blurted out was mumble jumble. Go back to sleep.

SHANG FEIQIONG: Ai, the man of my dream! (*Sings.*)

> The man in the jade hall is hard to become intimate with,
> In vain I changed into a butterfly seeking the roaming clouds.
> Who will be the needle to pull the thread along,
> And deliver good news to the eastern wall?
> This dream is especially annoying. (*Exits.*)

LI QINGYAN: (*Enters.*) I am traveling. (*Sings.*)

> Returning at midnight, the moon is at its brightest.
> Chang'e 嫦娥[46] is cold and alone by heaven's edge.
> Although Duke Xiang has entered the dream of the Witch Mountain,
> The alluring goddess is far away on the ninth peak.
> I can't stop playing with the jade hairpin.

(*His soul enters his body; speaks.*) My lady,

---

46. Goddess of the moon.

DONG YIN: Aiya, Old Li is talking gibberish—let me fool around with him. Good sir, I can't bear to part from you.

LI QINGYAN: (*Approaches in a hurry.*) Aiya, my lady!

DONG YIN: It's actually an old lady here. Old Li, so I have answered your calls for a young lady all this time. See how you like this humble lady's face?

LI QINGYAN: Elder Brother Dong, please don't be upset. Younger brother was just dreaming. I dreamt of the young lady I met in the garden. I dreamt that I went to her home. It turns out my purple gold fish was picked up by her, so I gave it to her, and she gave the jade hairpin to me. We vowed a hundred-year marital bond to each other in the dream.

DONG YIN: This is really dreaming! Who's ever heard of getting engaged in a dream? If you are right, I wouldn't have to do anything else any more—I'd just dream on. I'd dream that I am in the imperial court. I'd pick my brides from the royal ladies in the three palaces and six harems. Next, I'd dream that I'd become the chief examiner and I'd preside over your exam. What need would I have for you to write the exam essays for me?

LI QINGYAN: I've related my dream to a fool. It's still early, let's go back to sleep.

DONG YIN: You go ahead but I can't sleep any more—in case you should mistake me for your young lady to burrow and grab.

LI QINGYAN: You are really pulling my leg. I am going to get a good rest. Tomorrow I will go to the garden and meet the lady in my dream. (*He sleeps.*)

DONG YIN: Old Li said that he'll go meet his dream lady tomorrow. Am I supposed to foot his travel bills while waiting for him? Might as well get the boat going while he is sound asleep. By the time he wakes up, Zhenjiang would be so far away that he could only move on—so that's my plan. Hey, Boatman!

BOATMAN: Right here, good sir. What's your wish?

DONG YIN: The wind is favorable tonight. Why not be on our way?

BOATMAN: It's completely up to you. Let me pull up the anchor. One push with the pole and we're off.

DONG YIN: (*Sings.*)
How ludicrously unbearable Old Li is,
So you plan to have fun at my expense.
One push with the pole, we've left the bank of Zhenjiang,

How can Fan Li 范蠡 embark on Xishi's 西施 boat[47] now?

Traveling with a favorable wind, the boat is swift as an arrow.

LI QINGYAN: (*Wakes up.*) Elder Brother Dong, I was going to meet with my dream lady tomorrow. Why did you set the boat going overnight?

DONG YIN: We are going to the capital for our civil service exams, not for you to dream on.

(*Off stage: Is Mr. Yaotian on that boat? Please wait for me.*)

SERVANT: (*Enters.*) Your humble servant kowtows to Master Li. My master is serving a post in Jiangnan and dispatched your humble servant to deliver a letter to you. He said it's very important for you to follow the words in the letter.

LI QINGYAN: You go back and send my regards to your master. I won't reply in writing then.

SERVANT: Your humble servant understands. (*Exits.*)

DONG YIN: Open the letter right away. See how much travel money your official friend has sent you.

LI QINGYAN: (*Reads the letter; speaks.*) Is that so.

DONG YIN: Is what so?

LI QINGYAN: Elder Brother Dong, the daughter of Censor Cui of Xingyang 新陽 has just come of age. I have been asked to go there to become his son-in-law.

DONG YIN: You're so lucky everywhere you go.

LI QINGYAN: I just want to meet my dream lady. Who cares about that other marriage? Elder Brother Dong, look at this beautiful scenery along the bank. Let me go for a visit.

DONG YIN: You are going for a visit again? Go ahead, but don't end up in people's gardens any more. It's not good for you to have too many good dreams.

LI QINGYAN: (*Disembarks and recites.*)

After seeing the ocean, it's hard to deal with mere water.

Out of the Witch Mountain, nothing can be called clouds. (*Exits.*)

DONG YIN: I've no idea what Old Li recites at all. Eh, Old Li dropped his white jade hairpin and left his letter here too. Let me put them away for him. (*Off stage: Ahoy, friends on that boat. Are you going to the capital?*) Yes. (*Off stage: You don't need to go there any more. The civil service exams have been canceled.*) Oh no! I've wasted all

---

47. Xishi is one of the most famous beauties in Chinese history. She was presented as a gift from one sovereign to another during the Warring States period during the end of the Zhou dynasty, and she supposedly fell in love with Fan Li, the emissary who accompanied her to her destination.

this travel expense on someone for nothing! Now that the exams are canceled, I won't need Old Li any more. Who cares what he is up to? Oh yes, I have a great idea! I've got Old Li's jade hairpin and letter in my hands. Why not set the boat back to Zhenjiang? I'll disembark there and keep my ears open. If anyone is looking for a dream-gentleman, I'll use his name and sign up for the marriage. I know all about their dreams, and I've got the white jade hairpin as proof too. There is no worry that the marriages won't be on. Ah, Old Li, (*Sings.*)

> Essays you'll do for me,
> Marriages I'll do for you.
> I for you and you for me,
> It's all a bunch of baloney.

Ah, Old Li, you've just had the wrong dream! (*Exits.*)

Scene 5: The Impostor Seeks Marriage

SHANG ZHI: (*Enters and recites.*)
> Before the courtyard, the cassia of Mt. Yan 燕山 blooms no more,
> In the house, the orchid of Master Xie 謝公[48] will wilt soon.

(*Speaks.*) I am Shang Zhi. My daughter has become seriously ill on account of a strange dream. In desperation, I have asked matchmakers to look for the man in her dream. I wonder if they will be able to find him.

MONK: (*Enters with an officer.*) Let's go! (*Recites.*)
> This mandate descends from the Ninth Heaven,
> Its sound startles the Four Seas.

SHANG ZHI: Where is this Imperial Priest from?

MONK: This must be the venerable Shang Zhi. Don't be afraid. Do you have a daughter?

SHANG ZHI: I have a young girl.

MONK: The living Buddha is performing an auspicious ceremony for the Son of Heaven and wants your daughter to hold a banner under the platform. She should leave immediately, without fail.

SHANG ZHI: My daughter has presently taken ill. I beg for the Imperial Priest's compassion.

---

48. Cassias and orchids are plants which represent auspiciousness. Mt. Yan is a mountain in the northern plains of Hebei. Master Xie refers to Xie Lingyun 謝靈運 (385–443), a great poet of the Six Dynasties famed for his poems on nature.

MONK: You are obviously making excuses and should be beheaded.

SHANG ZHI: If only such were not the case—I will send her over within three days.

MONK: All right, I'll give you three days. If you stall, you'll be severely punished. (*Exits with the officer.*)

SHANG ZHI: Bad news! Maid, bring your young mistress out quickly.

SHANG FEIQIONG: (*Enters with the maid.*) Daddy, what is the matter?

SHANG ZHI: My child, you wouldn't have known. An imperial messenger has just come and said that a living Buddha is performing some sort of magic and wants my child to hold a banner under the platform. You'll have to leave within three days. (*Shang Feiqiong faints.*) Wake up, my child!

SHANG FEIQIONG: Alas! (*Sings.*)

> Hearing these words, my soul floats away from fright.
> Unwittingly, my eyes are brim full with tears.
> I blame the emperor and the prime minister
> For favoring and spoiling that monk so.
> Now that calamity has descended from Heaven,
> I call again and again for the man in my dream.
> If you and I had paid the debts from our previous lives,
> How would there be this mess right now?
> Ever since we leaned on each other in the dream,
> Why has there been no news for so long?
> If you won't come to unite the mirror of Lechang 樂昌,
> How will I be able to steal the incense for Hanshou 韓壽?[49]
> Aiya, I'd rather die than destroy my name and chastity,
> It would be better for me to take a rock and jump into the Yangzi River 揚子江.

SHANG ZHI: Don't kill yourself, my child. We will think of a good plan.

MATCHMAKER: (*Enters and recites.*)

---

49. The uniting of the mirror of Lechang refers to the reuniting of couples who were separated unwillingly. According to "*Benshishi:qinggan* 本事詩:情感" by Meng Qi 孟棨 (Tang dynasty; 618–907), when the Chen dynasty (557–589) of the Six Dynasties was about to fall, Xu Deyan 徐德言, the husband of Princess Lechang, broke a mirror in two, and they each kept one half. Years later the princess was taken as wife by Yang Su 楊素 (544–603), a renowned general of the Sui dynasty (589–618). Xu was so heartbroken when he found his wife's half of the mirror at a market that he wrote a poem about it. When the princess read his poem, she wept and refused to eat. Yang Su eventually allowed the couple to reunite. The incense for Han Shou refers to secret love affairs. Han Shou carried on a secret liaison with Jia Wu 賈午, daughter of the high official, Jia Chong 賈充, of the Jin dynasty (265–420). Jia Wu stole from her father a rare incense which had been bestowed upon Jia Chong by the emperor and gave it to Han Shou. When Jia Chong discovered the theft, he married his daughter to Han Shou ("Biography of Jia Chong" in *Jinshu* 晉書).

Wearing out shoes of iron, without finding a trace of it,
Here it now comes to me, without any effort at all.
(*Speaks.*) Congratulations, squire.

SHANG ZHI: Why are you congratulating me?

MATCHMAKER: Squire, the man in her dream has come.

SHANG FEIQIONG: He has come? Where is he?

MATCHMAKER: I've brought him to the study. The description of his dream matches what the miss had said word for word. He also has the white jade hairpin as proof.

SHANG FEIQIONG: Daddy, this is my white jade hairpin. It's him for sure!

SHANG ZHI: Is he a scholar?

MATCHMAKER: A licentiate on his way to the capital—of course he is a scholar!

SHANG FEIQIONG: Daddy, he is a scholar.

SHANG ZHI: Where is he from?

MATCHMAKER: He is a native of Jurong County in Jiangning. His name is Li Qingyan.

SHANG FEIQIONG: It is he, it is he! His surname is Li. Daddy, please decide on my behalf.

SHANG ZHI: But that monk is so powerful. What should we do?

SHANG FEIQIONG: If I could only meet the man of my dream, I would die without regrets.

SHANG ZHI: So be it! Your father is so old, what do I have to be afraid of? Matchmaker, you go ahead and tell him. He doesn't need to bring any dowry, just come over and bow to the ancestral tablet.

MATCHMAKER: Yes. Isn't this a speedy affair! (*Exits.*)

SHANG ZHI: Maid, help your mistress dress up. (*Maid exits and re-enters. Dong Yin kowtows to the ancestral tablets.*) Ahem, how did my child pick such a character?

MAID: (*Enters with Shang Feiqiong.*) Don't rush so, Miss. Is the man in your dream the man we saw in the garden?

SHANG FEIQIONG: Yes.

MAID: The face doesn't quite match.

SHANG FEIQIONG: The dream is already old. Are people not allowed to change? Let me kowtow with him, let me do it!

MAID: Miss, take a look. It's not right.

SHANG FEIQIONG: (*Looks.*) Oh no! (*Sings.*)
I only thought that I had finally escaped from disaster today,
Who would have known that another problem is created through the rush?
Trying to use my jade hairpin to trick me,
But how would I be willing to marry you?

(*Speaks.*) Ah, the man in my dream. (*Sings.*)
> You and I, the double-flowered pistols, will be torn.
> You and I, the heart-sharing silk belt, will be shorn.
> In the future when you look for me here,
> You will only find the goddess of River Xiang 湘娥 to mourn by
> the bank.

(*Speaks.*) Ah, the man in my dream, the man in my dream! (*Sings.*)
> In the past, we imitated sea swallows in the yellow millet dream,
> From now on, we will be the mandarin ducks of the Azure Tomb
> Tower 青陵臺.[50]
> I throw my body into the Yangzi and give death to my life.
> It is the end! (*She plunges into the river.*)

SHANG ZHI: Oh, my child! (*He kneels and falls.*)

DONG YIN: Darn, what a bummer! Didn't get to enjoy the lamb, but got to smell foul and muttony. Of the thirty-six tactics, running away is the easiest! (*Exits.*)

MONK: (*Enters and recites.*)
> Riding noble horses all day long,
> I pick beauteous flowers[51] everywhere.

(*Speaks.*) This is Old Man Shang Zhi. How come you haven't delivered your daughter yet? And why are you crying on the riverbank?

SHANG ZHI: I was just going to report to the Imperial Priest. There is a licentiate on his way to the capital by the name of Li Qingyan. He tried to force my daughter into marrying him. My daughter jumped into the river instead and died.

MONK: Hm. I have an imperial edict to gather beautiful girls. Who dared to cheat me?

SOLDIER: He was the one who slighted your reverence.

MONK: Well, well. Attendants, dispatch brocade-robed guards to the riverbank immediately. Arrest Li Qingyan and send him to the capital for sentencing. (*Recites.*)
> Even if that arrogant youth should have sky-soaring wings,

---

50. The yellow millet dream, *huangliangmeng* 黃粱夢, refers to a fantastic dream. Shen Jiji's 沈既濟 (750?–800) "*Zhenzhongji* 枕中記" relates the story of a traveler who sleeps on the pillow of a Daoist priest and goes through an entire life of success, glory, and decline. When he wakes up from the dream, he realizes that the millet the innkeeper was cooking is not even done. According to *Taiping yulan* 太平御覽 178 and Gan Bao 干寶 (Eastern Jin; 317–420)'s *Soushenji* 搜神記 10, the Azure Tomb Tower was built during the Warring States period (403–221 b.c.). Duke Kang 康王 of the state of Song 宋 lusted after the beautiful wife of Han Ping 韓凭. He ordered Han Ping to build the Azure Tomb Tower and then had him killed after its completion. Han's wife, however, refused the king's advances and subsequently committed suicide at the tower.

51. Picking flowers has the connotation of having amorous relationships.

It will be difficult for him to escape his mortal enemy in a narrow path. (*They exit.*)

MAID: Master, let's go home.

SHANG ZHI: My child! (*They exit.*)

Scene 6: Getting Rescued

LÜ SICHENG: (*Enters and recites.*)
> Not shirking from hardship but avoiding fools,
> Willingly I roam with the stags and deer.

(*Speaks.*) I am the official Lü Sicheng. When Sali Tiemuer 撒里帖木耳 wanted to abolish the civil service examinations, some of us petitioned against it and unexpectedly angered Yan Bo 顔伯. He demoted me to become a secretary to a board at Guangling 廣陵. There is no need to mention this. Censor Cui of Taichang 太倉 passed his exams the same year I did. Unfortunately, he passed away at his official post. His wife will move the family back home. I will visit them today. (*Off stage: Guys, looks like a body floating from upstream. Quick, pull it out!*)

BOATMAN: (*Enters.*) I report to my lord. We managed to save a person floating down the river.

LÜ SICHENG: Is it a man or a woman?

BOATMAN: Her hair's a mess, but she's wearing a brightly colored dress—looks like a bride.

LÜ SICHENG: Give her dry clothes and bring her here.

BOATMAN: Miss, pull yourself together.

SHANG FEIQIONG: (*Kneels.*) Aiya, have pity and save me, my lord!

LÜ SICHENG: Whose daughter are you? Why did you jump into the river?

SHANG FEIQIONG: I am a native of Zhenjiang. My father's name is Shang Zhi.

LÜ SICHENG: So, you are Shang Zhi's daughter. Get up.

SHANG FEIQIONG: My lord is most generous. May I ask how my lord became acquainted with my father?

LÜ SICHENG: He was an old friend of mine. I recommended him to an official post once, but he insistently declined.

SHANG FEIQIONG: Then, my lord must be Uncle Lü.

LÜ SICHENG: That is correct.

SHANG FEIQIONG: Since my lord is an old friend of my father, I would be happy to treat you as a father.

LÜ SICHENG: What a clever daughter! Attendants, buy a maid to take good care of your young mistress. My child, let us go to the back cabin. You can tell me all about the incident of your drowning there.

SHANG FEIQIONG: Your child obeys.

LÜ SICHENG: (*Recites.*)

  Trees on the mountain peaks block the view for one thousand miles,

SHANG FEIQIONG: (*Continues.*)

  The river meanders like the nine bends of winding intestines. (*They exit.*)

LI QINGYAN: (*Enters.*) Cursed Dong Yin, you inferior person, hateful through and through! (*Recites.*)

  You made me into a complete beggar,

  Pitiful as Su Jizi 蘇季子 when his fur coat was gone and his gold exhausted.[52]

  Who will be the washerwoman willing to feed the "royal scion"?[53]

  Pulling my hair, I want to demand justice from the azure Heaven.

(*Speaks.*) The other day I disembarked to go sightseeing along the bank. When I returned, I couldn't find where Dong Yin had taken the boat to. I was completely stuck, as I didn't have a penny with me. I ended up in dire straits, writing poems by people's gates to get by. Ah, my dream lady, when will I be able to reach town and see you again?

OFFICER: (*Enters.*) Heavenly justice may be loose and invisible, but the carp can't get away from the hook. Here is Li Qingyan up ahead. Go and arrest him.

LI QINGYAN: Why are you arresting me?

OFFICER: You forced the Shang family girl to drown herself in the river. We have orders from the Great Imperial Priest to take you to the capital and have you tried for the crime.

LI QINGYAN: I am completely wronged. (*Sings.*)

  Heaven has dropped this senseless calamity but nowhere can I protest.

---

52. According to *Zhanguoce* 戰國策 "*Qince* 秦策 1," Su Jizi lost everything in the process of trying to work for the king of the state of Qin 秦.

53. Royal scion, *wangsun* 王孫, was a polite way for a person to address another person. Han Xin 韓信, the general who helped found the Han dynasty, was in dire straits in his earlier days. A washerwoman at the city moat took pity on him and fed him. When he told the woman that he would repay her handsomely, she answered him with an angry retort, "A grown man like you can't even feed yourself. I give you food (*wangsun*) out of pity. How would it be for repayment!" When Han Xin became rich and mighty, he sent a thousand taels of gold to the washerwoman (*Shiji* 史記 "The Biographies of the Marquises of Huaiyin 淮陰").

This is indeed a heaven-defying snare but I can find no reason for
it.

Yes, obviously that monk fabricated something from naught,
And invented this to avenge the personal humiliation and grievance.

Villain! Heaven will not bless vicious devils like you.

OFFICER: Go! (*They exit.*)

Scene 7: Poking a Hole in the Wall

SHANG FEIQIONG: (*Recites.*)
Half a waning moon hidden behind the western mountains,
Along the river by the city, willows are mist-like.
The sun has set, but where is the village home?
I'm just glad that the trip will end in a couple of days.

SOLDIER: Where is the innkeeper?

INNKEEPER: Coming.

SOLDIER: My lord Censor Lü and his family will need two clean rooms.

INNKEEPER: If you please, my lord. (*They exit.*)

OFFICER: (*Enters.*) Come here, innkeeper!

INNKEEPER: Coming. What red-hot business! What is it?

OFFICER: On orders from the Great Imperial Priest, we have an important prisoner in custody. We need a quiet and secluded room to lock
him in and will be on our way at the fifth watch[54] in the morning.

INNKEEPER: I've got three good rooms. Lord Lü took one; his family
took another. The last one is separated from the family by a paper
wall—it may be awkward.

OFFICER: We'll lock him up in that room. Innkeeper, this is an important
murder criminal—you've got to be careful! (*All exit.*)

SHANG FEIQIONG: (*Enters and sings.*)
Slowly, I pull the wick of the dimming lamp next to the small
window,
Instead of longing for my love, I now resent him.
Ten thousand melancholic thoughts in my heart,
Why do I only feel the endlessness of this night?

LI QINGYAN: I, Li Qingyan, am so anguished! (*Sings.*)
I had truly hoped to climb atop the blue clouds in one stride,
To eliminate heresy and uphold morality for the world.

---

54. About 4 a.m.

Who would have thought that I would fall into the scoundrel's snare?

Incessantly, I appeal to Heaven over and over again.

(*Speaks.*) Ah, my dream damsel. (*Sings.*)

We two communicated in the dream,

Just like a pair of mandarin ducks born to be so.

You are there awaiting for our auspicious day,

How would you have known about my present fate?

I can't help but weep aloud in my sorrow.

SHANG FEIQIONG: (*Sings.*)

Suddenly I hear loud weeping from the other side,

Lightly I move my lotus feet to the paper wall.

Wetting a tiny hole to take a good look at him,

How could it be precisely the man of my dream!

I see him with iron chains around the neck,

His hair disheveled, his face sallow.

How did you end up in this shape?

Unwittingly, my winding intestines are torn asunder.

Ai, my poor dear, ai ai ai.

There may be other people going in and out of the inn,

I weep but dare not raise my voice.

(*Speaks.*) I believe he is a man of letters and would surely know the rites and laws. How did he get ensnared in the criminal's rope? Some scoundrel must have victimized him. (*Sings.*)

A scholar like you must fear the law,

So, how did you become another Gongye Chang 公冶長?[55]

(*Speaks.*) Man of my dream, oh, man of my dream! (*Sings.*)

For you, I was bedridden within my spring brocade curtains.

For you, I also jumped into the Yangzi River.

By fortune, we get to see each other today,

In regret, we are separated by this extraneous piece of paper.

We two are ill-fated in the same way,

Each has embraced grievances of a different sort.

I am the Woman of Qi 齊婦 whose grief caused three years of draught,

You are Zou Yan 鄒衍 whose wrongful imprisonment brought frost in August.[56]

---

55. Gongye Chang was a son-in-law of Confucius. He was supposed to have been able to understand bird language. However, I have not been able to find any reference to his being wrongfully imprisoned.

56. In both the tale of the Woman of Qi and Zou Yan, the integrity of these characters was manifested through abnormal weather conditions which indicated the displeasure of Heaven.

124

The more I think, the more disenchanted I become.

(*Speaks.*) I had made a terrible mistake. The white jade hairpin I gave him before must have been stolen by the deceptive monster. Now it is back in my hand, why don't I give it to him again to use as evidence for our future meeting? Jade hairpin, oh, jade hairpin, (*Sings.*)

For your sake, I nearly lost my life.

Back to my beloved, I now deliver you.

To become husband and wife in this life, I no longer expect.

I only hope you will bring Duke Xiang to me in my dreams.

LI QINGYAN: Ah, what is that sound? Let me have a look. So, it's a white jade hairpin. Oh, it's the jade hairpin! (*Sings.*)

I remember losing it at Zhenjiang,

How did it show up today in this inn?

This has been a completely confusing mess,

Unless I am still in the land of dreams.

(*Speaks.*) There is a small hole in the paper wall. It must have come from there. Let me take a peek. Ah, isn't that the lady in my dream? Let me ask her. Oh no, I can't. If anyone should hear us, it would be a case of passing disaster to the pond fish when the city watchtower catches fire. (*Sings.*)

I want to tell her the causes and effects,

But am apprehensive of bringing her misfortune and disaster.

Oh, my lady, I will most likely lose my life,

There will be no more good dreams of entering Gaotang 高唐.[57]

When you paint your eyebrows, don't look for Zhang Chang 張敞.[58]

And at Tiantai 天臺, don't hope to remember Mr. Ruan 阮郎.[59]

The Woman of Qi was a young widow of the Han dynasty who refused to remarry. Although she served her mother-in-law most filially, she was wrongfully indicted for murdering the woman. The region suffered three years of draught after she was executed (*Hanshu* 漢書 "Biography of Yu Dingguo 于定國"). Zou Yan was a philosopher during the end of the Warring States period. According to *Huainanzi* 淮南子 and *Taiping yulan*, Zou Yan served Duke Hui most loyally but was slandered by his enemies and executed by the duke. When he died, frost covered the ground during the Sixth Month. Both these stories influenced the most famous Yuan playwright, Guan Hanqing 關漢卿's (13th century) renowned play, *Dou'e yuan* 竇娥冤.
57. Gaotang refers to Song Yu's "*Gaotangfu* 高唐賦" in which the protagonist meets a goddess and has an amorous affair with her. See footnote 42.
58. Zhang Chang was known for helping his wife paint her eyebrows (*Hanshu* "Biography of Zhang Chang"). This act has come to represent conjugal felicity.
59. Mr. Ruan, *Ruanlang*, refers to Ruan Zhao 阮肇 who, along with Liu Chen 劉晨 supposedly visited with a couple of beautiful immortals at Mount Tiantai 天台 while picking herbs in the mountain. Seven generations had elapsed when they returned after half a year with the fairy la-

OFFICER: (*Enters.*) Put the cangue on and let's go.

LI QINGYAN: Our debt is over as of tonight.[60] (*Exits with the soldier.*)

SHANG FEIQIONG: (*Peeks from the hole in the wall.*) Ah, the man of my dream! (*Sings.*)

> In a blink, he is taken away, leaving no trace.
> Suddenly, the pair of mandarin ducks are scattered apart.
> I thought we would be together for the rest of our lives,
> Who would have known I was burning a broken joss-stick?
> My soul in dream would like to go with you,
> If only it knew where you would be tonight.

MAID: My lady, time to sleep.

SHANG FEIQIONG: (*Sings.*)

> I suddenly hear the golden rooster crowing next to my ears. (*Exits.*)

Scene 8: Saving the Scholar

SU TIANJUE: (*Enters and chants.*)

> Moss-covered platform and old trail show no human trace,
> Cold creeks and frigid springs murmur endlessly.
> Still remembering the highest twin peaks,
> I wish my feelings could match those of the ancients.

(*Speaks.*) I, Su Tianjue, am returning to the capital after completing an inspection circuit decreed by the emperor.

OFFICER: (*Enters with Li Qingyan in custody.*) Move!

LI QINGYAN: (*Sings.*)

> Everything topsy-turvy, how I hate Heaven and earth;
> Tigers and leopards are bullied by dogs and sheep.
> Scoundrel, I'll make sure your head and body will end up east and west.

YAMEN RUNNER: I report to my lord. It looks like Master Li Qingyan up the road. For some reason, he is in shackles.

SU TIANJUE: This is very strange! Summon the escorting officer here.

YAMEN RUNNER: Hello, escorting officer, my lord summons you.

OFFICER: Yes, attending to my lord.

---

dies. This popular story is included in Liu Yiqing 劉義慶's (403–444) *Youminglu: shenxianji* 幽明錄: 神仙記.

60. This refers to the belief that marriages and love affairs are results of debts incurred during one's previous life.

SU TIANJUE: Release the shackles on Master Li. I have questions for him.

OFFICER: We don't dare. He is an important murder criminal.

SU TIANJUE: What, an important murder criminal? Just release him—I will take full responsibility.

OFFICER: We are afraid of the monk's punishment.

SU TIANJUE: Tut, such brazenness! You are afraid of the monk's punishment, are you not afraid of mine?

OFFICER: Of course, I'll unshackle him. (*Exits.*)

SU TIANJUE: Attendants, help Master Li to a change of clothes.

LI QINGYAN: (*Exits and re-enters.*) Thank you, elder brother, for saving my life!

SU TIANJUE: For what reason was my wise younger brother ensnared by the villains?

LI QINGYAN: Elder brother, I am not clear about this myself. I was touring Zhenjiang the other day when my traveling companion, Dong Yin, found out that the civil service exams were canceled. He took off with the boat and left me destitute with nowhere to turn. Just then that baldy had me arrested, claiming that I had forced a certain daughter of a Shang family to drown herself in the river. Actually, I have no idea as to the root to this calamity.

SU TIANJUE: So how did the calamity start?

LI QINGYAN: Elder brother, please listen. (*Sings.*)

> That baldy misused an imperial edict to tyrannize the river basin,
> All gentry and officials gathered to welcome him, bowing and burning incense.

SU TIANJUE: Did my wise younger brother go?

LI QINGYAN: (*Sings.*)

> An upright man should always be adamant in supporting orthodox teachings.[61]
> That day I gave the baldy a thorough scolding,
> For that he remembers me with vengence in his heart.
> And now he has trumped up this charge,
> To elder brother I will relate in detail from beginning to end.

SU TIANJUE: I sent you a letter the other day. Did you go visit my aunt?

LI QINGYAN: I have read the letter but haven't gone there yet.

SU TIANJUE: That's all right. Now that Yan Bo has died, the Prime Minister of the Left, Tuota 脱塔, and the Prime Minister of the Right, Tie-

---

61. Confucianism.

muer—both wise ministers—have petitioned to the throne and had the exams revived. Follow me to the capital now and take the exams first. Once you've achieved fame, you and I can jointly petition to the throne to get rid that monk and vent our anger.

LI QINGYAN: Thank you, elder brother, for your assistance.

SU TIANJUE: Attendants, come. Lead the horse for Master Li. (*Sings.*)

> If Xiong 雄's literary works had been recommended earlier—

LI QINGYAN: (*Continues.*)

> Your old friend might already have written the "Changyangfu" 長楊賦.[62] (*They exit.*)

Scene 9: Clarification of the Hairpin

DONG YIN: (*Enters and sings.*)

> Who could've guessed that my lucky affair would come to naught?
> To no purpose I've ruined a life.
> My luggage was completely lost,
> My flight was—like a waft of wind—fast.

(*Speaks.*) Ahem. I only wanted to use his name and get a wife. I didn't expect that the woman would toss herself into the river. In my rush up the bank to duck into the woods, I even lost all my luggage. Where should I go now? Yes, I've got it. I still have Hanlin[63] Su's 蘇翰林 recommendation letter to Li with me. Why don't I go to Xinyang and try to get married again? Maybe my marital star awaits me there—so this will be my plan! (*Sings.*)

> You win some and you lose some.
> If it doesn't work here, try there. (*Exits.*)

MADAM CUI: (*Sings.*)

> Su Tianjue said that the man is as talented as Ban 班 and Ma 馬.[64]
> Su had already written for him to visit us.
> As it has been quite a while without any news, I am worried
> That it could be another case of a moon in the water or a flower in the mirror.

---

62. Xiong refers to Yang Xiong 揚(楊)雄 (63–18 b.c.), a Han dynasty scholar who wrote the rhyme-prose "*Changyangfu.*"

63. The highest literary degree.

64. Ban refers to Ban Gu 班固 (32–92), writer of *Hanshu*, and Ma refers to Sima Qian 司馬遷 (145? or 135?–87? b.c.), author of *Shiji* 史記. Both of them are famous historians.

How can one not be uneasy?

BUTLER: I report to madam. The lord Censor Lü has arrived.

MADAM CUI: Invite him in.

BUTLER: Lord Lü is invited to come in.

LÜ SICHENG: (*Enters with Shang Feiqiong; recites.*)
> Things remain but the person is dead, never to meet again.
> Tying up my horse in an empty court, I am overcome with grief.

SHANG FEIQIONG: (*Recites.*)
> The green bamboos before the window thrive in an open yard,
> The azure mountain outside the gate looks the same as ever.

LÜ SICHENG: Sister-in-law Nian 年嫂, greetings to your well-being and prosperity.

MADAM CUI: Thanks for your concern, Brother-in-law Lü. Please take a seat.

LÜ SICHENG: Thank you. Bow to your auntie, my child.

SHANG FEIQIONG: Yes. I wish auntie ten thousand fortunes.

MADAM CUI: Don't stand on formalities. Please take a seat.

SHANG FEIQIONG: Thank you very much.

MADAM CUI: Where did this child come from?

LÜ SICHENG: You would not have guessed, sister-in-law. This is the daughter of Shang Zhi in Zhenjiang. She tried to drown herself on account of a marriage proposal. I saved her and adopted her as my foster daughter. I am going to Guangxi for my post. Not only is the way far and treacherous, but it also makes the communication between her and her father very difficult. I would like to leave her with Sister-in-law Nian for a while; she can keep your daughter company.

MADAM CUI: That would be fine.

SHANG FEIQIONG: How could I bear to part with you, daddy?

LÜ SICHENG: Don't be upset, my child. I'll dispatch people to send a message to your father and also to look for the man in your dream for you. You stay here and serve your auntie.

SHANG FEIQIONG: Your child obeys.

LÜ SICHENG: Sister-in-law Nian, I have a deadline to meet and dare not to stay for too long. I bid you farewell.

MADAM CUI: If such is the case, I would not detain you any further. Butler, see Lord Lü out.

BUTLER: Yes, Madam.

LÜ SICHENG: There is no need. (*Recites.*)
> There is no three-foot boy to see guests off,
> Remembering the past, I take pity on the deceased. (*Exits.*)

MADAM CUI: Maid, send for your young mistress. Tell her that her elder sister is here.

CUI SHUANGLIN: (*Enters.*) Where is the elder sister? Where is the elder sister? Who are you, elder sister?

MADAM CUI: Elder sister is elder sister. How can you ask who she is?

CUI SHUANGLIN: I need to find out for sure. I can't muddle-headedly call just anybody elder sister!

MADAM CUI: Miss, give us, mother and daughter, a detailed account of yourself: your name, place of origin, the incident of your drowning, etc.

SHANG FEIQIONG: Auntie and young mistress will laugh if I tell you.

CUI SHUANGLIN: I won't laugh, I won't laugh. No way will I not laugh at anyone!

MADAM CUI: Nonsense! She will not laugh at anyone.

SHANG FEIQIONG: Auntie and young mistress, please listen to me. (*Sings.*)

> My home is at the mouth of Zhenjiang, a rustic village in a wild country.
>
> I am a daughter of the Shang family, my name is Feiqiong.

CUI SHUANGLIN: Aiya! Elder sister has such an elegant name! Xu Feiqiong 許飛瓊 is a goddess; elder sister is more beautiful than she.

MADAM CUI: What an impertinent young miss. Don't interrupt her.

SHANG FEIQIONG: (*Sings.*)

> My father is a retired scholar, his reputation spreads throughout the two rivers.
>
> To get away from the mundane world to enjoy the woods and springs, he gave up the official hairpin and tassels.

CUI SHUANGLIN: If uncle is a retired scholar, elder sister must also be literate.

SHANG FEIQIONG: (*Sings.*)

> No more than messy scribbling to make do at social occasions,
>
> I cannot compare with talented women of old like Ban 班 and Xie 謝.[65]
>
> One day, to dispel boredom, I took a stroll in the garden,
>
> Under the landscape lake rock, I chanced to meet a young scholar.

CUI SHUANGLIN: Elder sister is so lucky!

MADAM CUI: Ahem! What nonsense from you.

SHANG FEIQIONG: (*Sings.*)

> For five hundred years, we two shared a love deep and strong.

---

65. Ban refers to Ban Zhao 班昭 (49?–120?), a female historian and scholar of the Han dynasty who also served as an instructor for the empress and imperial consorts. Xie refers to Xie Daoyun 謝道韞 (an Eastern Jin figure; 317–420), a famous female poet.

During that night, we met again in a dream of Nanke 南柯.[66]

CUI SHUANGLIN: Guess you two got married in the dream.

MADAM CUI: Enough talk!

SHANG FEIQIONG: (*Sings.*)

> White jade hairpin and purple gold fish we presented to each other,
> But only a heavy sigh was I left with when I woke.
> Every day I toyed with the gold fish—mind and soul unsettled.
> Gradually, my robe and belt became loose—I fell seriously ill.

CUI SHUANGLIN: It was only natural that you'd get sick. Anyone would have gotten sick under those circumstances!

MADAM CUI: It was not up to you.

CUI SHUANGLIN: It was not up to you—who asked you anyway?

MADAM CUI: Later on, why did you try to drown yourself?

SHANG FEIQIONG: Ah, auntie! (*Sings.*)

> There was a big monk, full of tyranny,
> Who chose me to be some banner-bearing jade maiden.
> Then suddenly a matchmaker arrived with a message,
> She claimed to have found him—the man in my dream.
> He presented the white jade hairpin as the obvious proof,
> And described the dream word-for-word just as I did.

CUI SHUANGLIN: If so, he must have been the real brother-in-law!

MADAM CUI: Aren't you ashamed of being so talkative?

SHANG FEIQIONG: But it was not him at all! (*Sings.*)

> I do not know who it was that used his name.
> I only realized that he was a monster at the wedding.

CUI SHUANGLIN: So what happened? Who was it in your dream? And who got married to you?

SHANG FEIQIONG: (*Sings.*)

> One can only blame myself for being an ill-fated beauty.
> For a dream, I have brought onto myself such a disaster.
> Life no longer valued, I threw myself into the river,
> But then, fortunately, at the end of my rope, bright flowers and dense willows appeared.
> I was saved by Uncle Lü; to him I'm forever grateful.

MADAM CUI: What was the name of the person who forced you to die?

SHANG FEIQIONG: His name was Li Qingyan.

---

66. A dream which represented an alternative existence. According to the renowned Tang *chuanqi* 傳奇 story by Li Gongzuo 李公佐 (8th–9th centuries), "Biography of the Magistrate of Nanke" (*Nanke taishouzhuan* 南柯太守傳), a man falls asleep beneath a tree and dreams a life of glory and eventual downfall. He wakes up and realizes that he entered the realm of a nation of ants which inhabit the base of the tree.

CUI SHUANGLIN: Elder sister, how did he look?

SHANG FEIQIONG: Incredibly ugly.

CUI SHUANGLIN: Ah, ah, ah! My good cousin, a good match you've made for me!

MADAM CUI: Su Tianjue, you little rogue, fine nephew of mine!

CUI SHUANGLIN: (*Sings.*)
> Hearing this, my heart becomes flaming mad.
> I blame my old lady, the fault is all yours.

MADAM CUI: Idiot, you're going to kill me from shaking me!

CUI SHUANGLIN: (*Sings.*)
> You have but one single precious daughter,
> Why ask everyone you meet to consign me randomly?
> You can't wait to be rid of your child,
> You don't care if I live or die afterwards.
> This daughter of yours may be a money-losing investment,
> But I'd rather die than marry that creature.
> My dear elder sister, ah!
> It's now my turn to jump into the river,
> It's now my turn!

SHANG FEIQIONG: Auntie, why is young mistress so upset?

MADAM CUI: You wouldn't have known, miss, but the Li Qingyan you mentioned was recommended by my nephew, Hanlin Su, as a talented beau for my daughter.

SHANG FEIQIONG: If your nephew is a Hanlin, he wouldn't have recommended someone like that. There may be another Li Qingyan.

CUI SHUANGLIN: Elder sister, how many Li Qingyans do you think there are in this world?

MADAM CUI: There must be a hundred.

CUI SHUANGLIN: There must be ten thousand—who asked you?

SHANG FEIQIONG: I think that monster is not Li Qingyan for sure. I think the man in my dream is Li Qingyan. Auntie, just think. If that monster could steal my white jade hairpin, why couldn't he have also assumed someone else's name?

MADAM CUI: That makes sense. But if the Li Qingyan recommended by my nephew is the man in your dream and you two had already made a hundred-year engagement, then there is no hope for my daughter's marriage.

SHANG FEIQIONG: Auntie, if he is indeed the one recommended by your nephew, then young mistress and I can reenact the story of Ying

Huang 英皇.[67] I do not know how my wise younger sister feels about it?

CUI SHUANGLIN: If elder sister can put up with me, why would I have any reason to be unwilling. I'm willing, I'm willing!

MADAM CUI: Don't you ever feel embarrassed?

CUI SHUANGLIN: Aiya, of course I am not embarrassed! You should mind your own business!

BUTLER: I report to madam. A sworn brother of Master Su by the name of Li Qingyan, of Jurong County in Jiangning, has come to visit. He has a recommendation letter from Master Su.

MADAM CUI: Good timing.

CUI SHUANGLIN: Oh no! He has a letter—maybe he is the real one.

SHANG FEIQIONG: If he could steal my jade hairpin, why couldn't he have stolen your letter? You and I will stand behind the screen to see if he is the Li Qingyan of my dream or the Li Qingyan who forced me to death. Let us take a good look before we decide on a course of action.

CUI SHUANGLIN: Follow me then, elder sister. (*They exit.*)

MADAM CUI: Tell him to come in.

DONG YIN: Widows are easy to trick. I'll most likely succeed this time around. Mother-in-law above, your student, Dong—

BUTLER: What Dong?

DONG YIN: Dong! Don't know the customs here.

BUTLER: How can a scholar not know? Bow and kowtow when you meet someone.

DONG YIN: It's the same then. Mother-in-law above, your student, Li Qingyan bows and salutes you.

MADAM CUI: Ahem.

SHANG FEIQIONG: Younger sister, it's the monster that forced me to jump into the river.

CUI SHUANGLIN: Why don't we go out and order the servants to beat the truth out of him. That'll also help solve our puzzle.

SHANG FEIQIONG: Butler, lock the gate.

DONG YIN: What? They locked the gate. The local custom is certainly different—they welcome their son-in-law by closing the gate. Are you looking for chicken eggs?[68]

BUTLER: No chicken eggs—only chicken beaters.

SHANG FEIQIONG: Ugly thief, do you recognize me?

---

67. Ying and Huang refer to the two daughters of the legendary sage king, Yao (r. 2356–2255 b.c.) who married both of them to his heir, Shun (r. 2255–2205 b.c.).

68. People used to close the door so that egg-laying hens would not get away before they laid their eggs.

DONG YIN: Oh no! Beat the ghost, beat the ghost! Young lady, I shouldn't have forced you to die.

SHANG FEIQIONG: Ugly thief, how did you learn about our dream? How did the white jade hairpin end up in your hand? What is your name? Tell the truth!

BUTLER: Are you talking or not? (*He beats Dong.*)

DONG YIN: Don't beat me. I'll tell the truth. (*Sings.*)
>Li Qingyan is a classmate of mine,
>For the examinations, we traveled to the capital.
>My name is Dong Yin, we shared the same boat,
>He is in fact the man in your dream.
>Due to our friendship he told me all about it.
>The jade hairpin he dropped on the boat deck.
>That day when ashore he went,
>He left with me his name to abuse and his bride-list to use.

MADAM CUI: Miss, ask him how Hanlin Su's recommendation letter ended up in his hands?

DONG YIN: No need to ask. The letter and the jade hairpin are from the same trick book.

SHANG FEIQIONG: Butler, drive him out. (*Butler beats Dong. They exit.*)

CUI SHUANGLIN: Elder sister has predicted everything like a god. You are so wise!

MADAM CUI: Well, well, well. Now we can relax. (*Recites.*)
>Talented scholar—happily we receive true news concerning him,
>Frail damsel—when will she match the fine son-in-law?

SHANG FEIQIONG: (*Sings.*)
>Now we can only wait for the luan-bird to settle,
>And watch the phoenixes perch on the same branch. (*They exit.*)

DONG YIN: (*Enters.*) Aiya, aiya! Strange, very strange! I saw with my own eyes the Shang daughter drown in the river. Why is she here? She can't be Censor Cui's daughter. What do I care who she is? The bottom line is that I didn't get the beauty, and I did get a beating for nothing today. How can I settle the score? Yes, why don't I report her to the monk as a way to get even? That wench is nasty, really nasty! She even had me beaten, badly beaten! I'll borrow the knife of another to kill the enemy to vent my anger. I'll vent my anger! It'll definitely be difficult for her to escape from this trap—this clever trap! (*Exits.*)

Scene 10: Executing the Monk

SU TIANJUE: (*Enters with an officer and Li Qingyan; recites.*)
  A decree arrives from the Weiyang Palace 未央宫,
  He climbs the platform flanked by imperial guards.
  When Heaven bestows a seat atop the three terraces,
  The man should be able to soar ten thousand miles.[69]
  (*Speaks.*) I am the official Su Tianjue.
LI QINGYAN: I am the official Li Qingyan. It was my good fortune to be saved by elder brother the other day. Upon arriving at the capital, I received top ranking at the exams and was appointed as a Hanlin scholar by the emperor. Elder brother and I jointly petitioned a memorial against that monk. His Majesty was furious and bestowed upon us an Imperial Treasured Sword with which to execute the monk immediately. The selected jade maidens are to be sent home. This is so exhilarating!
SU TIANJUE: Wise younger brother, I fear that the scoundrel may escape. We need to expedite our trip.
LI QINGYAN: Exactly. Send the order that we will advance speedily for Zhenjiang day and night. (*They exit.*)
MONK: (*Enters with Dong Yin; recites.*)
  Prayer halls are always appreciated from beyond the clouds,
  Incense pavilions are indeed a passion of this world.
  (*Speaks.*) Master Dong, the Censor Cui's daughter you reported yesterday—how does she compare with Shang Zhi's daughter?
DONG YIN: Good, good. Don't know if my heart has gone astray, but the two looked exactly the same.
SOLDIER: I report to the Great Imperial Priest. We have brought Censor Cui's daughter.
MONK: Tell her to come in.
SOLDIER: You are ordered to enter.
SHANG FEIQIONG: Here I am.
  Today, my resentment surges against the lotus seat,
  In the future the voice of the wronged will be heard at Changmen 长门.
SOLDIER: Kneel!
SHANG FEIQIONG: I will not kneel to him.
MONK: Such brazenness deserves death!

---

69. Heaven refers to the emperor. This poem suggests that he [Li Qingyan] is well regarded by the emperor and hence should enjoy great success.

SHANG FEIQIONG: This ladyship of yours has come especially to die, baldy. (*Sings.*)

> This ladyship of yours is full of daring since childhood,
> Who's afraid of your forest of swords and mountain of knives?
> I only regret that I cannot chop off the baldy's head right away,
> How can Buddhism tolerate your heaven-pervading sins and crimes?

DONG YIN: Ai, this place is not like your home where you can lock the gate and beat people up.

SHANG FEIQIONG: Dong Yin, you thief! (*Sings.*)

> Willing to be dog to the hawk of a scoundrel monk,
> How would you know of unexpected changes in the future?
> I see your crimes and sins are full to the brim this very day,
> I will wait for you in front of the mirror of retribution.[70]
> Take the head of this ladyship of yours right away.

MONK: Who's going to kill you? Attendants, tie her up on the side. (*She is taken away.*)

SOLDIER: I report to the Great Imperial Priest. An imperial envoy has arrived.

MONK: Let me go to welcome him.

LI QINGYAN: (*Enters with Su Tianjue and four soldiers.*) You, Nianzhenchila. Look and see who I am.

MONK: You are Master Li.

LI QINGYAN: No, I am not Master Li. I am the fifth King of Hades here to fetch that dog head of yours! Attendants, off with the rascal's head! (*They kill him.*) Behead all his follower monks, too. (*Soldier exits and re-enters.*)

SOLDIER: I report to my lord. I caught a licentiate among the monks.

LI QINGYAN: Bring him up. (*Dong Yin enters, escorted by the soldier.*) Dong Yin, I finally see you again.

DONG YIN: Who is this? (*He looks.*) Oh, it's you, Old Li.

LI QINGYAN: Pull this dog hide to one side and tie him up.

SHANG FEIQIONG: (*Off stage: Oh, what misery!*)

LI QINGYAN: Dong Yin, who is the woman that's crying?

DONG YIN: That's Censor Cui's daughter.

SU TIANJUE: Why, that's my cousin! Untie her quickly! (*Soldier exits then re-enters with Shang Feiqiong.*) Oh, dear cousin—why, this is not she!

LI QINGYAN: Why, it is she!

---

70. This mirror is found in the Chinese purgatory or Hell, at the first court of judgment.

SHANG FEIQIONG: Is that the man in my dream? Let me ask him. No, I
cannot. He was a prisoner—how did he become a high official? There
are many people who look alike in this world—I could be mistaken.
That mysterious event in my dream was not totally credible. Let me
see how he questions me. My lord, save me.

LI QINGYAN: Whose daughter are you? Why are you here? Describe in
detail.

SHANG FEIQIONG: Let me report to my lord.

DONG YIN: Oh, no!

SHANG FEIQIONG: (*Sings.*)
> This humble woman Shang Feiqiong resides along the river-
> bank,
> My father's name is Shang Zhi, his style is Letian.

LI QINGYAN: Does your place have a garden?

SU TIANJUE: Wise younger brother, why do you ask such irrelevant
questions?

LI QINGYAN: Elder brother, you don't understand.

DONG YIN: But I do understand.

SHANG FEIQIONG: His question is getting to the point. I think I'll tell
him. (*Sings.*)
> The other day I was strolling in the garden with my maid,
> When I met a dashing young man under the garden rocks.
> He and I—

LI QINGYAN: What did he and you do?

SHANG FEIQIONG: It was obviously him. What do I have to be shy
about? Ah, my lord,
> He and I had affections for each other, we fell deeply in love,
> In a dream we exchanged tokens of love to be engaged forever.

SU TIANJUE: Isn't that the strangest thing? Ha, ha, ha! Who's ever heard
of getting engaged through a dream?

LI QINGYAN: Elder brother, strange things may happen in this world.

DONG YIN: It obviously happened, so what's this "may happen" business?

SU TIANJUE: What happened later?

SHANG FEIQIONG: My lord. (*Sings.*)
> My father was quite willing about this affair,
> But who would have expected all the mishaps later on?

(*Speaks.*) A licentiate heading for the capital arrived one day. He described a dream that was exactly the same as mine and also brought
my white jade hairpin as proof. Oh, my lord, (*Sings.*)

Hence, believing that he was the real one, a wedding feast was held in the east pavilion,

And the cowherd was brought next to the bridge of magpies.[71]

LI QINGYAN: What was his name?

SHANG FEIQIONG: (*Sings.*)

His home was in Jurong County at the mouth of Zhenjiang,

The licentiate was named Li Qingyan, his style was Yaotian.

LI QINGYAN: Attendants, leave us.

SU TIANJUE: Wise younger brother, no wonder you didn't go to my aunt's house.

LI QINGYAN: Elder brother, it wasn't I. Let us continue with the questioning.

SHANG FEIQIONG: It was in fact not my lord, it was that monster.

LI QINGYAN: Dong Yin, my good friend!

DONG YIN: Hey! I was footing your travel bills all the way.

SOLDIER: Who needs you to pay for the travel bills?

DONG YIN: I won't say no more.

LI QINGYAN: Continue with the story.

SHANG FEIQIONG: My lord, (*Sings.*)

For the man in my dream, I retained my chastity,

Reaching the end of my wits, I jumped into the Yangzi River to return to the Nine Springs.[72]

LI QINGYAN: Elder brother, this is why that baldy accused me of having forced someone's daughter to her death.

SU TIANJUE: That explains it.

LI QINGYAN: How did you regain life then?

SHANG FEIQIONG: (*Sings.*)

It was thanks to the fact that Lord Lü's boat passed by the shore

That I was saved from the abode of crabs and the pool for dragons.

LI QINGYAN: Where is your white jade hairpin now?

SHANG FEIQIONG: My lord, (*Sings.*)

One night I chanced to see him at an inn,

In the middle of the night, I tossed it to him across a paper wall.

LI QINGYAN: My poor, suffering lady! See what this is?

SHANG FEIQIONG: My lord—

SU TIANJUE: What's all this about? I don't understand at all.

---

71. The stars, Cowherd and Weaving Girl are an unfortunate couple who only get to meet once a year on the seventh day of the Seventh Month. Residing on opposite banks of the Milky Way, the Cowherd gets to visit his wife by crossing a bridge formed by magpies. Here the implication is that Dong Yin almost got married to Shang Feiqiong.

72. The Nine Springs refers to the land of the deceased.

DONG YIN: I do understand.

LI QINGYAN: You wouldn't have known, elder brother. This jade hairpin was given to me by the lady, and then stolen by Dong Yin. He then used it along with my name to solicit marriage with her, so it ended up in her hands again. The other day she presented it to me again at the inn, so I have it again.

SU TIANJUE: So she is indeed your wife. Please rise to speak.

SHANG FEIQIONG: Thank you my lord for your graciousness.

SU TIANJUE: You're poking fun at me, elder brother. But let me continue to ask—so where did you live afterwards?

SHANG FEIQIONG: My lord—

DONG YIN: What's there to ask?

SHANG FEIQIONG: (*Sings.*)

> There is a Censor Cui who lived not far from here,
> He and Lord Lü passed their exams during the same year.
> Lord Lü had to travel far and thought the trip too treacherous,
> So he left me temporarily in the safe custody of the Cui residence.

SU TIANJUE: So she ended up staying at my aunt's place.

SHANG FEIQIONG: Would this lord happen to be Lord Su?

SU TIANJUE: Yes.

SHANG FEIQIONG: Lord Su, (*Sings.*)

> How your cousin blamed you behind your back,
> One letter of yours almost ruined her entire marital life.

SU TIANJUE: What happened?

DONG YIN: Oh no. I am stuck!

SHANG FEIQIONG: The other day a licentiate came to the Cui residence armed with a letter to solicit marriage. Ah, my lord! (*Sings.*)

> He said he was recommended by Lord Su,
> He also said he was Li Qingyan, styled Yaotian.

SU TIANJUE: Wise younger brother, so did you or didn't you go to my aunt's place?

SHANG FEIQIONG: Again it was not this lord. It was that monster!

LI QINGYAN: Dong Yin, a fine job you did!

DONG YIN: Both sides didn't pan out, so Dong Yin doesn't count.

SU TIANJUE: What happened next?

SHANG FEIQIONG: My lord, (*Sings.*)

> Fortunately I was there and saw through his trick,
> We had the maids and servants beat him into confessing.
> Who would have known that bearing a grudge, he shot an arrow behind our backs?
> Reporting to the monk, he again created a heaven-sized huge problem.

Wickedly, an imperial envoy arrived, as fierce as thunder and lightening,

Immediately he ordered Miss Cui to bear the banner under the platform.

Hearing that, both mother and daughter wept incessantly,

Making me, ever so ill at ease, within my heart.

Knowing clearly that the ugly scoundrel had contrived this plot,

It was I who came in her stead, exchanging a plum for a peach.

DONG YIN: You were an imposter too. So why just blame me?

SHANG FEIQIONG: (*Sings.*)

Arriving here, I scolded the monk till he was speechless.

He had me tied on the side, I was truly pitiable.

If my lords had not arrived, my life would have been in danger.

To meet again, it would have only been possible through dream.

SU TIANJUE: Attendants, prepare a small palanquin. Take the lady to the Cui residence and tell them that we will be there shortly.

SOLDIER: Yes, sir.

SHANG FEIQIONG: (*Recites.*)

Only when the water recedes are the sizes of the stones visible,

Only when snow melts is the condition of the road revealed.

(*Exits.*)

SU TIANJUE: Attendants, go to Zhenjiang to inform Mr. Shang that his daughter is presently at the Cui residence. Ask him to come and meet her.

SOLDIER: Yes, sir. (*Exits.*)

SU TIANJUE: Attendants, give Dong Yin the knife.

DONG YIN: My lord, my lord, I have a plea. My lord, in the past, Fan Sui 范雎 didn't kill Xu Jia 須賈 because the latter had given him a robe as present.[73] How could Master Li bear to kill me, Dong Yin, today? Don't you remember all the trouble I went through providing for your trip?

LI QINGYAN: What a glib mouth! Attendants, give this shameless rogue forty heavy slashes and drive him out of here. (*They beat him and drive him out.*)

---

73. The playscript mistakenly has Xu Jia as Jia Xu. According to *Shiji's* "Biographies of Fan Sui and Cai Ze 蔡澤," Fan Sui was maligned by Xu Jia; he was driven out by the duke of the state of Wei and suffered much hardship. When he became prime minister of the state of Qin, Xu Jia went to Qin as an envoy from the state of Wei. Fan Sui pretended to be a poor man and visited Xu Jia who presented him with a robe. When Xu Jia found out that Fan Sui had become the prime minister of his host state, he went naked to see Fan Sui to ask for forgiveness. Fan Sui excused him on account of the robe.

SU TIANJUE: Since my wise younger brother is here today, we should go the Cui residence to complete the business in my letter.

LI QINGYAN: Of course I should go to pay my respects and thank them.

SU TIANJUE: (*Recites.*)

    If you had not ranked top scholar of the world—

LI QINGYAN: (*Continues.*)

    How could I get to meet the beauty in the moon? (*They exit together.*)

MADAM CUI: (*Continues.*)

    The haggard face blames the fragrant plants—

CUI SHUANGLIN: (*Continues.*)

    My amorous thoughts are tied to the weeping willows.

SHANG FEIQIONG: (*Continues.*)

    If it were not for the bone-piercing cold,

    How could one get the embracing fragrance of plum blossoms?

CUI SHUANGLIN: Elder sister, you have returned.

SHANG FEIQIONG: If he had not come, I would not have survived.

CUI SHUANGLIN: Elder sister, who are you talking about?

SHANG FEIQIONG: He was your cousin's sworn brother.

MADAM CUI: This has worked out fine.

BUTLER: I report to madam. Master Shang of Zhenjiang has arrived.

MADAM CUI: Invite him in.

SHANG ZHI: Yesterday someone sent a message—I thought I was dreaming. Hai—my child!

SHANG FEIQIONG: Daddy!

SHANG ZHI: Madam, this old man salutes you for your beneficence of adopting my daughter.

MADAM CUI: Not at all, not at all!

BUTLER: Madam, Lord Lü has regained his original post and is here on his way back to the capital.

MADAM CUI: Invite him in.

LÜ SICHENG: Greetings to you, Sister-in-law Nian.

MADAM CUI: Greetings to you, Brother-in-law Lü.

SHANG FEIQIONG: I hope daddy had a propitious trip.

LÜ SICHENG: My child, no need for formalities. Has Mr. Shang also arrived?

SHANG ZHI: Permit this old man to salute you for saving my daughter's life.

LÜ SICHENG: Not at all.

BUTLER: Master Su and Master Li have arrived.

MADAM CUI: My daughters, leave us.

CUI SHUANGLIN and SHANG FEIQIONG: Yes. (*They exit.*)

MADAM CUI: Invite them in.

LI QINGYAN: (*Enters and bows.*) Ten thousand felicities, auntie.

MADAM CUI: Please rise. You are indeed an exceptional fellow. I am very pleased. I am very pleased.

SU TIANJUE: Li Qingyan and I have to go to the capital to report to the emperor. We can't stay long.

SHANG ZHI and LÜ SICHENG: Today is an auspicious day. We can have them bow to the ancestral tablets and get married.

MADAM CUI: Very well. Maid, get your young mistress and Miss Shang ready. Servants, set up a banquet in the courtyard. (*Shang Feiqiong, Cui Shuanglin, and Li Qingyan enter to bow to the ancestral tablets. They exit together.*) Please come to the banquet. (*All exits.*)

The End

11: *The Coral Pagoda.* Shadow figures are from Yang Fei's collection. Photo: Huo Zhanping.

12: *The Coral Pagoda.* Photo: author.

The Coral Pagoda
珊瑚塔

Introduction

The Coral Pagoda, an Eastern style *wanwanqiang* from Shaanxi, was as popular as *The Jade Swallow Hairpin*, but it was not written by an intellectual. Because it is filled with homophonous and other types of incorrect character-words, this anonymous shadow play was probably composed and rewritten by semi-literate performers and copyists who based the drama on a host of orally transmitted folk stories.

The main story in *The Coral Pagoda* bears certain resemblances to the renowned Yuan dynasty *yuanzaju* 元雜劇 play, *Chen Lin Carries a Box at the Bridge of the Golden River* (*Jinshuiqiao Chen Lin baozhuanghe zaju* 金水橋陳琳抱粧盒雜劇; Zang 1983 reprint, Vol. 4) and the Peking opera (Beijing opera), *Exchanging the Crown Prince with a Raccoon* (*Limao huan taizi* 貍貓換太子; Dun n.d., Vols. 33–36). In fact, people living in Shaanxi told me that *The Coral Pagoda* was a version of *Exchanging the Crown Prince with a Raccoon*. But the influence exerted by these literary plays is minimal. A comparison of *The Coral Pagoda* with the more refined operas on the same topic highlights the sharp contrast between literary tastes and the mentality and inclination of peasants in northwestern China. Feisty and dynamic, *The Coral Pagoda* not only displays bloodthirstiness and satisfying court inquisitions but also includes a humorous romantic encounter rarely found in human actors' operas, on-stage military encounters, and tragic scenes—all bundled into one play. Indeed, although far from having conceived a perfect play, the creators of *The Coral Pagoda* seem to have mastered the psychological needs of their audience. They have interwoven a variety of popular elements from the shadow theatre and other performing art traditions to form a tightly knit and immensely satisfying opera.

The attempted murder of a historical emperor as a baby is a fictitious construct based on a few shaky facts. Historically, Empress Liu 劉皇后

143

(968–1033) raised Consort Li's 李妃 son as her own and ruled as a regent when he became emperor as a child. The fact that Consort Li was his birth mother was not revealed to him until quite some time after he had grown up and Consort Li had already died. The emperor granted the title of empress dowager to Consort Li posthumously (Dun n.d., 33:2). Hence, none of the plays on this topic are historically correct. However, their similarities demonstrate the complexity of influence among different performing traditions. Although drawing from various written and oral traditions, each play stands on its own as an entity with its own theme and agenda.

The *yuanzaju* play, *Chen Lin Carries a Box at the Bridge of the Golden River* forms the backbone of the first part of *The Coral Pagoda*. In the Yuan play, Empress Liu has her palace maid, Kou Chengyu 寇承御 trick Consort Li (Li Meiren 李美人) into giving the maid her newborn baby on the pretext that the maid will take him to show the emperor. Kou is ordered to drown the baby in a river, but she has second thoughts. Just then the eunuch, Chen Lin 陳琳 arrives carrying a box for picking fruits. Kou places the baby in his box, despite his protests, and claims that she will take all responsibility. Empress Liu arrives, suspects there is something wrong about the box, and creates a moment of intense suspense before she is called away by an imperial edict.

Chen Lin takes the baby to the Eighth Prince, Zhao Defang 趙德芳, who later arranges for the child to meet the emperor. Suspecting that this child is Consort Li's son, Empress Liu interrogates Kou and summons Chen Lin to beat her in order to exact a confession. Kou remains loyal and commits suicide by throwing herself down the stone stairs. Chen Lin himself is about to be interrogated, but he is saved by an imperial summons.

Twenty years later the "childless" emperor dies and bequeaths the throne to a son of his brother, the Eighth Prince, not knowing that the heir is in fact his own son. The new ruler, Emperor Renzong 仁宗, then summons Chen Lin to find out the circumstances surrounding his past. Although Empress Dowager Liu is not punished, because of a desire to "preserve the virtues of the deceased emperor," Consort Li, Chen Lin, and the spirit of deceased Kou are all amply rewarded.

By contrast, the Peking opera *Exchanging the Crown Prince with a Raccoon* is a sprawling play of four acts/volumes with forty to fifty scenes per volume. Interweaving stories from at least three novels and another Yuan play,[1] this drama is more akin than most Peking operas to the extensive *chuanqi* operas of the Ming and early Qing dynasties. It is basically a

---

1. According to Dun Gen 鈍根, the novels include *Baogong'an* 包公案, *Qixia wuyi* 七俠五義 and *Wanhualou* 萬花樓, and the *yuanzaju* play includes *Tianqimiao Baogong fangliang* 天齊廟 包公放糧 (Dun n.d., 33:1). I think the proper title of the *yuanzaju* should be *Baodaizhi Chenzhou tiaomi* 包待制陳州糶米. See Volume 1 of Zang 1983 reprint for a copy of the play.

play about events in the imperial court as well as various exploits related to Judge Bao. The opera in fact begins with legendary exploits of Judge Bao as a baby and then connects his stories with intrigues at the court. Unlike the hot-tempered and down-to-earth Judge Bao in *The Coral Pagoda,* who uses his own power to exact truth from the suspects, Bao in the Peking opera is a refined gentleman frequently aided by spirits in solving cases. He is even ordered by the emperor to help with exorcising evil spirits. But in the Peking opera, Bao is so weak that he cannot withstand the powerful magic of a Daoist priest and would have died if it were not for the intervention of a friend.

Many of the numerous characters in the Peking opera are incorporated from popular traditional novels and the Yuan play which influenced it. The main culprit, for example, in the *yuanzaju* drama *Judge Bao Sells Rice at Chenzhou (Baodaizhi Chenzhou tiaomi* 包待制陳州糶米) becomes a son of Pang Ji 龐吉 in *Exchanging the Crown Prince.* While such measures help to integrate the numerous branching episodes of the play, they do not eliminate the feeling of its being an immense sprawling opera. Indeed, the stories unrelated to the topic of exchanging of the Crown Prince are so numerous that the core tale is not altogether apparent.

The main villain in *Exchanging the Crown Prince* is Empress Liu, formerly Consort Liu. When both Consort Liu and Consort Li are found pregnant at the beginning of the opera, the emperor decrees that the first to bear a son will be named empress. Consort Li gives birth to a son first. Consort Liu who gives birth later to a daughter offers to help Consort Li and then exchanges the baby for a skinned raccoon. Palace maid Kou Chengyu, whom Consort Liu orders to dispose of the baby, hands him over instead to the eunuch Chen Lin. The baby is then substituted for the baby girl born to Consort Liu. Liu becomes empress and raises Consort Li's baby as the Crown Prince, without knowing that the boy whom she substituted for her daughter was the baby she had ordered to be drowned. At one point Empress Liu suspects that Kou has not followed her orders and that Consort Li's boy has survived and might create problems for her. She interrogates the palace maid and has her beaten to death. Kou's spirit continues to aid the "good" characters—Judge Bao, Chen Lin, and the Eighth Prince.

Fearing that the Crown Prince will find out about the past, Empress Liu commits a series of crimes which begins with the murder of Consort Li and the burning of her palace, and continues after she has become the empress dowager. But justice prevails through supernatural intervention; Consort Li is saved by deities and moved to a hovel in the countryside. Intent upon increasing her sphere of influence, Empress Dowager Liu draws Minister Pang Ji into her faction by arranging for his daughter to marry the emperor and then making Pang into the prime minister. However, Prime Minister Pang Ji and his consort daughter are not as influential and evil in this play as they are in *The Coral Pagoda*. Pang Ji's main crime is having a magic curse placed on Judge Bao. He is eventually punished by being degraded to a commoner, while his consort daughter is not condemned at all. The play ends with a grand court scene presided over by the emperor in which all the evil characters are punished. Empress Dowager Liu is exiled to the "cold palace," but when she finds out that Consort Li has been reunited with her son, the emperor, she is so overcome by shame that she hangs herself.

Although *Exchanging the Crown Prince* involves many of the same characters as *The Coral Pagoda*, including the fictitious Prime Minister Pang Ji, his imperial consort daughter, and the guards Wang Chao 王朝 and Ma Han 馬汗, it is fundamentally different from the shadow play. By linking Prime Minister Pang and his daughter with murder attempts on the life of the Crown Prince, and by having Judge Bao execute justice subsequently, the original creator of *The Coral Pagoda* in fact produces a tighter knit and more satisfying story. The historical Empress Dowager Liu and her imperial son's reluctance to punish her disappear from the story. And the blood-thirsty executions of powerful, evil characters in *The Coral Pagoda* must have gratified the ordinary public immensely.

Deliberately building up Pang Ji and his daughter as power-hungry, ruthless characters, the shadow play contrasts members of this family with their victims. Rather than following literary values, *The Coral Pagoda* perpetuates popular themes frequently found in shadow plays: the bloody execution of evil characters and the attainment of wealth and status through rebellion. Young men of the victimized clan typically collect many beautiful martial wives who are the sisters or daughters of marginalized groups. In *The Coral Pagoda*, Hu Yanlong and Hu Yanqing meet Madam Zhao, a woman warrior who, unbeknownst to them, married their father. This wife has raised two warrior daughters who now join the cause. Hu Yanqing marries a mere village girl, but even she manages to save the day by bringing a magic weapon, the coral pagoda, to her husband and his family. By attaching themselves to members of the victimized clan, common folks as well as marginalized people find an avenue to gaining power and status. The fact that members of the victimized clan also get to save members of the imperial clan, as happens in *The Coral Pagoda*, helps to eliminate the stigma attached to instigating a rebellion. Reflecting peasant taste and mentality, the Judge Bao in *The Coral Pagoda* is despotic and arrogant. Hot-tempered, forthright, and bloodthirsty, he is impressive in his ability to tell the truth. When he interrogates suspects, he already has a clear sense of who the good and bad people are before they are questioned. He knows exactly how to force the truth out of the suspects, even if that means taking advantage of the love between father and daughter. Judge Bao's integrity and intelligence have become so accepted by tradition that he can do whatever he likes. He is a hero because the evil and ruthlessness of his victims have been amply demonstrated. He is a kind of "perfect" judge who is unafraid to flout the wishes of the emperor and will have a prime minister cut into half at the waist to satisfy the justice-demanding audience.

Cast

BEAR SPIRIT 熊精: *a celestial messenger.*

BOY SERVANT

CHEN LIN 陳琳: *a eunuch; also referred to as Chen Gonggong* 陳公公.

CONSORT PANG 龐妃: *an imperial consort; daughter of Prime Minister Pang Qi.*

CROWN PRINCE (ZHAO PING 趙平): *lost son of the emperor and empress.*

EMPEROR: *Renzong* 仁宗 *of the Song Dynasty (r. 1023–1064).*

JUDGE BAO 包公 (BAO WENCHENG 包文丞): *a minister; also known as Scholar Bao.*

KOU ZHIYU 寇直御: *a palace maid.*

LIU YONG 劉勇: *a eunuch; also referred to as Liu Gonggong* 劉公公.

LORD OF THE EAST SEA (Donghaigong 東海公): *an immortal.*

MA HAN 馬汗: *a palace guard.*

MADAM ZHAO 趙氏: *wife of the deceased minister Hu Shouyong.*

MAID

MINISTERS: *Zhao Pu and Bao Wencheng.*

PALACE ATTENDANTS

PALACE MAIDS

PANG MAOHU 龐毛虎: *paternal cousin of Consort Pang; son of Pang Qi's younger brother.*

PANG QI 龐齊: *prime minister; father of Consort Pang (referred to as Pang Ji* 龐集 *in parts of the manuscript).*

QI GUOBAO 齊國保: *chieftain of a mountainous territory; maternal grandfather of Hu Yanlong.*

SOLDIERS

TWO SISTERS: *women warriors; daughters of Madam Zhao and Hu Shouyong.*

WANG CHAO 王朝: *a palace guard under Judge Pao.*

YANLONG (HU YANLONG 胡彥龍): *paternal cousin of Hu Yanqing but referred to as his brother in the play; son of Hu Shouxin* 胡守信.

YANQING (HU YANQING 胡彥慶): *paternal cousin of Yanlong; son of the deceased minister, Hu Shouyong* 胡守永.

ZHAO DEFANG 趙德芳 (EIGHTH PRINCE; Bawang 八王): *a younger brother of the emperor.*

ZHAO PU 趙普: *a minister.*

ZHAO WENJI 趙文姬: *daughter of Zhao Pu.*

ZHU RENLONG 祝仁龍: *a warrior in Village Zhu.*
ZHU SANNIANG 祝三娘: *a woman warrior; daughter of Zhu Renlong.*
ZHU YING 祝英: *a warrior; son of Zhu Renlong.*

Scene 1

YANQING: (*Enters and recites.*)
>My ambition soars, my bravery roars,
>Skilled in both literary and martial arts, my ambition is high.
>If I could reach the imperial ancestral temple one day,
>I would assist the Son of Heaven at the imperial court.

(*Speaks.*) I, Hu Yanqing, am a native of Shanhou 山後. My father's name is Hu Shouyong and my brother's name is Yanlong. Our family was victimized by the treacherous scoundrel, Pang Qi, but I escaped with a Daoist priest by the name of Wang Chan 王禪. He gave me a magic stone which can turn the painting of a tiger into a beast for riding, and an inch-long piece of iron ore, which can transform into a weapon. I intend to travel to the Central Plain[2] to find out the latest events. Let me call my brother and discuss this with him. Come here, my brother.

YANLONG: (*Enters.*) I suddenly hear my elder brother calling for me. I rush to meet him. Elder brother, your younger brother greets you.

YANQING: No need for formality, brother. Sit down and we'll talk.

YANLONG: Your brother has seated himself. May I ask why elder brother has summoned me here?

YANQING: Brother, you wouldn't have known. I intend to go to the capital to scout out the latest. Would my brother like to come with me?

YANLONG: I would like to go, but the place is far away and the travel is inconvenient.

YANQING: Don't worry, my brother. We'll walk slowly where there are people and ride the tiger where there aren't. Pack your luggage, we'll leave immediately. (*Sings.*)
>I hate Pang Qi so much that my teeth grind,
>He robbed my family of its peace and safety.
>Brother and I will go to the capital to scout out the latest,
>We'll kill the scoundrel and bring security to the emperor. (*They exit.*)

---

2. The Central Plain refers to the main part of China, the part under the influence of the central government.

Scene 2

EIGHTH PRINCE: (*Enters.*) His Majesty has been away on a military expedition for about ten years.[3] Thank goodness that smoke of the wolves in Eastern Liao 東遼[4] has finally subsided. I am Zhao Defang, the Eighth Prince. Yesterday, His Majesty returned to the court. We are having a welcoming banquet for him at my residence, the Nanjin Palace 南進宮. I plan to return the Crown Prince to him. I have invited Zhao Pu and Judge Bao to accompany us, but I don't see them yet.

MINISTERS ZHAO PU and JUDGE BAO: (*Enter.*) We, court ministers, prostrate ourselves before your highness.

EIGHTH PRINCE: Ministers, please rise.

MINISTERS: Your highness is most gracious.

ATTENDANT: I report to your highness. His Majesty has arrived.

MINISTERS: Let's welcome him. (*They exit and re-enter with the emperor.*) Your subjects prostrate themselves before Your Majesty.

EMPEROR: Favored ministers, please rise.

MINISTERS: We thank Your Majesty for the imperial favor.

EMPEROR: Favored ministers, sit down so that we may talk.

MINISTERS: We thank Your Majesty for offering us seats.

EIGHTH PRINCE: Your Majesty, your royal subject found a baby in bloody swaddling clothes in the Golden River and has raised him at my palace for some ten years by now. Would it be permissible for your royal subject to present him to Your Majesty?

EMPEROR: But of course. Order him to face his emperor.

EIGHTH PRINCE: Attendants, summon his highness[5] to pay respect to His Majesty.

CROWN PRINCE: I receive the imperial command. (*Sings.*)
> All these years I have been wary of showing my face,
> Today I can finally disperse the clouds and see Heaven.[6]

EIGHTH PRINCE: I kowtow to His Majesty.

CROWN PRINCE: (*Sings.*)
> I quickly kneel before the emperor and dare not be negligent.

---

3. The original says *shushinian* 數十年, several tens of years, which would have made it impossible for his son to have been merely ten years old.

4. Until the arrival of the Mongols, the Kingdom of Liao was one of the most formidable enemies of China during the Song dynasty. Here the Liao people are referred to as wolves and the smoke implies war. Hence, he is saying that war with the Kingdom of Liao has finally ceased.

5. Since the identity of the prince is not yet revealed, the Eight Prince should not have addressed him as "your highness," *dianxia* 殿下, in public; but I follow the original manuscript here.

6. Heaven refers to both the sky and the emperor here.

What is in my heart will remain hidden and unsaid.

EIGHTH PRINCE: Greet the ministers.

CROWN PRINCE: (*Sings.*)

I bow to the ministers and inquire of them about their health.

MINISTERS: Your ministers are much obliged.

CROWN PRINCE: Bowing my head and remaining silent, I stand before the banquet.

EMPEROR: My! (*Sings.*)

This child's deportment is noble and his face exudes auspiciousness.

A closer look shows a heavenly forehead broad and full:

Propitiously round where it should be round,

Propitiously square where it should be square.

How did one so full of auspicious character come so near to death?

We wish that our imperial brother would explain it to us.

EIGHTH PRINCE: (*Sings.*)

The details behind this story are so very strange,

Your royal subject fears that he might upset the imperial air.

Believing that Your Majesty may have guessed most of it,

Could it be possible to have someone else's son at the imperial palace?

ZHAO PU: (*Sings.*)

All this while I have been scrutinizing him carefully:

Indeed his hands reach below his knees and his ear lobes extend to his shoulders.[7]

JUDGE BAO: (*Sings.*)

I estimate his age by a calculation with my fingers,

His Majesty has been away for about ten years.

(*Speaks.*) Eighth Prince, I have this dire event figured out.

EIGHTH PRINCE: Judge Bao, please don't say anything yet. Your highness, please withdraw.

CROWN PRINCE: I obey your will. (*He exits.*)

EMPEROR: Our imperial brother, why don't you tell us plainly?

EIGHTH PRINCE: Your Majesty, if your subject tells it plainly, many people would be implicated. If Your Majesty wishes a clear explanation, ask Consort Pang at the palace about what transpired when the empress gave birth many years ago.

JUDGE BAO: Eighth Prince, I have been back at the court for several years by now. Why didn't you tell me about this?

---

7. He has the physiognomy of a prince.

EIGHTH PRINCE: Ai, because you are too hot-tempered. Besides, with the emperor away from the court, I was afraid that it would be inconvenient.

JUDGE BAO: Oh, how infuriating! (*Sings.*)

> Hearing this, Bao Wencheng's liver and bile explode in anger.
>
> I resent the fact that Your Majesty has trusted the treacherous and evil.
>
> If it weren't for the singleminded loyalty of the Eighth Prince,
>
> This dragon[8] bloodline would have long gone to the Yellow Springs.[9]
>
> I request that Your Majesty entrust the affair to this subject's judgment.
>
> In the fatal moment before the guillotine[10] falls, the truth will usually emerge.
>
> If the case is not solved, have this subject of yours chopped into ten thousand pieces.
>
> How can we tolerate such an evil traitor in the court of the Song dynasty?

EMPEROR: (*Sings.*)

> Our favored Minister Bao, please calm down and cease blaming us.
>
> Leading an expedition against the Liao, we have been away for ten years.
>
> Once we return to the palace, we will investigate thoroughly.
>
> If we cannot clarify the case, we will then trouble you, our dear minister.

EIGHTH PRINCE: (*Sings.*)

> Scholar Bao, you are indeed replete with loyalty.
>
> In terms of talent, you are also at once intelligent and brave.
>
> Let's hide the Crown Prince in Nanjin Palace for the time being,
>
> We will take him to the royal palace eventually and stabilize the state.

EMPEROR: (*Sings.*)

> Thanks to our royal brother for explaining this to us,
>
> You have caused us to clap our hands and laugh in happiness.
>
> Tell the palace attendants to prepare our imperial carriage,
>
> This time we will for sure question the evil consort closely.

---

8. The dragon refers to the emperor.

9. The Nine Springs, like the Yellow Spring, refers to the realm of the deceased.

10. According to shadow figures and pictures, this torture instrument known as *tongzha* 銅鍘 is a huge bronze chopper fastened on one end and has a handle on the other end to facilitate execution. It was used to chop criminals right across the waist.

We bid farewell to you all.

MINISTER: We will see Your Majesty off.

EMPEROR: That won't be necessary. (*They exit; except for the emperor all re-enter.*)

JUDGE BAO: Eighth Prince, you should have told your subject about this.

EIGHTH PRINCE: Favored minister, you wouldn't have known. Back then when the empress gave birth, the evil consort covertly exchanged it with a baby girl. Taking pity on the boy, Chen Lin brought him to me. If it weren't for that, the life of our young lord would have gone to the Nine Springs.[11]

JUDGE BAO: What an evil consort! If you ever land in my hands, you'll be sure to end up in the bronze guillotine.

ZHAO PU: My lord, this is bound to come to pass in the future. Let's take our leave now.

EIGHTH PRINCE: I will see you off.

MINISTERS: We are much obliged.

EIGHTH PRINCE: I am delighted that the country will have a future sovereign. We will see to it that the evil consort's time comes to an end. (*They exit.*)

Scene 3

CONSORT PANG: (*Enters and recites.*)
Spring wind blows into the garden, the sun rises slowly.
It is my favorite time to visit the court.
(*Speaks.*) I am Consort Pang of the Western Palace 西宫.[12] His Majesty returned to the imperial court yesterday; the Eighth Prince welcomed him with a banquet. It's late but he hasn't returned to the palace yet.

PALACE ATTENDANT: I report to your ladyship. His Majesty has arrived.

CONSORT PANG: Let me go welcome him. Your consort greets Your Majesty.

EMPEROR: (*Enters with Consort Pang.*) We are so infuriated!

CONSORT PANG: Your Majesty has returned to the palace. Why do you look so angry?

EMPEROR: Ho! You are asking us? Let us ask you instead: did the empress give birth to a boy or a girl? Why did it disappear completely?

---

11. Same as the above.
12. The consort who resides in the Western Palace is a queen only lower in rank than the empress.

CONSORT PANG: Your consort doesn't know a thing about it. I did hear that it was a girl who died at birth.

EMPEROR: We are afraid that it wasn't a girl but a boy. He didn't die at birth but floated away to safety instead. Evil consort, don't you try to deceive us any more! The Crown Prince is now ten years old and has been hiding at Nanjin Palace. You thought we wouldn't know. We will assemble all the civil and military ministers tomorrow to interrogate both you and your father. (*Off stage: I report to Your Majesty. Generalissimo Di has forwarded a memorial to the throne.*) Present it to us. (*Off stage: We obey the imperial will.*) Let us take a look at it. Ho! So the Liao people are creating havoc again and have invaded our borderland. Attendants, dispatch our edict: Order Zhao Pu to raise an army of one hundred thousand and leave immediately. (*Off stage: We obey the imperial will.*)

CONSORT PANG: (*Tugging at the emperor.*) Your Majesty, your consort knows nothing about the affair concerning the Crown Prince.

EMPEROR: Evil consort, we are not going to discuss this today. We will interrogate you and your father when we return to the court. How infuriating! (*He exits.*)

CONSORT PANG: How did His Majesty find out about this matter? How did the Crown Prince get into Nanjin Palace? I know it! Palace maid. (*Off stage: Yes.*) Summon Kou Zhenyu into the palace.

PALACE MAID: Kou Zhenyu, enter the palace.

KOU ZHENYU: (*Enters.*) I am hurrying. (*Sings.*)

>Just now I heard a boisterous commotion in the palace.
>His Majesty wanted details about the Crown Prince and was angry.
>I expect that I can't escape suffering and calamity this time around.
>Having come this far, I'd be at peace even if I should die right now.

(*Speaks.*) Your maid kowtows to my lady.

CONSORT PANG: You scoundrel! (*Sings.*)

>To hide the Crown Prince, you and I discussed it carefully.
>How is it that he has been hiding in Nanjin Palace for the past ten years?
>Tell me quickly the particulars of this affair in minute detail,
>If you deceive me, I'll have you beaten until you meet King Yama![13]

KOU ZHENYU: Ah! My lady! (*Sings.*)

>As I remember, the Golden River was gusty and turbulent,

---

13. The king of Hell judges whether the deceased should be punished in Hell or reincarnated.

When I tossed the Crown Prince into the river, he drowned immediately.

To date, it has been ten years without a single trace of him,

Who would have thought that he had left Hell and returned to
Heaven?[14]

CONSORT PANG: This is infuriating! (*Sings.*)

You little slut, you are so bold that you still dare to dispute,

Now that the crime is unveiled, who would believe your fudging?

You have caused me to offend the ruling emperor,

Who cares if I have you beaten to death this very day!

I call for the palace maids—you all know how to lash,

Lash pitilessly, just keep on at it, without questioning. (*The palace
maids beat Kou Zhenyu.*)

KOU ZHENYU: Ah, my lady! (*Sings.*)

I ask my lady to consider this matter carefully:

Can a woman like me jump over the palace walls?

Would a minor maid like me have contact with the Nanjin Court?

Are we to assume that the tiny Crown Prince grew wings and flew
over the walls?

CONSORT PANG: (*Sings.*)

Hearing this, my anger flares up ten thousand feet,

I'll have you beaten until your skin and flesh are frayed and you
die instantly.

There must have been an accomplice who was in it with you,

Confess quickly to avoid suffering this calamity alone.

KOU ZHENYU: Ah, my lady! (*Sings.*)

Carrying the Crown Prince to the river, I was so very rushed.

How would I have time to scheme with anyone in secret?

Everyone within the palace owed favors to my lady,

Who dared to take the Crown Prince and hide him privately?

CONSORT PANG: Stubborn slut! (*Sings.*)

There must have been an accomplice to help him escape from this
palace.

I hadn't realized at all that this affair is so highly irregular.

I have suddenly remembered how frequently Chen Lin used to
visit,

I'll have him summoned and will definitely get to the root of this.

(*Speaks.*) Palace maid.

PALACE MAID: Yes.

CONSORT PANG: Give her a solid lashing!

---

14. Heaven here refers both to paradise and to the emperor.

PALACE MAID: Your maid obeys the command. Kou Zhenyu, take this! (*She lashes.*)

CONSORT PANG: Summon Chen Lin to the palace.

(*Off stage: Chen Lin, enter the palace.*)

CHEN LIN: I'm coming. I'm coming. (*Sings.*)

> Hearing the summons suddenly, my soul flies and floats away in fright.
>
> It is most likely that Kou Zhenyu has met with calamity in the palace.
>
> Arriving at the palace gate, let me stop and take a peek inside,
>
> I see Palace Maid Kou lying on one side.
>
> The secret we harbored for ten years is out, the dam has been breached.
>
> It makes me so very flustered and so very scared.
>
> I wish I didn't have to enter the palace; I wish I could escape from this snare.
>
> Ah! They keep on calling for me, I can't turn around now.
>
> So be it! I'll enter the palace with courage to face the wind and waves,
>
> Not knowing whether this will lead to fortune or catastrophe.

(*Speaks.*) Chen Lin greets my lady.

CONSORT PANG: Chen Lin, when Kou Zhenyu stole the Crown Prince out of the palace, she must have had an accomplice. Take the imperial cane and interrogate her for me.

CHEN LIN: My lady! Your subject is only good for holding a broomstick in the palace; I don't know how to use a lashing cane.

CONSORT PANG: Go! Chen Lin, how dare you make excuses?

CHEN LIN: Ho! Your subject accepts your command. Palace Maid Kou Zhengyu, who was your accomplice? Confess right now.

KOU ZHENYU: (*Sings.*)

> Bathed in blood, I fell upon the dust and fainted for quite a while.
>
> Opening my eyes, I see Chen Lin standing fiercely by my side.
>
> Viciously he holds that ruthless cane.
>
> I can't help but turn away, my eyes brimming with tears.
>
> I expect that one dares not lie about it any more.
>
> Why don't I harden my heart and shoulder it all?
>
> Loyal and heroic, I am by nature a woman of iron will,
>
> Who fears that my blood might stain the yellow sand in an instant.

CHEN LIN: Kou Zhenyu, Palace Maid Kou, who was your accomplice? If you don't confess, the cane will fall.

CONSORT PANG: Go! Chen Lin, I ordered you to interrogate her. What kind of interrogation is this?

CHEN LIN: Please calm your anger, my lady. This place is quite close to the imperial bed, which makes it awkward to interrogate. Allow me to drag her to the courtyard where I can interrogate her to the full extent.

CONSORT PANG: I'll leave it up to you then.

CHEN LIN: (*Dragging Kou.*) Kou Zhenyu, do speak out! Kou Zhenyu, who was your accomplice? If you won't tell the truth, watch out for the cane! (*He lashes at her.*)

KOU ZHENYU: Ah! I curse you evil consort! (*Sings.*)
> Evil consort, you are far too uncurbed in the palace.
> Your face may look human, but your heart is like that of jackals and wolves.
> Father and daughter, you two devised schemes to deceive the emperor,
> Pitiable were the three generations of loyal subjects of the Hu family.
> Kidnapping the Crown Prince is as wicked as assassinating His Majesty,
> You are utterly unafraid of Heaven's justice at the end.
> This maid here is loyal to His Majesty, I'm not one of your faction;
> Today I suffer your viperous hand and endure the wrong in vain.
> As for hiding the Crown Prince, I admit to going there by myself.
> Why should I not dare to say what I dared to do?
> I am willing to plunge into this snare set by you slut.
> To give up my life, I'd even jump into fire and boiling water.
> When I reach the underworld and see King Yama, I will tell everything;
> I expect you won't escape from the penalties and regulations in Hell.

CONSORT PANG: You cheap slut! (*Sings.*)
> How dare you talk about me in such a perverse and spiteful manner?
> Uncontrollably, my chest bursts with anger.
> I am resolved to uncover with whom you have been in alliance,
> Who cares if you rave like a flowing creek or like churning sea and wild river?

(*Speaks.*) Chen Lin, lash her for me!

CHEN LIN: Ai, yes. Kou Zhenyu, who was your accomplice?

KOU ZHENYU: You were.

CONSORT PANG: Palace maids, tie up Chen Lin for me.

CHEN LIN: Aiya, my lady. Kou Zhenyu was so confused from my beating that she falsely blamed me. If my lady won't believe me, you can ask her yourself.

CONSORT PANG: Fine, let me ask her. Kou Zhenyu, who was your accomplice?

CHEN LIN: Kou Zhenyu, her ladyship is here. Tell her quickly who your accomplice was. Don't blame the innocent.

CONSORT PANG: Was it Chen Lin?

KOU ZHENYU: It wasn't Chen Lin.

CONSORT PANG: Who was it then?

KOU ZHENYU: It was you.

CHEN LIN: Ah! Now she has your ladyship implicated too!

CONSORT PANG: So he was right. Palace maids.

PALACE MAIDS: Yes.

CONSORT PANG: Untie Chen Lin.

PALACE MAIDS: He is untied.

CONSORT PANG: Interrogate her for me.

CHEN LIN: I was scared to death! (*Sings.*)
　　Suddenly, the palace maids came and tied me up,[15]
　　Shaking from fright, I knew not what to do.
　　Obliterating my conscience, let me strike her right on the head.
　　A quick death will save her from enduring this torment any further.
　　(*Speaks.*) Kou Zhenyu, Palace Maid Kou, I'm going to hit you. Loyal subjects are not scared of death.

KOU ZHENYU: How can the loyal be scared of death? Go ahead and strike!

CHEN LIN: Hai, don't you dodge. Take my cane!

KOU ZHENYU: Ah! (*She dies.*)

CHEN LIN: Aiya, my lady, your subject slipped and killed Kou Zhenyu with one blow.

CONSORT PANG: Chen Lin, I saw right through you. You must have been a part of that incident back then. Now that you have killed her, her dead body won't be able to testify against you. Am I right or not?

CHEN LIN: Aiya, my lady! There is no need to press this matter any further. Now that Kou Zhenyu is dead and I am blamed, this foolish Chen Lin is willing to go to the Yellow Springs with Kou Zhenyu.

PALACE ATTENDANT: (*Enters.*) I report to my lady. His Majesty has dispatched an edict while on his way to the campaign. He has summoned Chen Lin to serve him in the army. Leave right away, Chen Lin.

CHEN LIN: Yes.

---

15. The original text said "tied" rather than "untied" which may have been an unwitting mistake on the part of the copier.

CONSORT PANG: Chen Lin, when you see His Majesty, you must not say anything about what happened here today.

CHEN LIN: Your subject prostrates himself before you. So be it. Ah, Palace Maid Kou!

(*He exits.*)

CONSORT PANG: Palace maids!

PALACE MAIDS: At your service.

CONSORT PANG: Throw Kou Zhenyu's corpse into the Golden River.

PALACE MAIDS: We obey your command.

CONSORT PANG: When the emperor returns, I am sure there won't be an end to this affair. It is almost the Mid-Autumn Festival; I will have to get someone I trust to lure the Crown Prince out of the palace and have my brother kill him. So, this is the plan. Ah, let me tell you, Crown Prince, I'll teach you that a spear thrust in the open is easy to dodge, but an arrow shot at the back is most difficult to guard against. (*She exits.*)

Scene 4

HU YANQING: (*Enters with Hu Yanlong; both riding on a tiger.*) We brothers are climbing up a rock. (*Sings.*)

On Mount Tianding 天定山 we bid farewell to our parents.
In an instant we've passed the Xiong Pass 雄關.
Traveling faster than galloping horses and as swift as an arrow,
In a twinkling we've traversed ten thousand mountain ranges.
Ah, my brother! Close your eyes tightly and be brave,
The ground under your feet will feel as secure as Mount Tai 泰山.
Being impatient, I'm only resentful of the long road ahead.

(*He stands up and speaks.*) Ho! There is a large banner here with four words, "Avenge Our Ancestor's Grievance." I wonder who set this up here? They must have been wronged the same way our family was. Even as I speak, I see an older lady approaching.

MADAM ZHAO: (*Enters.*) I am strolling along. (*Recites.*)

Too lazy to tend to sewing and embroidery,
My daughters prefer riding, fighting, and wielding broadswords.

HU YANQING: Greetings, auntie!

MADAM ZHAO: Are you travelers asking for information?

HU YANQING: Yes we are. Please tell me, auntie. Who has erected this large banner?

MADAM ZHAO: My family did.

HU YANQING: Who is your ancestor, auntie, and what is the grievance you wish to avenge?

MADAM ZHAO: Where are you gentlemen from?

HU YANQING: We are natives of Shanhou 山後. My name is Hu Yanqing and my brother here is Hu Yanlong.

MADAM ZHAO: Are you members of Hu Yanshou's family?

HU YANQING: He is my father.

MADAM ZHAO: Is your mother named Jinlian 金蓮?

HU YANQING: Yes, she is. How did you know that, auntie?

MADAM ZHAO: Follow me home first.

HU YANQING: Please go ahead. (*He sits down.*) Auntie, please explain.

MADAM ZHAO: Ah, my dear son! (*Sings.*)

> Before I speak, tears flow profusely.
> My son, do sit down and listen to me.
> Ever since your family suffered the calamity,
> Your father escaped and left Henan.
> Fleeing from trouble, he went to the Village of the Wang's,
> With the evil traitor at his heel.
> Disguised as a maiden, he stayed with a girl to evade his pursuers.
> After that Judge Bao offered to be matchmaker for their marriage,
> Only then did your mother marry your father.
> It was a pity that before three days had passed,
> The evil traitor arrived at their home,
> Riding on a horse, your father traversed high mountains,
> When will they reunite again?[16]

HU YANQING: So who are you, auntie?

MADAM ZHAO: (*Sings.*)

> I was originally a daughter of the Zhao at Houshan 後山.
> My elder brother was Zhao Ding 趙定, a real bravo.
> After your father killed Pang Heihu 龐黑虎, we got engaged.
> When his family met great calamity,[17] we were also terrified.
> With my brother and his wife, I left Henan.
> Arriving at this location, we took over this high mountain.
> Gathering followers and raising horses, we reside here temporarily.
> Awaiting solely for news from your father.

HU YANQING: Has my father ever come here?

MADAM ZHAO: (*Sings.*)

---

16. This is a synopsis of a romance which may have been elaborated in a play on the previous generation. It was probably a popular tale familiar to the audience. A detailed enactment of the same motif is found in one of the episodes in *Reunion of the Five Swords*, one of the most famous serial shadow plays of Hebei and Northeast China. Here it is merely mentioned to show the teller's familiarity with the family.

17. Revenge from the Pang family.

One day when I was taking an excursion,
I met your father and brought him up the mountain,
Only then did we consummate our marriage.
HU YANQING: Oh, so you are my mother![18] Allow your child to kowtow
to you. Where did my father go?
MADAM ZHAO: (*Sings.*)
He lived here for ten days,
When suddenly the evil traitor showed up here.
Your uncle, hair propping up his cap,[19] leapt into his saddle,
In one battle, he had them all scattered.
Then they brought the four tigers of the Eastern Sea Immortal to
burn our mountain;
Fortunately, the spirit of your deceased grandfather came to our
aid,
So that the life of this family was spared.
After that your father went to seek out his relatives,
While we continued to live at this Mount of Five Hegemonies 五霸
山.
We have not seen him since.
HU YANQING: Where are my uncle and aunt?[20]
MADAM ZHAO: (*Sings.*)
Pitiably, they took ill and went to the Yellow Springs together,
Leaving me behind, all by myself.
Since it is inconvenient for me to live high up in the mountains,
I live right here with my daughters.
Too lazy to work with needle and thread,
We ride horses and shoot arrows instead.
Preparing to avenge the injustices suffered,
I have been drilling a large army.
Waiting for the arrival of your father,
Who would have thought that I'd meet with you, my son, first?
HU YANQING: So I have sisters? Can I meet them?
MADAM ZHAO: Boy!
BOY SERVANT: Yes.
MADAM ZHAO: Ask the two young mistresses to come meet their broth-
ers.
TWO SISTERS: (*Enter and sing.*)

---

18. Polygamy was so prevalent that characters in shadow plays are frequently pleasantly sur-
prised by the discovery of helpful alliances in the form of mothers and siblings they hadn't
known about.
19. Infuriated.
20. Her brother and sister-in-law.

Practicing archery in our garden,
We hear suddenly a summons from our mother.
Entering the screen door, we take a look,
From where did these two young men come?
Majestic and awesome, they look quite handsome.
(*Speak.*) For what did our mother summon us?

MADAM ZHAO: These are your elder brothers. Come greet them.

YOUNGER SISTER: Yes. I bow to my brothers. Who are you, my brothers?

MADAM ZHAO: Fool! It's enough that they are your brothers—why ask who they are!

YOUNGER SISTER: Aiya! So who are they? Am I to call anyone brother without checking him out?

MADAM ZHAO: Get back there. My son, why not tell us about yourself?

HU YANQING: My dear mother, listen to me. (*Sings.*)
In the past when my father was escaping from calamity,
It was thanks to a scheme devised by my mother.
Disguised as a woman, he entered her boudoir,
And stayed there as her companion.
Judge Bao distinguished the male from the female,
My maternal grandfather then chased the knaves away.
But barely three days after their wedding,
The bridegroom had to leave and did not return.
I am the legacy of that marriage.
At my maternal grandparents' home, mother and I stayed.
When my grandparents went to the Yellow Springs,
Mother and son stayed alone and kept the estate.

YOUNGER SISTER: It sounds like elder brother is a bad-luck star!

MADAM ZHAO: Fool, you talk too much. Continue with the story, my son.

HU YANQING: Ah, my dear mother. (*Sings.*)
I have lived under a pseudonym for eighteen years,
Then one day a Daoist priest came by the name of Wang Chan.
He came in order to transmit special powers to me,
Hence I followed him to the Dengyang Pass 登陽關.
I am going straight away to revive the country, without any delay.[21]

YOUNGER SISTER: Elder brother, what kind of magic did the Daoist teach you that you will be able to revive the country?

---

21. Since the protagonists believe that the country is being corrupted by their enemy, Prime Minister Pang, reviving the nation refers to their raising a rebellion against the state for its benefit.

HU YANQING: Ah, younger sister. (*Sings.*)

> He gave me a piece of rock that can turn into a tiger for riding,
> And an inch-long piece of iron that can turn into a staff.
> I speak the truth, there is not a shred of falsehood.
> In an instant, I can traverse ten thousand miles[22] of mountains.

YOUNGER SISTER: The way you put it, elder brother, you are a divine boy!

HU YANQING: (*Sings.*)

> When my mother and I passed by Mount Tianding,
> We reunited with my father's younger brother
> Who was taken as son-in-law at the mountain camp,
> It has been more than ten years to date.
> My brother here is named Yanlong,
> He is not only strong but also brave.
> Together we are making our way to China,[23]
> In no time great armies will enter the Xiong Pass.

MADAM ZHAO: Have you had any news of your father?

HU YANQING: (*Sings.*)

> The other day we did dispatch scouts into barbarian lands,
> But to date no news has yet arrived.
> I expect that my father is raising an army in order to restore the country,
> My uncle will meet him, so that their armies can jointly raise a resistance.

MADAM ZHAO: Wonderful! (*Sings.*)

> Hearing this, my knitted brows relax.
> Today my heart can finally rest at ease.
> These two boys are both brave souls,
> No fear for the evil traitor's army of ten thousand.
> Yanlong, my son, listen to me.
> Stay here to practice your military skills,
> So that your brother wouldn't have any concern during his travel.
> He'll be able to come and go quickly, without any difficulties.

HU YANLONG: Ah, dear auntie! (*Sings.*)

> Although I am but a young man,
> My mind is set to avenge grandfather's grievance.
> I intend to create havoc the way a tiger does among sheep.

YOUNGER SISTER: (*Sings.*)

---

22. I have translated *li* 里, a distance of 360 paces or 1890 feet, as miles whenever the word is used liberally.

23. China refers to the central plain where the government had control. The various mountainous and other fringe areas seem not to be considered parts of China.

I am so happy that flesh and blood are reunited today,
And that they are both men of great daring.
Ah, dear mother.
Your daughters have bows and arrows,
What's wrong with our going together with them?
MADAM ZHAO: How can I allow it?
YOUNGER SISTER: Ah, our dear mother! (*Sings.*)
Although your children are mere women,
We, too, want to avenge grandfather's grievance.
Today, by fortune, an opportunity has arisen,
We can go together to kill the evil and treacherous.
MADAM ZHAO: You can't go.
HU YANQING: Ah, our dear mother! (*Sings.*)
The courage of our sisters is truly admirable,
Why not let them join us? What's the problem?
HU YANLONG: (*Sings.*)
Since both sisters are willing,
What more is there to consider, dear mother?
The sword is drawn from its sheath, the arrow is cocked on its bow,
We'll take the evil traitor and gouge out his heart and liver.
MADAM ZHAO: How do you intend to travel?
HU YANQING: We'll disguise ourselves as refugees and get into the city incognito.
MADAM ZHAO: That'll be all right then.
HU YANQING: In that case, we'll pack our things and leave tomorrow. When there's no one around, we'll ride on the tiger but where there are people, we'll walk slowly.
YOUNGER SISTER: Thank you, big brother, for letting us tag along.
HU YANQING: There's no need to thank me.
MADAM ZHAO: (*Recites.*)
For years no one came to visit,
But one morning relatives from far away are here.
HU YANQING: (*Continues.*)
Flesh and blood from a thousand miles away get to meet,
OLDER SISTER: (*Continues.*)
Our brothers and we are in fact members of the same family. (*They all exit.*)

Scene 5

PANG MAOHU: (*Enters and recites.*)
Having strength makes one tiger-like;

Without treachery, one is not a man.

(*Speaks.*) I am Pang Maohu. I've received an order from my paternal uncle and cousin to assassinate the Crown Prince. I'll go to a secluded place and wait for him. (*He exits.*)

CROWN PRINCE: (*Enters, led by a palace attendant and recites.*)
Wishing to see beautiful sights,
I slip out from the reclusive palace.

(*Speaks.*) I am Prince Zhao Ping. It is the night of the Mid-Autumn Festival. I heard that the city is bustling with activities. Palace attendant!

PALACE ATTENDANT: Yes.

CROWN PRINCE: I am going out of the palace to visit for a while.

PALACE ATTENDANT: My prince, the streets around here are not interesting. Let me take you east of the small stone bridge.

CROWN PRINCE: Lead the way then. (*Sings.*)
This night of the Mid-Autumn Festival is truly as bright as day.
The attendant has rushed away; let me wander at leisure.

HU YANQING: (*Enters with Hu Yanlong and his sisters.*) Follow me closely. (*Sings.*)
The capital city of Bianliang can indeed be called a world of gaiety.
The streets are full of bustling people, coming and going.

PALACE ATTENDANT: (*Enters.*) Get out of the way people, the prince is here! (*He talks to the assassin.*) Who's there? There's the prince, go kill him!

PANG MAOHU: (*Enters.*) Don't run away! Take my knife!

CROWN PRINCE: There is an assassin!

HU YANQING: Who are you?

CROWN PRINCE: I am the Crown Prince at Nanjin Palace. He is trying to kill me!

HU YANQING: All right, scoundrel; don't you dare to run away!
(*He drags Pang Maohu off stage.*)

YOUNGER SISTER: Do you know your way home?

CROWN PRINCE: Of course I do.

OLDER SISTER: We'll escort you back then.

CROWN PRINCE: Let's go quickly. (*They exit and re-enter.*) We are at the palace gate. Who's there?

PALACE ATTENDANT: Oh, it's the young prince. Who are those behind you?

CROWN PRINCE: Don't ask. Is his highness at the palace?

PALACE ATTENDANT: Judge Bao invited him to a banquet.

CROWN PRINCE: Young ladies, please come with me to meet the queen mother first. (*They exit.*)

(Offstage: I report to my lord—there is an assassin. Hu Yanqing and Pang Maohu fight. Pang gains the upper hand.)

Scene 6

HU YANLONG: (*Enters.*) I am Hu Yanlong. I was unexpectedly separated from my brother and sisters. What should I do? Oh, I know. I see a garden ahead. Let me climb the wall and get in. (*He exits and re-enters with flowers on him.*) I've got into the garden. Here's a cave in the rock, I'd better hide in there. (*He exits.*)

MAID: (*Enters with Zhao Wenji.*) Young mistress, let's go back.

ZHAO WENJI: (*Sings.*)
Taking advantage of the bright moonlight, I stroll aimlessly;
My feet tread the fragrant paths.
Suddenly, I hear the drum of the watchtower striking three.[24]
The fragrance of cassia flowers enfolds me,
I expect that the Goddess of the Moon 嫦娥 has already left the seclusion of her Palace of Pervasive Coldness 廣寒宮.

(*Speaks.*) I am a daughter of the Zhao's. My name is Wenji. My father, Zhao Pu, accompanied the emperor on the expedition to Liao. My mother died early. I had a dream last night that a blue dragon coiled itself around me. I don't know whether it portends well or ill. Today is the Mid-Autumn Festival, I am admiring the moon in our garden.

MAID: Young mistress, the gate to the rock cave has been unlatched. I suspect there's a thief. Let's call for help. Gardener, come here quickly!

HU YANLONG: (*Enters and grabs Zhao.*) Young lady, I'm not a thief.

ZHAO WENJI: Get away from me!

HU YANLONG: Yes.

MAID: What is your name, child? Why did you come here?

HU YANLONG: I am Hu Yanlong. (*Sings.*)
Trembling while standing in the garden, I present my petition.
I ask the young lady to excuse me and allow me to explain my situation.
My grandfather, Hu Bixian 胡必顯, was loyal and brave.
To uphold the law, he fought an evil minister and offended the imperial court.

ZHAO WENJI: Everyone knows that the Hu family was loyal and upright. Continue with your story.

HU YANLONG: (*Sings.*)

---

24. The third watch is struck at midnight.

My father Hu Shouxin escaped to barbarian territories.

At Mount Tianding, he was made husband of the princess and I was born.

With my brother and sisters, we came to the capital to pay respect to our ancestral graves.

We met robbers in the streets and got separated.

Somehow, I ended up at the cave in your garden.

I plead, young lady, that you will take pity on me and let me go.

ZHAO WENJI: Fine. (*Sings.*)

Last night, while fast asleep, a blue dragon came into my dream,

Now that I meet him, his name is exactly an elegant dragon.

MAID: Young mistress, when that boy embraced you just now, it corresponded to your dream!

ZHAO WENJI: Maid, you talk too much. Young man, you wouldn't have known, but I am Minister Zhao's daughter. I'd like to save you, but I cannot.

HU YANLONG: Oh? How can you want to save me but can't? Why so?

ZHAO WENJI: We are neither kin nor friend, how can I save you?

MAID: Young mistress, he's just a young man. Speak to him plainly.

ZHAO WENJI: I am too embarrassed to say.

MAID: You're embarrassed but I certainly am not. Fine, I'll speak for you. Young man, my young lady would like to marry you. Do you agree?

HU YANLONG: Sure, if she wants to get married, we'll get married. Let's kowtow to the ancestors right now.

MAID: You can go kowtow to the sesame candy![25] Young mistress, the boy has agreed to it. How do you want to do this?

ZHAO WENJI: Since you have agreed to it, here is a white jade hairpin. I'll present it to you as a token of our pledge.

HU YANLONG: Oh yes. I don't have anything so precious, I only have this pair of emerald jade bracelets. I'll give them to you, young lady, as my token.

ZHAO WENJI: Ah, my dear sir![26] (*Sings.*)

My father's name is Zhao Pu; he is a minister in the court.

Because of attacks by the Liao, he has followed the emperor on a military expedition.

When he returns, get a matchmaker and propose formally and properly.

---

25. The *tang* 堂, the "hall" part of *baiting* 拜堂 which refers to the marriage ritual of performing kowtows in the central hall of one's residence, is a homophone of *tang* 糖, sugar or candy. The maid here is making a joke out of the term by making the hall in *baitang* into a candy.

26. *Xianggong* 相公 which is literally "young gentleman," denotes endearment when used by women in romantic situations.

Don't forget the affection represented by the jade bracelets you offered.

HU YANLONG: (*Sings.*)
Here I thought that a promise is enough for getting married,
Who would have guessed that there's still all this rigmarole?
I hope, young lady, that you will save my life first.
Hide me in your boudoir and keep me there; then I'll be safe.

ZHAO WENJI: That won't work! (*Sings.*)
Our residence has too many people, there are too many eyes and ears.
Keeping you in my room, I am afraid, will ruin my reputation.
(*Speaks.*) Look, it's already dawn. Maid!

MAID: Yes.

ZHAO WENJI: See him off.

MAID: Leave! People are coming to catch you! (*He exits.*)

ZHAO WENJI: Oh, how wonderful!

MAID: Oh, how wonderful? Well, the best is yet to come! Now that your dream has come true, your marriage has been set, your hairpin has been given away, and you got yourself his bracelets—we can finally go back! (*They exit.*)

Scene 7

EIGHTH PRINCE: (*Enters and recites.*)
I hate the evil and slanderous so much that I grind my teeth.
I vow to avenge the wrongs suffered by the loyal and upright.
(*Speaks.*) I am the Eighth Prince, Zhao Defang. When I returned from the Bao residence, I saw the Crown Prince and talked at length with him and the two girls surnamed Hu. It was truly disheartening! Fortunately, the young warrior, who did not reveal his real identity, and the Hu girls exerted themselves to save the Crown Prince. I have already promised the girls in marriage to the Crown Prince. Since the emperor is not here, I wrote a memorial to the throne for the pardon of the Hu family. I have sent them away for now and will present the memorial when His Majesty returns. (*Sings.*)
In the midst of trouble, he met descendants of the loyal and upright,
It is as if dark clouds were parted to reveal the blue sky. (*He exits.*)

HU YANQING: (*Enters with Hu Yanlong and the sisters.*) My brother and sisters are together again. (*Sings.*)
Because I forgot to bring the magic rock,
We almost got ourselves into a great catastrophe.

If it weren't for the Eighth Prince's timely arrival,
The treacherous scoundrel would not have let me go.
Fortunately, we have not revealed our names and surname,
So the evil scoundrel, Pang Qi, still does not know about us yet.
Before we could pay respects at our grandfather's grave,
We brothers and sisters endured this misfortune in vain. (*They exit.*)

Scene 8

ZHU RENLONG: (*Enters and sings.*)
Transmitting through generation the arts of the sword, halberd, spear, and staff,
Martial skills have enabled us to preserve our village.
(*Speaks.*) I, Zhu Renlong, live in the Zhu Village. I have a son and a daughter. My son is called Zhu Ying and my daughter is called Zhu Sanniang. The other day the general defending the Xiong Pass by the name of something like Pang Maohu wanted to marry my daughter. Because he is the son of an evil minister, I did not agree to it. I fear that he may come again.

ZHU YING: (*Enters.*) I am strolling along. (*Recites.*)
Heaven suffers unpredictable winds and rain,
People experience unexpected fortunes and adversities.
(*Speaks.*) Father, we have a problem!

ZHU RENLONG: My son, why are you so flustered?

ZHU YING: Father, you wouldn't have known, but Pang Maohu has surrounded the village with his army and demands my sister's hand.

ZHU RENLONG: If that's the case, go fight the rascals with your sister.

ZHU YING: Yes. (*He exits.*)

ZHU RENLONG: (*Sings.*)
Proud and spirited though they are, waving spears and staff,
I fear that this time we are weak and enemy is strong.
Let me watch from a vantage point in the village,
And gauge the martial skills of our enemy. (*He exits.*)

PANG MAOHU: (*Enters.*) I am Pang Maohu. I brought a battalion to Village Zhu to kidnap my bride. Warriors, attack the village!

HU YANQING: (*Enters on a tiger.*) I, Hu Yanqing, am traveling here. How come there's a general carrying a banner of the Pang clan? Let me rescue his victims. (*He exits.*)

PANG MAOHU: (*Fights and is defeated.*) In the middle of the battle, a man riding on a tiger appeared out of nowhere and fought in all directions. My army had to retreat forty miles. I'd better stop fighting for now and mobilize all the armies from the three passes before we engage in battle again. (*He exits.*)

HU YANQING: Don't you run away, you thug!

ZHU RENLONG: (*Enters with his son and daughter.*) Please come to our home, benefactor. Zhu Ying, thank our benefactor with your sister.

ZHU YING and ZHU SANNIANG: Benefactor, please accept our bows.

HU YANQING: I return your bow. Who was that just now? What grievance does he harbor against your family?

ZHU RENLONG: Benefactor, you wouldn't have known. Please listen to me. (*Sings.*)

> This old man, Zhu Renlong, doesn't own much family estate;
> We live in Village Zhu, planting only mulberry and hemp.
> Pang Maohu, the wicked, treacherous little brute,
> Wished to marry my girl Zhu Sanniang by coercion.
> Not agreeing to it from the start, I told him the fact.
> The little brute got so angry that he resorted to his army.
> Luckily, you, our great hero descended from Heaven,
> Routing them, they had to flee like fallen flowers on flowing current.

(*Speaks.*) What is our benefactor's name and where are you from?

HU YANQING: My name is Hu Yanqing. (*Sings.*)

> My grandfather, the duke of Zhongxiao 忠孝王, was exalted and great.
> Suffering an injustice, he has not yet been vindicated.

ZHU RENLONG: So you are old General Hu's descendant! Where did you come from?

HU YANQING: (*Sings.*)

> At Mount Tianding, my uncle[27] married a chieftain's princess,
> He sent me to go to the capital to scout the best route.
> When I saw so many men and horses in your village,
> I decided to kill the bandits; I don't expect them to bother us again.

ZHU RENLONG: You are indeed a hero deserving to be the descendant of a warrior family.

HU YANQING: You are too kind in your praises.

ZHU RENLONG: Warrior sir, I have a fifteen-year-old daughter who is also skilled in the martial arts. I would like to marry her to you. Since the status of your family is high, we hope that you won't disdain the match.

HU YANQING: Ah! I ought to obey uncle's will, but please allow me to inform my parents before making the engagement.

---

27. The original said "grandfather" which seems to be a mistake.

ZHU RENLONG: Warrior sir, you're quite right. I will send my daughter over soon. I am sure that your father will be delighted.

HU YANQING: In that case, please allow your son-in-law to kowtow to you

ZHU RENLONG: My fine son-in-law, please rise.

HU YANQING: Father-in-law is most gracious. Please accept my bow, elder brother.

ZHU YING: I return your bow.

HU YANQING: I bid you farewell.

ZHU SANNIANG: Daddy, ask him where he's going. He should make it clear.

HU YANQING: I'm heading to—(*Sings.*)

> On Mount Tianding, my maternal grandfather has been gathering an army and raising horses,
>
> My father and uncle are stationed at the foot of that mountain.
>
> Not long from now, our army will arrive at the city walls to avenge the grievance;
>
> When that happens, I will ask a matchmaker to come to your home.

(*Speaks.*) Your son-in-law bids you farewell.

ZHU RENLONG: We will see you off. (*Hu exits.*) My dear child! (*Sings.*)

> It is our good fortune today that we met a gallant warrior.
>
> He is no less a match for your beauty, intelligence, and wisdom.
>
> We still have to guard against Pang Maohu, who may send more forces;
>
> At the worst, we'll give up our lives in order to have him slaughtered. (*They exit.*)

Scene 9

PANG MAOHU: (*Enters.*) I'm Pang Maohu. I've mobilized all the troops from the three passes to take Village Zhu. Warriors, set fire to the village! (*Fire is lit; Bear Spirit saves Zhu Sanniang and they exit.*) The Zhu Village is completely torched.

SOLDIER: The prime minister has dispatched an order. All the troops from the three passes are to be mobilized to the foot of Mount Tianding for further orders.

PANG MAOHU: In that case, let's march to Mount Tianding! (*They exit.*)

BEAR SPIRIT: (*Enters with Zhu Sanniang.*) I am the Hairy-Headed Bear Spirit, sent by an immortal in Heaven to deliver a magic coral pagoda to you. Go to Mount Tianding today to avenge your family and help the Hu family smash the enemy's military formation.

ZHU SANNIANG: I am a mere woman. How can I ever get there in time?

BEAR SPIRIT: Here is a blue silk handkerchief. Wrap it around your feet and you'll be able to fly with the winds. This pagoda can expel evil spirits and shatter their military formations. Guard this treasure and do not lose it. Heed my words! I must leave now. (*He exits.*)

ZHU SANNIANG: I must have passed out! Oh, so an immortal did come to me in a dream—the treasures are indeed here! I'd better go there then. (*Sings.*)

> In an instant, I am engulfed in space—my body feels like a cloud,
> This must be how the immortals feel.
> My entire family was annihilated by fire, with no one to take pity on us;
> I'll go beyond the passes and avenge my family's grievance first.
> (*She exits.*)

Scene 10

QI GUOBAO: (*Seated inside a military tent. Recites.*)

> I have just returned from the outside,
> Daily, my armies display our might at the Xiong Pass.

(*Speaks.*) I, General Qi Guobao, am delighted that the Hu family has brought their armies here.

SOLDIER: I report to the Chief.[28] The lord of the Eastern Sea has surrounded the city.

QI GUOBAO: Ho! Tell our soldiers to be vanguard and have the Hus, father and son, guard them from behind. Let's fight our way out of the siege. (*He exits; fighting ensues. The Lord of the Eastern Sea is defeated.*)

LORD OF THE EASTERN SEA: (*Enters and speaks.*) How disheartening! I'll have to set up my Great Military Formation of the Five Elements 五行大陣. (*Hu Yanqing kills Pang Maohu. The Lord of the Eastern Sea uses a magic hammer; Zhu Sanniang uses the coral pagoda.*) What an awesome fight! Oh no, something devastated my magic military formation! Let me make my escape!

HU YANQING: (*Enters.*) Watch my staff, old rogue! I've killed the Lord of the Eastern Sea, but his two sons have escaped. Let me recall my troops. (*He exits.*)

QI GUOBAO: (*Enters and recites.*)

> My eyes espy brandishing banners,

---

28. *Dawang* 大王, literally, Great King, is a common appellation for bandit leaders.

My ears hear good news.

(*Speaks.*) The scoundrels captured my soldiers, but fortunately they've all been returned.

HU YANQING: I report to grandfather. Sanniang requests an audience with you.

QI GUOBAO: Tell her to come in.

ZHU SANNIANG: I kowtow to grandfather.

QI GUOBAO: Raise yourself.

ZHU SANNIANG: Grandfather is most gracious.

QI GUOBAO: What are you holding?

ZHU SANNIANG: The magic coral pagoda.

QI GUOBAO: We'll hold the wedding for you and Yanqing today and attack the Xiong Pass tomorrow. (*They exit.*)

HU YANQING: (*Re-enters with Zhu Sanniang.*) My wife, you and I can both display our military skills. (*Sings.*)

> To flaunt our skills, we cannot dawdle.
> In an instant, we've both crossed ten thousand mountains—
> Faster than wind and cloud, and swift as an arrow.
> We'll bring my mother here and reunite with her. (*They exit.*)

Scene 11

JUDGE BAO: (*Enters and recites.*)

> With singleminded loyalty, I support the emperor of the Song Dynasty;
> Iron-faced and pitiless, even gods and spirits fear me.

(*Speaks.*) I, Scholar Bao Wencheng, have received an imperial edict to interrogate the evil scoundrel with utmost severity. I have ordered him summoned, but he has not yet arrived.

SOLDIER: I report to my lord. Prime Minister Pang has arrived.

JUDGE BAO: Hang up the edict and have him go through a side entrance.

SOLDIER: Prime Minister Pang, please use this entrance.

PANG QI: Why should I use a side entrance? No matter, I'll let it go this time. Go announce me. Greetings, Scholar Bao.

JUDGE BAO: You evil scoundrel! How dare you stand and not kneel down when you see me?

PANG QI: Ha! I am father-in-law of the emperor, and my position is that of prime minister. How can it be that I should kneel to you?

JUDGE BAO: Ho! You traitor! Take a look at what's hanging up there! Wang Chao, tear off the scoundrel's dog skin and lash him!

PANG QI: Aiya! How ghastly!

JUDGE BAO: All right traitor. Tell me how the entire clan of the Hu family was wiped out? Who exchanged the Crown Prince? And how did the Crown Prince get out of Nanjin Palace the night of the Mid-Autumn Festival? Tell the truth and save yourself from the guillotine.

PANG QI: My lord, Hu Bixian offended His Majesty; it had nothing to do with me. As for the Crown Prince, I don't know anything about it.

JUDGE BAO: You are certainly good at evading questions. Wang Chao, request an imperial edict to bring Consort Pang of the Western Palace here for investigation. (*Wang exits; Judge Bao sings.*)

> Evil scoundrel! You father and daughter are like birds and beasts;
> Devising schemes, you inflict harm upon the loyal and upright.
> Loyal and upright warriors the Hus had been,
> But the entire clan of three hundred met with disaster.
> It was all on account of you, the prime minister and imperial father-in-law,
> Relying on the position of your daughter, you tyrannized the court.
> The Crown Prince, as a baby, you nearly drowned,
> Yet you dared to exercise your depravity a second time,
> In the streets the night of the Mid-Autumn Festival, you tried to assassinate him.
> Your heart and liver are like those of tigers and wolves.
> Today your crimes are brimful and you are caught in the net of law,
> Think no more of wealth and power by playing sycophant to the ruler.

(*Speaks.*) Ma Han!

SOLDIER: Yes.

JUDGE BAO: Bring the bronze guillotine to the court.

WANG CHAO: I report to my lord. The evil consort is brought in. There is an edict from His Majesty that the consort of the Western Palace is to be interrogated with lenience.

JUDGE BAO: (*Speaks angrily.*) Ahem! Emperor Renzhong of the Song— what a muddle-headed emperor! After all this, how can you still spoil her so? Wang Chao, drag the evil consort here!

WANG CHAO: Ho!

CONSORT PANG: (*Enters.*) Scholar Bao, please consider the will of His Majesty!

JUDGE BAO: Oh, you evil consort! (*Sings.*)

> Hearing this, my fury flares up three thousand yards,[29]
> Wave after wave, the fire of rage fills my chest.

---

29. I have translated the *zhang* 丈, 10 feet or 141 inches, as yard whenever it is used liberally.

When have you two ever considered the will of His Majesty,
You who tried to harm the life of the Crown Prince?
Raise your head and take a good look, you evil consort,
Lined up here in this court are twelve bronze guillotines.
Confess everything quickly, from the beginning to the end.
Don't you try to hide, not even a single bit.

CONSORT PANG: Ah, my lord! (*Sings.*)

Hu Bixian was too rash in his actions,
He shouldn't have complained about the sovereign behind the back.
It was His Majesty who decided to execute him,
When was it ever the idea of us, father and daughter?

JUDGE BAO: Oh? You were angry because the empress did not like you. When the emperor was away, you had the Hu residence demolished. Your father personally led the army in the attack. Your involvement was so obvious, how can you still deny it? Wang Chao, put the finger press on her.

CONSORT PANG: The pain is killing me! (*Sings.*)

The bronze finger press squeezes my ten fingers,
Never have I experienced such an ordeal in my life!
Daddy, please tell them the truth right away,
The pain inflicted upon your daughter is truly hard to bear.

PANG QI: Lord Bao, please release my child from torture; I am willing to confess.

JUDGE BAO: Release her. Now confess.

PANG QI: Ah, my lord! (*Sings.*)

Brimming with tears, I kneel at the court,
To Lord Bao I will recount all the details.
Hu Shouyong killed my son,
But I could not avenge this injustice.
Therefore I caused the ruin of his entire family,
In order to exact vengeance for the death of my son.

JUDGE BAO: This sounds reasonable enough. Now tell the truth about exchanging the Crown Prince.

PANG QI: Lord Bao! (*Sings.*)

Never have I been in contact with the palace of the empress,
How could I have known whether her baby was a girl or a boy?
This matter really had nothing to do with me,
I beg my lord to consider it carefully.

JUDGE BAO: When His Majesty went on the expedition against the barbarians, you went to the palace every day. You and your daughter schemed the plot together, so how could you not know about it? Wang Chao!

WANG CHAO: Yes.

JUDGE BAO: Take the traitor to the bronze guillotine!

CONSORT PANG: Aiya! Lord Bao, please don't put my father in the guillotine. I am willing to confess.

JUDGE BAO: Go ahead!

CONSORT PANG: Aiya, my father, I am scared to death! (*Sings.*)

> Suddenly he was taken to the bronze guillotine,
> In the blink of an eye, father and daughter would have been separated.
> Oh my lord, exchanging of the Crown Prince was to deceive His Majesty,
> Palace Maid Kou was the one who intended to jeopardize his life.
> On account of her poisonous, vile nature,
> She has already been beaten to death and has gone to the Yellow Springs.

JUDGE BAO: Your story does not ring true. What would a palace maid have against the Crown Prince? If it wasn't your idea, who would have dared to do anything so treacherous? Clearly, your faction of hounds was afraid that the imperial favor you had enjoyed would be displaced, if the empress gave birth to a son. So you ordered the palace maid to have the boy drowned. The palace maid must have had a conscience, so she saved the boy and delivered him out of the palace. If this weren't the case, why hadn't you interrogated the palace maid earlier? After His Majesty found out about it, you then had her beaten to death. What a treacherous consort!

CONSORT PANG: I have never harmed the Crown Prince.

JUDGE BAO: Don't you dispute it! Wang Chao!

WANG CHAO: Yes.

JUDGE BAO: Go to the palace and summon Chen Lin for interrogation.

WANG CHAO: Yes.

JUDGE BAO: You, treacherous bitch of a consort! (*Sings.*)

> How dare you be so stubborn about it, evil consort?
> I, Bao Wencheng, am none other than the Fifth King of Hell.
> How dare you lie in front of the mirror of your crimes?
> Do you think that Heaven no longer upholds justice?
> Familiar with treacherous factions of hounds like yours,
> I have investigated several thousand cases like this.
> Angrily, I sit at the court, waiting to ask Chen Lin for further details.

WANG CHAO: (*Enters.*) I report to my lord. Chen Gonggong[30] is here.

JUDGE BAO: Please invite him in.

CHEN LIN: Greetings, Lord Bao.

JUDGE BAO: Greetings! The imperial edict is hanging up there, so it is inappropriate for me to get up to greet you. Please excuse me, Gonggong sir.

CHEN LIN: You are too kind. My lord serves the state with utmost diligence. Of course the law must be abided by. I, your student, have come forward to be investigated.

JUDGE BAO: Gonggong sir, please tell the truth concerning the Crown Prince.

CHEN LIN: Lord Bao, allow me to present my tale. (*Sings.*)
>I see the evil traitor placed in the guillotine,
>And the evil consort, kneeling there, having had her fingers pressed.
>It proves that retribution indeed works,
>It's going to be difficult for them to elude disaster.

(*Speaks.*) Ah, my lord. (*Sings.*)
>Long ago when His Majesty went to the state of Liao,
>He charged me with visiting the harem frequently.
>One day I bumped into Palace Maid Kou,
>Carrying a baby at her bosom, her eyes brimming with tears.
>We two discussed saving the Crown Prince;
>At the Nanjin Palace, I sought help from the Eighth Prince.
>Thanks to his highness, the prince was raised and cared for.
>Having grown up after ten years, the Crown Prince is still in hiding.
>It was she who beat Kou Zhiyu to death—
>Pity the valiant lady with a heart of iron.
>Chen Lin could have lost his life too,
>If it weren't for the timely arrival of an imperial edict
>Summoning me to go serve in the army.
>Thus, I got to leave the capital and kept my safety.

JUDGE BAO: Gonggong sir, please return to the palace. I will memorialize to His Majesty right away to have Kou Zhiyu commemorated.

CHEN LIN: Yes. (*He exits.*)

JUDGE BAO: You traitor, what more do you have to say?

PANG QI: I have been wronged.

---

30. *Gonggong* 公 公 (miswritten as 宮宮 in the original) is a courteous appellation for eunuchs. Although it is the same appellation as that daughters-in-law call their fathers-in-law, the usage is very different here.

JUDGE BAO: How did you try to kill the Crown Prince the night of the Mid-Autumn Festival? Tell the truth to spare yourself from the guillotine.

PANG QI: I really know nothing about this affair concerning the Crown Prince. The Eighth Prince had the assassin taken away.

JUDGE BAO: Ho! You had sent an assassin, captured the person who rescued the Crown Prince, and still dare to deny! Wang Chao.

WANG CHAO: Yes.

JUDGE BAO: Go to Nanjin Palace and bring the person who attended the Crown Prince the night of the Mid-Autumn Festival.

WANG CHAO: Yes. (*He exits.*)

JUDGE BAO: You father and daughter team have made a clear-headed emperor into a muddle-headed one. The two of you invented a scheme in the palace to get rid of the Crown Prince.

WANG CHAO: (*Enters.*) I report to my lord. Liu Gonggong is here.

JUDGE BAO: Tear off his dog skin and drag him up here.

LIU YONG: At your service, my lord.

JUDGE BAO: What is your name?

LIU YONG: My name is Liu Yong.

JUDGE BAO: Liu Yong, did you accompany the Crown Prince out of Nanjin palace the night of the Mid-Autumn Festival?

LIU YONG: Yes.

JUDGE BAO: Speak the whole truth.

LIU YONG: My lord, you wouldn't have known about this. Lady Pang of the Western Palace sent me five hundred taels of gold and told me to coax the Crown Prince to leave the palace that night. She ordered her brother,[31] Pang Maohu, to kill him. This is the truth.

JUDGE BAO: Ha, ha, ha . . . That five hundred taels of gold was certainly easy money! Wang Chao!

WANG CHAO: Yes.

JUDGE BAO: Take Liu Yong to the bronze guillotine.

WANG CHAO: It's all set.

JUDGE BAO: Cut!

CONSORT PANG: I'm scared to death!

JUDGE BAO: That's settled. Considering the will of His Majesty, Wang Chao.

WANG CHAO: Yes.

JUDGE BAO: Take the evil consort to the strangling chain and strangle her three times until dead. (*They exit.*) Ma Han, tie up Pang Qi and remove him from the capital. Have Hu Shouyong kill this traitor at his father's

---

31. Paternal cousins were frequently considered to be siblings in traditional China.

grave; order Hu Yanqing to expose the corpses and scatter the bones of Pang Qi's ancestors from their graves. Let me proceed to the imperial court now and memorialize to the emperor. (*They exit.*)

Scene 12

EMPEROR: (*Enters.*) We, Emperor Renzhong of the Song, are the reigning sovereign. Yesterday the Pang father and daughter were thoroughly investigated and have been executed. Our brother, the Eighth Prince, has persuaded the Hu family to surrender. We are extremely pleased. Attendants, proclaim an edict that we wish an audience with all the civil and military ministers.

MINISTERS: (*Enter.*) We, the court ministers, accept the imperial will. We prostrate ourselves before the emperor!

EMPEROR: Our ministers, listen to our conferment of appointments. Qi Guobao is awarded the title of the Duke of Tianding. Hu Shouyong will be the Duke of Loyalty and Filial Piety. Hu Xinyong will be the Marquis of Righteous Valor. Their wives, Madam Zhao and Madam Qi, will both be ladies of the first rank. Hu Yanqing will be Marquis of National Defense; Hu Yanlong will be given the title of General of Imperial Defense. Zhu Ying will be given the title of Vanguard General. Considering her merit in diffusing the enemy's military formation, Zhu Sanniang will be granted the title of Lady of Military Valor. The two daughters of the Hu family will marry the Crown Prince, with Minister Bao as the matchmaker. Chen Lin was meritorious in saving the Crown Prince's life. He is granted the title of Loyal and Righteous Eunuch. Kou Zhiyu has already died, but to her we award the title of Martyred Loyal Palace Maid. Sacrifices will be performed for her every spring and fall. Raise yourselves, our favored ministers.

MINISTERS: Long live the emperor!

EMPEROR: Attendants, have a banquet prepared.

ATTENDANT: The banquet is ready.

EMPEROR: Let's go to the banquet.

The End

13: *Yang Long Draws the Bow.* Shadow figure from Yang Fei's collection. Photo: Huo Zhanping.

Yang Long Draws the Bow
楊龍開弓

Introduction

Yang Long Draws the Bow is a *xianbanqiang* shadow play from Shaanxi. Like most shadow plays, it is an anonymous work most likely written for a peasant audience by semi-literate performers. As a more traditional subgenre than *wanwanqiang, Yang Long Draws the Bow* is a fairly typical simple play which reflects the tastes and mentality of its audience. The preference for "military" over "civil" content, the fondness for independent, bandit-like male and female warriors, the distrust of muddle-headed emperors and evil courtiers (frequently the prime minister), and the desire to obtain titles, wealth, and marriage to the imperial family through raising a rebellion. The plot is immensely predictable, but its outcome is still highly satisfying—the culprit is decapitated and made into a "human candle," and the rebels all gain honors and titles, including a marriage to the Crown Prince.

The difference between retired generals controlling mountain stockades and "barbarian" chieftains or bandits is very slight. Although Yang Hong 楊宏 is supposed to be protecting the borderland, he is very much a lord of the "barbarians" and bandits of the region. Since he is beyond the control of the central government, even the emperor has to beg for his assistance—a situation which must have found favor with the audience.

Yang Hong's reluctance to go to the court is due to the intense animosity between himself and the prime minister. The emperor usually sides with the courtiers, who tend to be highly suspicious of the power of the generals, and with good reason. According to this shadow play, warriors and soldiers obey the commands of their generals rather than those of the emperor and his court. The warriors under the command of a Yang general do not budge when the emperor requests that they dismount. But one twirl of the general's whip, and all the officers respond.

In *Yang Long Draws the Bow*, the prime minister, Yan Song 閻嵩, repeatedly commits treachery. Ironically, however, it is the extra precaution taken by Yang Hong that ultimately allows Yan Song's schemes to lead his son to disaster. Fearing jealousy, he tells his son Yang Long 楊龍 not to accept titles and emoluments. This precaution, however, provides Yan Song with an opportunity to victimize the young warrior.

The name Yan Song seems to be a stock name for evil prime ministers in the popular tradition. He also appears in an anonymous Qing dynasty novel, *Haigong Dahongpao Quanzhuan* 海公大紅袍全傳 (The complete tale of the red robe of Lord Hai) as the father of an imperial consort and a most treacherous prime minister.[1] The Yan Song in *Yang Long Draws the Bow* is a simple villain. There is nothing subtle about his treachery. He consistently resorts to imprisoning family members of Yang Hong's daughter-in-law, Xu Zan 許贊, in an attempt to force Xu into negotiating with the Yangs. He has the distance and height of the target changed when Yang Long draws the bow. When Yang Long manages to hit the target anyway, he drops an imperial wine cup and blames it on the young man. His final evil act is to falsify an edict to ensure the timely execution of the hero.

The simplicity of the muddle-headed emperor matches the unlikely chicanery of his prime minister. Gullible and malleable, he is a puppet with neither will nor intelligence. Although such a characterization is not an anomaly for this genre, he is one of the worst. He is completely under Yan Song's control until Prince Xu (Xu Guogong 徐國公), the emperor's brother, enters the court in the guise of an imperial ancestor and turns him against the prime minister. Placing the portrait of a deceased ancestor on his head and swinging an ancestral hammer, Prince Xu manages to represent ancestral authority. This act is an ingenious invention that I've found in neither history nor any other fiction.

In the fringe world of independent warriors, familial ties and the bond between sworn brothers are stronger than the loyalty to one's state and emperor. The father, Yang Hong, is the only person who is reluctant to raise rebellion against the state after the wrongful execution of his son. His wife and the deceased's siblings are all quick to denounce the emperor and eager to raise an army to subdue the state and kill the prime minister responsible for Yang Long's death.

Women are the leaders of this insurrection, and they tend to be even more fierce and bloodthirsty than the men. The rebel army commander is

---

1. See Wu 1990, 37–38, for information on and a synopsis of the novel. The real Yan Song 嚴嵩 is a historical character who along with his son, Yan Shifan 嚴世蕃, created a most powerful faction within Xiaozong's 孝宗 (r. 1488–1506) court. He and his son were eventually defeated by another faction and condemned for committing great evils.

none other than Yang Long's widow, Xu Jinding 許金定. But however fiery-tempered and powerful the women warriors are, the world they inhabit is ultimately patrilineal and patriarchal. The debate between Xu Jinding and her father, who begs her to desist, indicates that a married woman's loyalty rightfully resides with her husband and his family rather than with her natal family. While filial piety is important, the love and loyalty of a woman for her husband is more important. Once married, a woman's father no longer has control over her.

Yang Long Draws the Bow has limited literary value. Both its language and its plot are quite plebeian. But precisely because it appeals to the common folk and represents their worldview and values, it provides insight into the desires and aspirations of the poor.

Cast

ATTENDANTS

BARBARIAN: *an emissary from the kingdom of Black Water* (Heishuiguo 黑水國).

EMPEROR: *a fictitious emperor of a real reign during the Ming dynasty (1368–1644 a.d.).*

GUARDS

LI YI 李義: *a warrior; a sworn brother of Yang Long* 楊龍.

LIU YING 劉英: *a general at the court.*

MADAM KANG 康氏: *mother of Yang Long.*

MAID

MINISTERS

PRINCE XU (XU GUOGONG 徐國公; XU ZHOU 徐周): *brother of the emperor, with a hereditary title.*

SERVANT

SOLDIERS

XU JINDING 許金定: *a woman warrior; wife of Yang Long; daughter of Xu Zan.*

XU ZAN 許贊: *a minister; father-in-law of Yang Long.*

YAN SONG 閻嵩: *Prime Minister; also referred to as the Secretary of State and Grand Tutor.*

YANG HONG 楊宏: *a renowned general guarding Mount Cock Crow* (Jimingshan 雞鳴山).

YANG HU 楊虎: *a warrior; Yang Hong's second son.*

YANG LONG 楊龍: *a warrior; Yang Hong's eldest son.*

YANG SUZHEN 楊素貞: *a woman warrior; Yang Hong's daughter.*

ZHANG REN 張仁: *a warrior; a sworn brother of Yang Long.*

Scene 1

EMPEROR: (*Enters and recites.*)

Treasured palace enjoys tiles of yellow gold,
Imperial soldiers wear armor of white jade.

(*Speaks.*) We are the emperor of Jiajing 嘉靖 reign (1522–1567) of the Ming dynasty. Our name is Zhu Hou 朱厚. Ever since we ascended the throne, peace has prevailed. The kingdom of Black Water has, however, unexpectedly presented us with an iron bow and challenged that should anyone be able to draw this bow, they will assume a subordinate status and pay a yearly tribute to us; but if no one can draw this bow, then they will topple our state and country. The day before, our brigade-general, Chou Luan 仇鸞, tried unsuccessfully to bend the bow; he dropped dead with blood gushing out of the seven apertures of his head. We then dispatched the censor, Liu Rong 劉榮, to go to Mount Cock Crow to summon Yang Hong. Who would have thought that Yang Hong would defy the imperial will three times and refuse to come to the capital? We feel so aggravated that we will have to discuss the problem with our secretary of state. Attendants, summon the secretary of state.

YAN SONG: Your Majesty on high, your minister, Yan Song, presents himself. (*He kowtows.*)

EMPEROR: Rise.

YAN SONG: Which military issues did Your Majesty summon your minister to discuss?

EMPEROR: It's only that Yang Hong has defied our imperial will thrice and there is no one else who can draw this bow. What is to be done?

YAN SONG: Please do not worry, Your Majesty. We have a minister by the name of Xu Zan who is a close relative of Yang Hong. Order him to summon Yang Hong and Yang will definitely come.

EMPEROR: What if he still refuses to come?

YAN SONG: If we imprison all the members of Xu Zan's family, then Xu will surely try hard to persuade Yang to come.

EMPEROR: So be it. Our favored minister, you may leave the court and pass on our edict.

YAN SONG: Your minister accepts the edict. (*He exits.*)

EMPEROR: (*Sings.*)
Let us consider it carefully in our heart:
Minister Xu Zan will persuade the valiant hero.
If only the iron bow is drawn,
Our state won't be overthrown,
And for us, this disaster will be gone. (*He exits.*)

Scene 2

XU ZAN: (*Enters with a group of ministers; sings.*)
I leave the capital, carrying the imperial edict.
Grief darkens the faces of all the ministers.
They fear that the old one will resist the imperial will,
Making this trip to Mount Cock Crow a waste
And no help will be rendered to avert the toppling of the state.

(*Speaks.*) I, Minister Xu Zan, lead five court ministers with me to Mount Cock Crow to summon the general. We have arrived at the foot of the mountain.

MINISTERS: Lord Xu, you go ahead, we will wait for you at the foot of the mountain.

XU ZAN: Why so?

MINISTERS: We are all guarantors. He may get upset if he sees us. But you are his in-law, so he won't mind you. We will come when he summons us.

XU ZAN: In that case, stay as you please. (*He exits.*)

MINISTERS: My lords, Minister Xu is more likely to fail than to succeed. Let's run away the moment we receive any bad news, lest we end up being humiliated. (*Sing.*)

> Old Yang Hong is so stubborn,
> Even worse than He Sanwang[2] 賀三王 of yesteryear.
> Leading an army atop Mount Cock Crow,
> One frown from him and down you'll go.

(*Speak.*) We will wait at the base of the mountain. This event is likely to be inauspicious. (*They exit.*)

Scene 3

YANG HONG: (*Enters and recites.*)

> Away from the capital, this general has subdued the barbarians;
> My awesome fame has long thundered at Mount Cock Crow.
> Leading generals and soldiers, we guard this borderland
> So that the safety of the state altar will be upheld.

(*Speaks.*) I, Yang Hong, styled Yantian 炎天, am from the Shanhai Fort 山海關. I have been granted a fiefdom and my might awes the three barbarian tribes so much that none of them dares to move without my permission. At the top of this mountain, I have erected a pole a hundred foot high on which hangs an iron plaque. When the plaque is lowered to the ground, all the tribes[3] will mobilize their armies and come here to receive my commands. If the plaque stays on the pole, they will stay put and guard their own territories. This is beside the point. The point

---

2. Literally, Third Chieftain He. He may have been a locally famous chief of a mountain.

3. The word used in the original is *guo* 國, literally, states or nations. Since they are more properly simply groups of independent peoples who exist mostly outside the influence of the central government, I have translated the word as tribes. Depending on the context and the playwright's point of the view, such groups in other plays are called barbarian tribes or mountain bandits.

is, Yan Song, who holds great sway at the imperial court does not get along with me, so all the members of my family stay here at Mount Cock Crow to guard the borderland. I am willing to fight for the state but unwilling to be summoned to the court. When the kingdom of Black Water presented the precious bow and His Majesty summoned me to court, I resisted the imperial will three times. I wonder how His Majesty felt about it? It's not that I refuse to assist His Majesty, it's just that the emperor trusts that treacherous Yan. As soon as I reach the capital, that evil scoundrel Yan will likely indict me for defying the imperial will. There won't be much I can do when he works his poisonous treachery on me. When I arrived at my military tent this morning, my generalissimo's banner fluttered without any wind—something must be afoot.[4]

SOLDIER: I report to my lord. Lord Xu has arrived with an imperial edict.

YANG HONG: Line up to welcome him. (*He exits and re-enters.*) Please forgive me for being ignorant of my in-law's arrival and, hence, failing to welcome you properly.

XU ZAN: The honor would have been too great for me. How is my lord's health?

YANG HONG: Fine, thank you. How are you, dear in-law?

XU ZAN: I am fine too.

YANG HONG: May I ask what has brought my dear in-law to this mountain?

XU ZAN: My lord wouldn't have known. Even though you have resisted his edict three times, His Majesty will not punish you. He still wants my lord to return to the capital and help preserve the state.

YANG HONG: Aiya! My dear in-law, you really shouldn't have brought up the subject of preserving the state. This subject of preserving the state truly pains me! (*Sings.*)

> I remember how in the past when Korea rebelled,
> My nephew led an army and subdued it.
> To the court he was invited for a warm cup of wine,
> Princes from the various fiefs were all scared stiff.
> The emperor lined up his guards and granted them a personal audience,
> All the civil and martial courtiers met them at the imperial gate.
> Imperial edicts were announced two or three times,
> The various generals, however, stayed fast in their saddles.
> Yet when my nephew but twirled the tip of his whip,

---

4. Generals in shadow plays typically know that someone is coming to visit before they arrive by noting that their banners flutter despite the absence of wind.

All the warriors and soldiers dismounted and knelt.
The evil scoundrel Yan Song was so blinded by rage,
That he presented a memorial accusing my nephew of insurrection.
Believing in this slander His Majesty acted rashly,
Thus my poor nephew lost his life to the Yellow Springs.[5]
And for his nation, he became a headless ghost;
That's the result, you see, for having protected the state.
Now the kingdom of Black Water has presented a single bow,
In the court there must be tens of thousands of civil and martial officials.
They receive emoluments from His Majesty; they should alleviate his problems,
Why instead summon me two or three times?
Why dispense with the near and seek the far?
It is commonly said that heroes emerge from among youths,
But I am already in my mid-seventies,
How will it be possible for me to go to the court and draw the bow?
The entire court must be full of cowardly rats,
Without a single courageous manly chap.
The more I speak the more aggravated I feel,
What good words do I have to say about them?
If it weren't for the high regard for my dear in-law,
I would at this instant have the messenger's head hung from a high pole.

XU ZAN: (*Sings.*)
I, Xu Zan, hear him talk and find it hard to contain my wrath,
He is too unkind in his condemnation of the officials.
I have a mind to argue with him,
But that won't do, as I'll fail in my mission.
I have no choice but to swallow my grief and suppress my anger,
And appeal to him again as a dear in-law.

(*Speaks.*) Your nephew's death is the fault of that evil scoundrel Yan and has nothing to do with all the civil and martial officials. Furthermore, my lord is the hero of our time, a general of loyalty and integrity well known to all the nations. If you don't draw this precious bow, won't you have essentially wasted your life-long glory and reputation? It makes sense for you to go to the capital.

YANG HONG: There's no valid excuse for me not to go. His Majesty, however, trusts the evil scoundrel Yan. If I go, the evil scoundrel Yan

---

5. A realm of the deceased.

will certainly indict me for disobeying the imperial will. Furthermore, I am old and weak, and fear that I may fail the state. I can send my son to go the capital instead. He is young and strong; I expect him to be able to handle the job. My only worry is injury from the evil scoundrel Yan. I'm not sure what to do. I will need ten court ministers to vouch for his safety, otherwise we will still have to defy the imperial will.

XU ZAN: His Majesty has already dispatched five court ministers to be guarantors. They are presently at the foot of the mountain.

YANG HONG: That is very good. Attendants, summon the five ministers immediately and settle them at the rest station.

SOLDIER: Yes, my lord.

YANG HONG: Dear in-law, please go to the study and wait for me while I make arrangements for sending someone to the capital.

XU ZAN: Please go ahead.

YANG HONG: Attendants, go to Mount Azure Opening 青口山 and summon the two young masters here. (*Sings.*)

> I order my men to go to Mount Azure Opening,
> To summon my sons to draw the bow in the capital.
> Drawing the bow to avert disasters from the state,
> And spare anguish from His Majesty's brow.
> The ferocious reputation of us, father and sons, who dares to ignore?

SOLDIER: The two young masters are waiting to see you.

YANG HONG: Tell them to come in.

YANG LONG and YANG HU: (*Enter.*) We kowtow to our august father.

YANG HONG: There's no need for formalities, my sons. Get up.

YANG LONG: Thank you, father, for you graciousness. For what errand has our father summoned us?

YANG HONG: My son, you wouldn't have known. The kingdom of Black Water has terrorized our country with an iron bow. His Majesty has summoned your father to the capital to draw the bow. Your father is old and weak and would like you to go in my stead. Are you willing?

YANG LONG: When the father gives an order, how dare your son not follow? I am only concerned about injury from the evil scoundrel Yan. What should I do?

YANG HONG: Don't worry, my son. We have five court ministers here, and you will also have the protection of your father-in-law. One expects no problems.

YANG LONG: If such is the case, your son is willing to go.

YANG HU: Father, I want to go, too.

YANG HONG: My son, you are young and weak. You won't be of assistance if you go.

YANG HU: Father, I may not be able to draw the bow, but I can keep my brother company. That's important too.

YANG HONG: Fine then, you two can go together. I will write a letter on your behalf to Prince Xu's residence. Your Uncle Xu will surely take good care of you. My sons, listen to your father's admonitions. (*Sings.*)

Be sure to deliver this short letter,
You two brothers will depend on him to make all the decisions.
As soon as the bow is drawn, return to Mount Cock Crow immediately,
To prevent your father from worrying day and night.
You must not accept any titles or emoluments;
When receiving rewards, pick the smallest,
Lest that evil scoundrel Yan shoot you with a stealthy arrow,
And create a calamity that will be hard for you to escape from.
Bid farewell to family members in the inner quarters and change your clothes,
So that you may accompany your father-in-law Xu to the court right away.

(*Speaks.*) Do heed your father's instructions. Leave immediately.

YANG LONG: We obey your orders. (*They all exit.*)

Scene 4

YANG LONG: (*Enters and sings.*)

Following my father's order to go to the capital, I am filled with delight.
Drawing the precious bow to help the emperor, I will exhibit my prowess.
I wish I could take on wings and fly to the capital—
Suddenly I fall from my horse and my eyes are hazy.

YANG HU: (*Enters with Xu Zan.*) Elder brother, wake up!

XU ZAN: My wise son-in-law, wake up!

YANG LONG: (*Sings.*)

Suddenly, I fell from my horse—I almost lost my life.
Careful consideration deems this a terrible omen rather than good.
It is probably better to return to the mountains than go to the capital.

XU ZAN: Wait. It was merely your horse stumbling. My wise son-in-law, please don't be suspicious.

YANG LONG: (*Sings.*)

What can I do with my father-in-law begging and urging me ahead?

(*Speaks.*) Ah, so be it! (*Sings.*)

    If I don't go, the lives of his entire family would be in jeopardy.

    Great men do not worry about life and death.

    Once I reach the capital, then I will decide what to do.

    If I don't go, I would have disobeyed my father and become un-filial. (*They exit.*)

Scene 5

PRINCE XU: (*Enters and sings.*)

    Having attended the imperial court, I descend from my golden carriage.

    A hereditary prince, I just came from the imperial morning court.

    The kingdom of Black Water has presented a bow,

    And sent the hundred civil and martial officials into a quandary.

    How can the knitted brow of His Majesty be relieved?

(*Speaks.*) I am Xu Zhou, a descendant of Xu Da 徐達. Due to the fact that Yang Hong has thrice defied the imperial will and refused to come to the capital, His Majesty has ordered Minister Xu Zan to summon him personally. Xu Zan has not yet returned to the court. It's so unsettling that I can neither sit nor sleep well.

SOLDIER: I report to your highness. Minister Xu Zan requests an audience.

PRINCE XU: Invite him to come in.

XU ZAN: (*Enters.*) I have brought with me two champions who can relieve the worries of the emperor and his ministers. Your highness on high, allow Xu Zan to make his obeisance.

PRINCE XU: Please raise yourself.

XU ZAN: Thank you. Your highness is most gracious.

PRINCE XU: Please take a seat, my dear minister.

XU ZAN: Thank you for the seat.

PRINCE ZAN: Allow me to inquire, my dear minister, whether the venerable General Yang has arrived?

XU ZAN: The venerable General Yang said that he is too old and fears that he might fail the state and has, therefore, dispatched his two young warrior sons to follow me to the capital. They are presently waiting at the gate for an audience with you.

PRINCE XU: Summon them in.

XU ZAN: His highness has ordered the two warriors for an audience.

YANG LONG and YANG HU: (*Enter.*) August uncle, your nephews kowtow to you.

PRINCE XU: Ho! Your father defied the imperial will three times, what kind of punishment should this crime deserve?

YANG LONG: Please calm your anger, uncle. My father is old, his breath is weak and strength small; he fears that he might fail the state. He finally decided to dispatch your young nephews to come to the capital to draw the bow. That is why it took so long. Please don't blame him, uncle. Here is a letter from my father, please read it, uncle.

PRINCE XU: Let me read it. Since such is the case, you two brothers can raise yourselves.

YANG LONG: Uncle is most gracious.

PRINCE XU: My dear minister, you may go home.

XU ZAN: Thank you, your highness. (*He exits.*)

PRINCE XU: My children, you two brothers can stay at my residence. I will go to the court tomorrow and ask the emperor to pardon your father's offense.

YANG LONG: Thank you very much, uncle.

PRINCE XU: Come attendants. Set up a banquet at the second hall to welcome these two warriors. (*Sings.*)

> Upon seeing the two warriors, I am filled with delight.
> Sporting the awesome deportment of champions of this world,
> They will draw the bow and avert our national disaster,
> And thus relieve the frown from His Majesty's brow.
> Let's prepare a memorial for the imperial court. (*They exit.*)

Scene 6

EMPEROR: (*Enters and sings.*)

> When will our tiger general come to the capital?
> For this, we, the emperor, have become sick from worrying.

ATTENDANT: I report to His Majesty. Young General Yang awaits at the imperial gate.

EMPEROR: Summon him to the court immediately.

YANG LONG: Your Majesty on high, your lowly subject, Yang Long, presents himself.

EMPEROR: Ho! Your father has defied the imperial will again and again. What kind of punishment should be dealt for this crime?

YANG LONG: Your Majesty, please allow me to memorialize concerning it. (*Sings.*)

> Please excuse your subject for arriving late at the capital,
> Guarding the borderland fort, the distance is far.
> My father, being advanced in age, is weak and unable to draw the bow;
> He fears the he might fail the state and become a laughingstock for the barbarians.

Your subject is at the court to draw the bow on my father's behalf,
To avert calamity from the state and to secure stability for Your
Majesty.
Please grant us amnesty so that no disaster will befall me.

EMPEROR: Such being the case, we will absolve you of the crime. Draw
the bow immediately.

YANG LONG: Let your subject take a look at the bow first.

EMPEROR: Attendant, take the general to the Temple of Pervasive Prosperity 廣祿寺 to examine the bow.

ATTENDANT: Yes, Your Majesty. Please come with me, general. (*They
exit and re-enter.*)

YANG LONG: Your subject has examined the bow and would like to know
whether Your Majesty prefers a civilized draw or a martial draw?

EMPEROR: What is the difference between the civilized and martial
styles?

YANG LONG: In a civilized draw, your subject would cock the bow in the
imperial court and shoot ten times consecutively. In a martial draw,
your subject will shoot from a galloping horse at a one-hundred-foot
pole erected outside the city walls.

EMPEROR: As long as it is drawn, the heroic fame of you and your father
won't have existed in vain. You, young general, have just arrived at the
capital. Both you and your horse must be exhausted. The civilized draw
would be preferable.

YAN SONG: (*Enters.*) Wait just one minute! This bow must be drawn the
martial style—a civilized draw is definitely unsuitable. For such an in-
comparable hero as this young warrior, how can a civilized draw be
worthy of spreading his fame throughout all under Heaven? A martial
style draw would definitely be the choice. When his success is made
known everywhere, no nation would dare to attack us recklessly.

EMPEROR: We will follow your advice then. Go don full military garb,
young warrior.

YANG LONG: I accept the imperial will. (*He exits.*)

YAN SONG: Your Majesty, who will be the presiding official in charge of
pacing the measurements at the bow drawing today?

EMPEROR: Could it be that you would like to be the presiding official?

YAN SONG: I accept the imperial will.

EMPEROR: You managed to talk your way into being the presiding official. You may now leave the court.

YAN SONG: Your subject accepts the imperial will. (*He exits.*)

EMPEROR: Attendants, prepare our carriage. (*Sings.*)
Our attendants will prepare our dragon carriage
To take us to the Benevolent Cloud Pavilion 惠雲樓.
Our state has produced such a heroic warrior,

Our realm will now attain peace and prosperity.
Other countries would not dare to attack us. (*He exits.*)

Scene 7

YAN SONG: (*Enters and sings.*)
> Yang Long, that abominable little beast,
> Will draw the iron bow at the instructional field today.
> Even if your talent should be great,
> It will be impossible for you to escape unscathed.
> I will devise a scheme to end your life.

(*Speaks.*) Ah, Yang Long, you suckling child! How much talent do you have that you dare to boast so? How can I stomach it? Attendants, make the pole a hundred and twenty feet high and take extra large steps—count more than sixty of them.

SOLDIER: My lord, why are we adding to the original measurements?

YAN SONG: Shut up! Just go and do it right away. Ah, Yang Long, Yang Long! I'll show you that although a spear hurled in the open is easy to dodge, an arrow shot in stealth is difficult to guard against. (*Sings.*)
> How hateful—little Yang Long is bolder than Heaven.
> You even dared to make preposterous claims at the imperial palace.
> Adding height and distance at the instructional field, I scheme secretly,
> To make sure that you, little bastard, will not live to a ripe age.
> I'll have you, little kid, delivered to meet with the king of Hades.[6]

(*He exits, re-enters and sits under the pole.*)

YANG LONG: (*Enters with Xu Zan and sings.*)
> Yang Long arrives at the instructional field in full military garb.
> Raising my head, I examine everything carefully;
> The distance has been stretched out; what is the matter?
> The height has been extended; what is the idea behind it?

XU ZAN: (*Sings.*)
> My dear son-in-law, do be cautious at the instructional field,
> Beware of stealthy arrows from the scoundrel Yan.
> Why not go see His Majesty in the Benevolent Cloud Pavilion?
> The heart of that evil scoundrel is worse than those of tigers and wolves.

---

6. King Yama, the main judge of Hell.

(*Speaks.*) Look, my wise son-in-law, the one sitting under the pole is scoundrel Yan. You must be careful.

YANG LONG: Ah, father-in-law, the pole is a hundred and twenty feet high, the distance is sixty some paces. This is obviously a scheme to hurt me, I have to go see His Majesty. Ah, wait a minute! If I go to His Majesty, the evil Yan will surely scoff at me. I'd better draw the bow before I settle this. Please go ahead, father-in-law.

XU ZAN: Do be very careful. (*He exits.*)

YANG LONG: Beat the drum. (*He draws the bow, shoots the target and exits.*)

YAN SONG: The little bastard is truly amazing!

BARBARIAN: Superb warrior! Aiya, what a superb warrior! Ha, ha, ha, ha ... (*He exits with Yan Song.*)

EMPEROR: (*Enters.*) Ah! What a superb warrior! (*Sings.*)

> Observing from the instructional field, our brow is filled with delight.
> Yang Long is indeed a wonder among warriors!
> We will seat ourselves in the dragon palace,
> And wait for Yang Long to deliver his memorial.
> Such a hero is incomparable in this world.

(*Speaks.*) We saw Yang Long draw the bow at the instructional field; it was as effortlessly as a roc snatching a sparrow. He is the supreme warrior of our age.

ATTENDANT: Your Majesty, Warrior Yang awaits at the imperial gate.

EMPEROR: Show him into the imperial court.

YANG LONG: (*Enters.*) Your Majesty [on high], your lowly subject, Yang Long, brings a memorial.

EMPEROR: You are a matchless hero! We bestow upon you the title of Governor of Gaoshi 高世節度使. You may leave the court.

YANG LONG: Your Majesty, my father has given me clear instructions. The Yang family already holds an office of the first rank; we dare not receive any further entitlements.

EMPEROR: Since you won't accept an official post. We will bestow upon you a thousand ounces of gold. You may leave the court and get it now.

YANG LONG: Your subject does not dare to receive any rewards.

EMPEROR: Young warrior, what is the meaning of this?

YANG LONG: Your Majesty, please allow me to explain. (*Sings.*)

> Please consider that your subject received orders from my father to serve the state.
> Having received emoluments from the state, it is but our duty to relieve Your Majesty of your worries.
> According to my father: our positions are high, we must not act pettily.

Therefore, I cannot accept a single morsel of the abundant imperial favors.

My only wish is to return early in order to perform my filial duties.

EMPEROR: You are truly both loyal and filial. Since you won't accept our rewards, we will present you with three cups of imperial wine to show our gratitude.

YANG LONG: In this case, your subject will be bold.

EMPEROR: Attendants, bring some wine. We will bestow the wine upon you personally.

YAN SONG: (*Enters.*) Wait, wait, wait a minute. Although Your Majesty is fond of the warrior, it is inconceivable for an emperor to serve wine with his own royal hand. Let me serve on behalf of Your Majesty.

EMPEROR: So be it. We will trouble you to serve it for us then.

YAN SONG: I obey the imperial will. (*Sings.*)

> I hold the wine cup for His Majesty and think to myself,
> If I don't get rid of this little rascal, my hateful anger will be intolerable.
> I'll use the trick of dropping the cup to end his life.
> Once this stealthy arrow is sent, he will not be able to defend himself.

(*Speaks.*) General Yang, please take the cup.

YANG LONG: Aiya! (*Sings.*)

> I, Yang Long, am about to receive the cup, I think to myself:
> The old scoundrel plans to harm me, he must have a devious scheme.
> But unable to do anything, I can only raise my hands and dare not look up.

YAN SONG: (*Sings.*)

> Taking advantage of the opportunity, I will smash the jade cup;
> He won't possibly be able to escape this snare set by Heaven.

(*Speaks.*) General Yang, please take the cup.

YANG LONG: Yes.

YAN SONG: (*He drops the cup and speaks.*) Your Majesty, Yang Long has smashed the jade cup. He means to insult both Your Majesty and myself. Please punish him.

EMPEROR: Ah! Yang Long. Why did you smash our jade cup?

YANG LONG: Aiya! Your Majesty. Your subject hadn't even touched it before the Grand Tutor threw the cup on the ground. He clearly intended to incriminate your subject. Your Majesty, please adjudicate this case for me.

YAN SONG: Liar! Your father defied the imperial will three times, yet His Majesty did not prosecute him. When you came to draw the bow in his stead and His Majesty rewarded you with an official post and gold, you actually dared make excuses and refuse them, you ungrateful beast. His Majesty's dragon heart felt so uneasy that he offered you three cups of imperial wine. To have me serving you wine should not have been considered an indignity to you, why, then, did you smash the jade cup? Your Majesty, Yang Long obviously has no respect for the Son of Heaven and should be beheaded.

EMPEROR: Stand aside for a moment.

YAN SONG: Yes, Your Majesty.

EMPEROR: Yang Long, you little rogue! As a recipient of imperial emoluments, it is your duty to assist the state and draw the bow. Why did you refuse our rewards of an official post and gold? Now that we bestowed imperial wine upon you and had the secretary of state to serve you—this was certainly no slight treatment—how then dare you smash the jade cup? You mock us because we have no one else to protect our state—how can we put up with this? Guards, come into the court and take Yang Long to the Gate of Displaying Righteousness 張 義門 for execution. (*He exits with guards.*)

XU ZAN: (*Enters.*) Spare him from the knife! Aiya! Your Majesty! The warrior accidentally dropped the cup but, considering his merit in drawing the bow, he must not be executed.

YAN SONG: Rubbish! Yang Long showed no respect for the Son of Heaven: he defied and then insulted His Majesty. He is not forgivable and must be executed. How dare you defend and cover up for him?

EMPEROR: Our dear Minister Xu, Yang Long's crime is not forgivable. There is no need to memorialize to guarantee for him.

XU ZAN: Aiya! Ah, Your Majesty! (*Sings.*)

> I, Xu Zan, prostrate myself in the golden palace, I plead grievously;
> Your Majesty, up there in the dragon throne, please listen carefully.
> Breaking the cup, it was just a slip of the hand on the part of the warrior.
> One should consider his drawing the iron bow to avert a national disaster.
> Executing Yang Long, I fear, will leave no one to guard our border.
> I dread that when the foreigners know, they will create more trouble.
> Please reconsider, Your Majesty, and allow your minister to memorialize.

EMPEROR: There's no need for you to plead. Yang Long's crime cannot be exonerated. Leave the court, our minister.

XU ZAN: Aiya! Your Majesty!

YAN SONG: Hush! If you make any more fuss, you'll be condemned along with Yang Long. Come guards, chase the minister out of the court!

XU ZAN: My fine son-in-law, I cannot save you! (*He exits.*)

YAN SONG: Your Majesty, who will preside over Yang Long's execution today?

EMPEROR: Is it possible that you are asking to be the presiding official?

YAN SONG: I thank His Majesty for this imperial favor.

EMPEROR: You have managed to talk your way into getting this position too!

YAN SONG: Since Your Majesty has commanded your minister to preside over the execution, please advise when the execution should be performed and when you would like his head to be presented?

EMPEROR: Perform the execution at four and present the head at five.

YAN SONG: Your Majesty, your minister is a civil official, but Yang Long is so incomparably strong, what am I to do should there be a mishap?

EMPEROR: We can order General Liu Ying to guard the execution ground. How do you feel about that?

YAN SONG: This way your subject will feel secure.

EMPEROR: You may now leave the court.

YAN SONG: I obey the imperial will. (*He exits.*)

EMPEROR: Attendants, roll up the audience curtains. (*He exits.*)

Scene 8

YANG LONG: (*Enters with Liu Ying and sings.*)

> I, Yang Long, lower my head and tears drench me.
> Raising my face, I ask Heaven for justice, but Heaven does not reply.
> If only I could have known about this disaster I am encountering today,
> I wouldn't have come to the court to perform this loyal deed.

(*Speaks.*) Oh my dear parents whom I'll never see again! (*Sings.*)

> I cry for my parents whom I'll never see again,
> And my sister, brother, wife, and children, whom I'll never meet again.
> Suddenly I think of my younger brother, Yang Hu.
> Irrepressibly, this brave soul weeps aloud.

(*Speaks while weeping.*) I call for my brother, ah my brother! You told our parents that you would accompany your big brother. Now that your big brother is getting executed, why aren't you here to save me? Why aren't you thinking of your big brother?[7]

LIU YING: Warrior, do not weep. I'm sure that there must be civil and military officials at the court today who will memorialize to have you exonerated.

YANG LONG: Don't you console me. Who are you anyway?

LIU YING: I am your junior, Liu Ying.[8]

YANG LONG: Oh, so it is Lord Liu. Come here, I have a secret to tell you.

LIU YING: Warrior Yang, what do you wish to say?

YANG LONG: Ah, you scoundrel! (*Sings.*)
 I wish I could end your life right here.
 I grind my teeth in anger and yell at Liu Ying,
 When has the Yang family ever done wrong to you?
 Why have you conspired in this plot against me?
 If I can't avenge myself today, I'll deal with you at the court in Hell.

LIU YING: Warrior, you are a victim of Yan's evil scheme. He requested at the imperial court for me to guard the execution ground. There is nothing I could do about it.

YANG LONG: If that's so, I won't blame you. Just take me to the execution platform.

LIU YING: All right. Executioner, take the young general to the execution platform.

SOLDIER: (*Taking him to the platform and speaks.*) Ai, young warrior Yang is on the platform, those who wish to see him should do so now, he will be executed momentarily.

XU ZAN: (*Enters.*) Aiya! (*Sings.*)
 Hearing this, my soul is almost scared out of me.
 My feet wish to fly, but I can barely walk.
 Arriving at the execution ground, I stumble all of a sudden;
 All I can see is my dear son-in-law up on the platform.
(*Speaks.*) Aiya, my fine son-in-law! (*Sings.*)
 Your father-in-law has caused your death;
 I regret having brought you to the imperial court.
 Drawing the iron bow, your merit was by no means minuscule;
 Who would have guessed that the loyal and good won't end up well?
 At the palace I did try hard to plead and beg;

---

7. The original says, "Why do you not wish to kill your brother" which I believe is a miscopy.
8. By calling himself a younger brother of Yang Long, he shows humbleness and indicates that he means well.

Risking my life, I also memorialized at the court.
The Son of Heaven got angry and banned guaranteeing for you.
Chased out of the imperial palace, I could only cry and weep.
I thought and thought but came up with no cunning schemes,
Only the sound of my wailing remained by the end of the audience.

LIU YING: Lord Xu, it's useless for you to cry here. Run quickly to Prince Xu's residence for help. Our young warrior may be saved yet.

XU ZAN: Yes. (*Sings.*)
The old dragon is still lying in his secluded, deep pool.[9]
These words suddenly wake me up from this nightmare.
Bear with the hardship, my fine son-in-law, for a few more moments,
I will plead with Prince Xu for him to seek an imperial audience.
(*He exits.*)

YAN SONG: Oh no! Xu Zan wept at the execution ground and then left in a hurry. He must have gone to mobilize the civil and military officials to offer to be guarantors for Yang. If His Majesty should accept the guarantors, then I would have wasted all this effort. Oh I know, I will present a false edict and get this rascal executed. I'm sure it won't hurt. Guards, execute Yang Long right away.

SOLDIER: It's still too early.

YAN SONG: I have an edict which says not to wait until the appointed time but to execute him immediately.

SOLDIER: Beat the drums. (*Yang Long's head is chopped off.*)

YAN SONG: Hang the head on top of the Gate of Displaying Righteousness. (*He exits.*)

LIU YING: (*Enters.*) Aiya! My young warrior! (*Sings.*)
The old scoundrel is truly too vicious,
He has killed the man before the appointed hour.
In vain, the minister seeks help at Prince Xu's,
Not knowing about this evil scoundrel's scheming deadliness.
The scoundrel is ten times more poisonous than snakes and scorpions. (*He exits.*)

Scene 9

YANG HU: (*Enters.*) I am taking a stroll. (*Sings.*)
We brothers have settled in at Prince Xu's residence;

---

9. This is a reference to Prince Xu.

In leisure, I play chess with the uncle.
My elder brother has quietly slipped out of the residence,
One whole day passed without any news from him.
I wonder where he had gone to enjoy himself.
(*Off stage: Listen everyone, have you heard that Yang Long from Mount Cock Crow achieved merit by drawing the bow? His Majesty was so pleased that he conferred upon him an official post, but he refused to take it. The emperor then bestowed upon him gold and, again, he refused to accept it. His Majesty thereupon presented upon him three cups of imperial wine. The sneaky scoundrel Yan Song offered to serve the wine for the emperor and schemed to incriminate the warrior by dropping the cup. His Majesty believed in Yan's slander and had Yang charged for insulting the emperor. He was executed at the Gate of Displaying Righteousness. This is the end to the loyal and upright who strove to save the state. Ai, it's sad, isn't it?*)*
YANG HU: Aiya! Ah, dear elder brother! (*He faints.*)
XU ZAN: (*Enters.*) Your highness, please hurry! (*Sings.*)
Your highness, please go to the palace right away,
You must help save young Yang Long!
If you are but one step too late,
Saving his life will be impossible!
Here the two of us are moving forward in haste,
Who is this dead man[10] in the middle of the road?
(*Speaks.*) Ah, it is the younger Warrior Yang.
PRINCE XU: Help him right away.
XU ZAN: Wake up, young warrior.
YANG HU: (*Sings.*)
We thought that drawing the bow would spread his fame,
Who would have expected the loyal and upright to end up at the Yellow Springs?
Slowly, slowly, I open my eyes to take a peek,
So it is my two uncles standing in front of me. (*He rises.*)
XU ZAN: Where are you going, young warrior?
YANG HU: (*Sings.*)
I am going to the palace gate to seek my elder brother,
Please do not stop me, my dear uncles.
(*Speaks.*) Take your hands off me!
PRINCE XU: Aiya! If this is the case, my dear minister, you proceed to the execution ground right away while I hurry to the palace. (*They all exit.*)

10. People who fainted are considered dead until they wake up again.

Scene 10

YANG HU: (*Enters.*) Aiya! My elder brother! (*Sings.*)
> Hanging high at the Gate of Displaying Righteousness is my brother's head,
> I wept so hard that my throat is choked and my face is drenched in tears.
> Kneeling on both knees, I bewail this rotting flesh and blood of mine.
> I regret that you have drawn the bow and alleviated the state's woe.
> The emperor had no regard whatsoever for your merits;
> He listened to slanders and treated the loyal and upright as foe.
> I can't stop cursing that treacherous scoundrel Yan Song.
> Bending the pole, I will first retrieve my brother's head;
> I'll carry the head back to Mount Cock Crow and talk to my father.
> We'll mobilize an army, flatten the capital—not leaving a single dog or chicken!
> Weeping loudly, I run along the road to Mount Cock Crow. (*He exits.*)

YAN SONG: (*Enters.*) I am Minister Yan Song. Just now a soldier reported that a young man bent the pole, took Yang Long's head, and left the capital. He must have been a member of the Yang family. We can't let him escape! Attendants, track down the one who took the head and bring him here. (*He exits.*)

YANG HU: (*Enters and sings.*)
> Carrying my brother's head in my bosom, I dare not look back.
> Painful tears flowing from my eyes, I weep until my entrails are torn.
> I loathe the treacherous minister Xu Zan for being in their faction.
> How will you be able to face my parents in the future?
> After leaving the city, I travel hastily and dare not look back.
> (*Yelling offstage.*)
> Turning my head, I see pursuing soldiers; they are forcing me off the road.

(*Speaks.*) Ho! The pursuing soldiers are catching up. I don't have any weapons—how am I going to evade them? Oh, I know. I'll hit them with my brother's head, snatch a horse and weapon, and then make my escape. (*Yang Hu fights with soldiers, escapes and exits.*)

SOLDIER: (*Enters with Yan Song; speaks.*) I report to my lord. The young man has escaped, but he left Yang Long's head behind.

YAN SONG: Recall the soldiers and return to the city. Hang the head back in front of the Gate of Displaying Righteousness. (*They exit.*)

YANG HU: (*Enters and sings.*)
>
> I almost lost my life back there,
> The whereabouts of my brother's head is unknown.
> One alone cannot defeat a multitude, so I made a quick escape,
> Worried that the life of this warrior would have been jeopardized.
> Urging on the horse, I snap my whip and climb up the mountain.
>
> (*He exits.*)

Scene 11

YANG HONG: (*Enters and sings.*)
>
> My two sons have gone to the capital and have not yet returned;
> This old man worries about them nearly every moment.
> Yan Song monopolizes the power in the court,
> I fear that the treacherous scoundrel will bring calamity upon them.

MAID: (*Enters and sings.*)
>
> My lord's brow is knitted today,
> On account of his two sons' trip to the capital.

YANG SUZHEN: (*Enters and sings.*)
>
> Last night I had a dream both singular and bizarre,
> I'll have to tell my parents about it.
> Good or bad, it is difficult for me to tell.
>
> (*Speaks.*) Papa and mama, I had a dream last night which seems unpropitious.

YANG HONG: What did you dream about, my child?

YANG SUZHEN: I dreamt that I was standing in the snow, wearing a gauze hat on my head and carrying a piece of wood against my chest. What kind of omen is it?

YANG HONG: Standing in the snow represents wearing funerary clothes.[11] Wearing a gauze hat[12] may signify danger. Carrying a piece of wood forms the character for "to rest."[13] This dream is a bad omen. Your brothers who went to the capital are probably in danger.

SERVANT: (*Enters.*) I report to my lord. Our Second Young Master is waiting to be seen.

YANG HONG: Tell him to come in.

YANG HU: (*Enters.*) My august papa and mama, your child greets you.

---

11. White is worn at Chinese funerals.
12. Gauze hats were worn by government officials.
13. The character for "to rest," *xiu* 休, consists of the graph for a person, *ren* 人, next to the graph for wood, *mu* 木.

YANG HONG: My son, it's good to see you back. Why isn't your brother here? Didn't he come back with you?

YANG HU: I, your child, am back.

YANG HONG: I know you are back, but where did your brother go?

YANG HU: My brother—

YANG HONG: What happened to your brother?

YANG HU: (*Speaks while weeping.*) Papa—

YANG HONG: Don't cry, take your time and tell me.

YANG HU: Papa, you wouldn't have known. After your sons took your order to go to the capital, elder brother drew the precious bow—

YANG HONG: So he did manage to draw the bow!

YANG HU: Yes, he did manage to draw the bow—

YANG HONG: That's good if he was able to draw the bow.

YANG HU: His Majesty was so delighted that he conferred the position of the governor of Gaoshi upon him and rewarded him with a thousand ounces of gold. My brother declined and accepted neither. The emperor then presented him with three cups of imperial wine. Yan Song served the wine and dropped the jade cup to incriminate him. His Majesty believed Yan's slander and indicted my brother for dishonoring him. He was pushed out to the Gate of Displaying Righteousness—

YANG HONG: Pushed out there for what?

YANG HU: He was pushed out to the Gate of Displaying Righteousness to be executed!

YANG HONG: Aiya! My son! (*He faints.*)

YANG HU and YAN SUZHEN: Wake up, papa, wake up!

YANG HONG: (*Sings.*)
> Hearing the news, I got so upset that I fainted on the floor,
> Leaving me, my three souls hover in mid-air.
> Hearing calls, I slowly open my eyes.
> My son, Yang Long, where are you now?

MADAM KANG: My dear child! (*Sings.*)
> I, Madam Kang, standing on the side, am drenched in tears.
> The pain tears my entrails, as if I am being stabbed by knives.
> The dim-witted emperor did not consider my son's immense contribution,
> He executed the wrong person, causing blood to stain the yellow sand.

YANG SUZHEN: Elder brother whom I'll never see again! (*Sings.*)
> I, Yang Suzhen, am so filled with anger that my chest hurts.
> The dim-witted emperor did not consider your immense merits—
> Who told you to go to the court to be loyal and upright?
> All of a sudden my killer instinct is aroused,
> I'll demolish the capital on my horse

And exact a life for a life from that scoundrel.

(*Speaks.*) Papa, the dim-witted emperor listened to slander and caused my elder brother's death. Why don't we rebel and avenge his death?

YANG HONG: My child, your brother died because of the treacherous scoundrel's scheme. How can we rebel?

YANG SUZHEN: Oh! (*She exits.*)

YANG HU: We still have the five court ministers here. Why don't we execute them to avenge my elder brother's death?

YANG HONG: Oh yes! Announce my order: beat the drums and prepare for holding court in my tent. (*They exit.*)

Scene 12

YANG HONG: (*Enters tent with Yang Hu; sings.*)
    Fuming with anger, I preside over my military court.
    Mourning grievously, I think of my son.
    If one wants me to smooth my sorrowful brow,
    Kill that evil scoundrel and chop him in two.
    Heavy-heartedly, I sit and ruminate at my desk.

YANG HU: Papa!

YANG HONG: What is it, my son?

YANG HU: Papa, you are in the military tent.

YANG HONG: Yes, I am in the military tent.

YANG HU: Do you know why are you in the military tent?

YANG HONG: So, why am I in the military tent?

YANG HU: Have the five court ministers executed so as to avenge my brother's grief.

YANG HONG: Oh yes! Order the five court ministers rounded up here!

MINISTERS: (*Enter.*) We await to serve my lord.

YANG HONG: Ho! You and your evil faction have conspired to murder my son. What kind of punishment do you deserve for such a crime?

MINISTERS: Our lord, you are gravely mistaken. We have stayed at Mount Cock Crow and have not been to the capital. If we had been there, we wouldn't have folded our arms and watched as the treacherous Yan murder your son. It's really not our fault. Please calm your anger, our lord. Even if you execute all five of us, you still wouldn't have avenged Yang Long's death.

YANG HONG: Yes, indeed. My son was murdered by Yan Song. It had nothing to do with you.

MINISTERS: No, it had nothing to do with us.

YANG HONG: Since it had nothing to do with you, you may leave the mountain and go back to the court.

MINISTERS: Thank you, our lord.

YANG HU: Papa, why didn't you execute the five court ministers?

YANG HONG: Since we know for sure that Yan Song was the murderer, why execute them instead?

YANG HU: Ah, papa! (*Sings.*)
> Papa, you don't seem to understand.
> My brother and I shouldn't have gone to the capital.
> Only because the five scoundrels came and tricked us,
> That we consented to go to the capital to draw the bow.
> They and that evil scoundrel are all in the same boat.

YANG HONG: But, ultimately, it wasn't the fault of these five court ministers.

YANG HU: I, Yang Hu, think to myself. Papa is not willing to avenge my Elder brother's death, why don't I go to the inner camp to talk to my younger sister. We'll raise an army in secret. (*Sings.*)
> Papa is old and his heart too loyal
> That my elder brother's grievous death cannot be avenged.
> I will discuss this matter with my sister at the inner camp;
> We will raise an army in secret and besiege the capital.
> We will flatten the scoundrel thieves in one big sweep. (*He exits.*)

YANG HONG: Yang Long, your papa's dear son! (*Sings.*)
> I, Yang Hong, lower my head and tears pour down.
> I call for you ten times, nine times without any response.
> My only wish was for you to be both loyal and filial,
> Who would have expected that you would end up in Hades?
> I resent Heaven and blame the earth; my heart is not at peace. (*He exits.*)

Scene 13

YANG HU: (*Enters.*) I am strolling. (*Sings.*)
> Papa stubbornly refuses to rebel,
> My elder brother's death will hence be hard to vindicate.
> I have just arrived at the inner camp,
> Let me quickly give my younger sister a shout.

(*Speaks.*) Younger Sister, come out quickly.

YANG SUZHEN: (*Enters.*) Here I am. Have the five court ministers been beheaded?

YANG HU: Not only were they not beheaded, but they were released and allowed to return to the capital!

YANG SUZHEN: When the tiger is released back to the mountains, it will do injury in the future. Brother, go report to our sister-in-law at Mount Azure Opening right away. We will rebel with her.

YANG HU: In that case, I'll leave right away. (*He exits.*)

YANG SUZHEN: Guards, get your weapons and be ready for action. (*Sings.*)

> At the inner camp, I, Yang Suzhen, am consumed with fury.
> I will trample the capital on horseback and annihilate the scoundrels.
> Taking my spear and mounting my steed in a forward charge,
> I will obliterate this pack of thugs with one big sweep. (*She exits.*)

Scene 14

ZHANG REN and LI YI: (*Enter and sing.*)

> We heard that our wise sworn brother was murdered,
> The news filled us warriors with irrepressible anger.
> When we do catch that treacherous scoundrel,
> We will interrogate him—one knife-cut with every question.

(*Speak.*) We are Zhang Ren and Li Yi at the camp of Iron Peak Fort 鐵嶺關. We are sworn brothers of Yang Long. Our wise younger brother was unexpectedly murdered at the capital by the scoundrel Yan. (*Horse neighs off stage.*) Someone is coming on a galloping horse.

YANG HU: (*Enters.*) I am in such a rush that I curse the distance and bemoan that my horse is not running fast enough.

ZHANG REN: Oh, so it is the Younger Warrior Yang!

YANG HU: Big brothers, where are you going?

ZHANG REN: We just heard that your elder brother was murdered by the scoundrel Yan. We have come up the mountain to talk to the venerable general about mobilizing a rebellion together.

YANG HU: My father won't rebel, so big brother need not go to him. I am going to my sister-in-law right now and we'll start an uprising from Mount Azure Opening.

ZHANG REN: We'll wait for the iron plaque to fall then. Goodbye! (*They exit.*)

YANG HU: (*Sings.*)

> The two sworn brothers, Zhang and Li, are willing to rebel
> To avenge the injustice suffered by my elder brother.
> Even they feel their duty to him as sworn brothers,
> How can I not feel the attachment of fraternal love?
> Hence, for the sake of my elder brother, my father will be disobeyed. (*He exits.*)

Scene 15

XU JINDING: (*Enters and sings.*)

> My warrior husband has left to preserve the state,
> There is no news of him here at Mount Azure Opening.
> Worrying that wind and frost are making his trip difficult,
> I can neither sit nor sleep and am consumed with anxiety.
> My mind and spirit feel so disturbed that I cannot stay calm.

YANG HU: (*Enters and sings.*)

> This is Mount Azure Opening, the territory guarded by my brother.
> Lined with banners, spears, and swords, the two rows align perfectly.
> Seeing my sister-in-law, my tears drop involuntarily.

XU JINDING: So you've come back, brother-in-law. How come I don't see your elder brother?

YANG HU: (*Sings.*)

> Here you are, sister-in-law, waiting for your husband inside the red brocade curtain,[14]
> How would you have known that conjugal love has forever ended for you?

XU JINDING: Brother-in-law, what on earth do you mean?

YANG LONG: (*Speaks while weeping.*) Sister-in-law, after my elder brother drew the precious bow at the capital, His Majesty was so pleased that he bestowed upon him an official position and gold, both of which my brother declined. The emperor thereupon presented three cups of imperial wine to him. That evil scoundrel, Yan Song, served the wine at the court and dropped the jade cup to incriminate him. The stupid emperor listened to Yan's slander and found elder brother guilty of slighting him. Elder brother was taken to the Gate of Displaying Righteousness and executed there.

XU JINDING: Aiya! My poor husband! (*She faints.*)

YANG HU: Wake up, Sister-in-law!

> XU JINDING: (*Sings.*)
>
> Hearing the news, I was so outraged that my throat choked.
> I feel my soul disperse and my four limbs are totally limp.
>
> (*Speaks.*) Ah! My dear husband! (*Sings.*)
>
> Never again will you be able to take your bow and arrow to hunt in the countryside;

---

14. The bed curtain.

Never again will you be able to show off your awesome gallantry;
Never again will you be able to strategize to impress all under Heaven;
Never again will you be able to subdue the three barbarian tribes and protect the state.
Your death has caused my life to have beginning but no continuation,
Your death has severed me from love, half way down the road.
Suddenly I am jolted by the evil treachery of that scoundrel Yan Song—
Why have you always plotted poisonous schemes to ruin the Yangs?
If I capture that scoundrel, I will be sure to hack him ten thousand times.
Even that Jiajing Emperor himself, I will not spare.
I order my brother-in-law, go quickly, lower the iron plaque immediately. (*Yang Hu exits.*)

XU JINDING: (*Sings.*)
Leading the three barbarian tribes,[15] I will for sure trample the capital with our steeds.

YANG HU: (*Enters.*) I report to sister-in-law. The iron plaque has been lowered.

XU JINDING: Instruct everyone to mount! (*They exit. Offstage: The iron plaque has been lowered to the ground!*)

XU JINDING: (*Enters with Yang Hu and barbarian army; sings.*)
The Tartar chiefs of the three barbarian tribes will lead the way;
The two warriors, Zhang and Li, will be the vanguard;
Younger brother, Yang Hu, will stay in the center;
Younger sister, Suzhen, will guard the rear.
The banners glitter brightly, the mountains and rivers tremble,
The men are as fierce as tigers, the horses are as noble as dragons.
As the army proceeds, suddenly a soldier reports.

SOLDIER: We have arrived at the capital.

XU JINDING: Then, set up camp here. Come, don't let the scoundrel Yan Song get away. (*Sings.*)
Ordering camps set up at all four gates,
I'll make sure that the scoundrel, Yan Song, will not escape.
If I catch that treacherous scoundrel, I'll stab him a thousand times
And chop him into ten thousand pieces with no mercy.
Should anyone dare to disobey this command,

---

15. The Yang family apparently has the allegiance of the barbarian tribes in the region.

My three-foot-long precious sword will show no pity. (*They exit.*)

Scene 16

XU ZAN: (*Enters and sings.*)
> The Yangs have brought an army and besieged the capital city,
> The treacherous scoundrel has presented a memorial to the throne.
> Condemning my entire family to the imperial dungeon,
> He will have us all beheaded if the army does not retreat.
> Clearly, he is stifling this life of mine.

(*Speaks.*) Ai! I, Xu Zan, have arrived outside the city gate. I wonder where the Junior General Yang's camp is? Let me ask. You there!

SOLDIER: What do you want?

XU ZAN: Where is Junior General Yang's camp?

SOLDIER: This is it.

XU ZAN: May I bother you to pass on the message that Xu Zan asks to see him.

SOLDIER: Stand back. Wait for me to report the message. (*He exits and speaks off stage: The minister Lord Xu Zan wishes to see you. Yang Hu, display the banners.*)

YANG HU: (*Enters.*) Oh! So, it's Uncle Xu. What is your business at the camp?

XU ZAN: Because your army has besieged the city, the treacherous scoundrel memorialized to the throne secretly and had my entire family imprisoned. If your army retreats, we'll be released; if not, my entire clan will be executed. Young general, in consideration of our kinship, please get the army to retreat and save my family!

YANG HU: Aiya! Come, come. When you brought us with you to the capital, you said that you would guarantee our safety. To date all the guarantor-ministers are still alive, but where is my brother? Now that I have rebelled to avenge his death, how dare you show your face and ask us to retreat? This is utterly ridiculous! (*Sings.*)
> What the uncle says is totally unreasonable;
> He fills me, Yang Hu, with rage.
> That you did not keep the guarantee, I could somewhat understand,
> But what face do you have to ask for a retreat?

(*Speaks.*) Drive him out of here. (*They exit.*)

XU ZAN: (*Re-enters.*) Ai! How stupid of me! My daughter Jinding is stationed at the western gate. There was no need to implore him. (*Sings.*)
> Yang Hu stubbornly refuses to retreat;
> I leave his camp, my head lowered in shame.

It is only on account of the lives of my entire clan,
That I proceed to the western gate to see my daughter. (*He exits.*)

Scene 17

XU JINDING: (*Enters and sings.*)
> Avenging my husband's death, I mobilized a large army.
> Besieging the capital, I intend to nail the treacherous rogue.
> If I manage to capture this territory of the capital city,
> I will wipe out the evil faction and bring about stability.
> Only then, will I be able to heal the affliction in my heart.
> (*Speaks.*) I am none other than Xu Jinding. Just now I heard that my father came out of the capital; I wonder what he is up to? Let me wait for him by my camp gate.

XU ZAN: (*Enters and sings.*)
> I, Xu Zan, lower my head and tears pour down.
> Yang Hu is not willing to do me a favor,
> The lives of my entire family is now at stake.
> Seeing no alternative, I will now beg my little daughter.
> If her army retreats, it'll be my great fortune.

XU JINDING: Papa, here you are, please accept your child's greeting!

XU ZAN: Please dispense with the formalities, my child.

XU JINDING: Papa, why did you come here?

XU ZAN: My child, you wouldn't have known; but because your army has besieged the city, the treacherous scoundrel secretly memorialized to the throne and had our entire clan imprisoned. He has ordered your father to come here to ask the army to retreat. That's why I have come to your camp.

XU JINDING: Papa, you came here to get my army to retreat? Do you mean that the injustice done to my husband is not to be avenged?

XU ZAN: My child! (*Sings.*)
> Because you led an army and besieged the city,
> The evil scoundrel memorialized to the throne.
> Our entire clan was imprisoned inside the ministry of punishment.
> They ordered your father to come outside the city to implore a retreat.
> If the army cannot be persuaded to withdraw,
> Our entire family, young and old, will suffer execution.
> (*Speaks.*) Ai, my child, ah! (*Sings.*)
> Please, you must consider the love between father and daughter,
> And have the army retreated temporarily, for my sake!

XU JINDING: Ah! Papa! (*Sings.*)

You only talk about saving your family,
Is the injustice suffered by my husband not to be avenged?
In the past, when Black Water presented the precious bow,
Papa came to Mount Cock Crow to enlist the warrior.
Entering the capital and drawing the bow, the warrior's merit was
    great.
Yet this meritorious subject ended up at the City of Wronged
    Souls—
You certainly did a great job as his guarantor!
What face do you have to come and ask for a retreat?

XU ZAN: Ah! My child! (*Sings.*)

Fool, your words show a total lack of sense.
Listen to the stories of ancients your father has to tell:
For her father, Gao Cainü 高才女 scraped the bottom of the sea;[16]
And Cao E 曹娥, too, carried her father out of a deep pool.[17]
It was not that they did not value their lives,
It was because their love for their father was as immense as moun-
    tains.

XU JINDING: Ah! Papa! (*Sings.*)

You have brought up ancient examples for my elucidation,
Let your child, too, enumerate tales from the past for your sake:
Gongjiang 公姜 remained chaste, her love for her husband never
    wavered;[18]
The tale of Rongfeng 榮風 carrying an elixir on her back has been
    passed down for ten thousand years.[19]
There was also Meng Jiangnü 孟姜女, the most virtuous among
    women;[20]
Her weeping moved Heaven and crumbled the great wall.

XU ZAN: Ah! You fool! (*Sings.*)

Although foolish, you may make sense,

---

16. I have not been able to find out more about this folk tale.
17. Cao E was a young girl of fourteen who tried to find the lost body of her father who had drowned in a river. "Night and day her voice did not stop. After seventeen days she threw herself into the river and drowned." (Fan Ye 范曄 (398–446), *HouHanshu* 後漢書 114/3b:3079; quoted in Bodde 1975, 311). In the Wuyue 吳越 region of the east, she was worshipped as the Cao E river goddess on the 21st day of the Fifth Month (Jiang 1992, 367). The way Xu Zan uses this example, however, suggests a mistaken understanding that Cao E was successful in saving her father.
18. I have not been able to find out more about this folktale.
19. I have not been able to find out more about this folktale either.
20. The Meng Jiangnü tale is popular all over China. Meng's husband was drafted as a corvée laborer to build the Great Wall. When Meng finally located him, he had already died and his bones were buried within the wall. Meng wept so pitifully that Heaven caused the wall to crumble and exposed his bones for her.

But in this world attacking one's sovereign is a rarity.

XU JINDING: Oh? Papa, (*Sings.*)

>King Wu led an army to attack King Zhou, his sovereign;
>Could it be possible that the sage made a mistake?

XU ZAN: Ah! My child! (*Sings.*)

>King Wu attacked Zhou because the latter lacked principles.

XU JINDING: (*Sings.*)

>Your sovereign has no principles, either.

XU ZAN: (*Sings.*)

>When did my sovereign ever lack principles?

XU JINDING: (*Sings.*)

>Then why did he unjustly execute my husband?

XU ZAN: (*Sings.*)

>He defied the emperor, who could not forgive him.

XU JINDING: (*Sings.*)

>Don't tell me that the emperor was made of wood!

XU ZAN: (*Sings.*)

>I exhort you to order your army to withdraw.

XU JINDING: (*Sings.*)

>I won't do that until the capital is subdued.

XU ZAN: (*Sings.*)

>Please consider the fact that I, your father, have come here.

XU JINDING (*Sings.*)

>So you have come, but where is your son-in-law?

XU ZAN: (*Sings.*)

>Our entire family is imprisoned in the dungeon.

XU JINDING: (*Sings.*)

>But I can't afford to mind your problem.

XU ZAN: (*Sings.*)

>You fool! Which family are you a daughter of?

XU JINDING: (*Sings.*)

>I am now a daughter of the Yangs.

XU ZAN: (*Sings.*)

>The tongue of this fool is truly sharp,
>I try to talk but am rendered speechless.
>My entire family is imprisoned in the dungeon,
>But pleading with my daughter has proven useless.

XU JINDING: (*Sings.*)

>It is not that your child is heartless,
>You really shouldn't have come to the camp of the Yangs.
>Since you can't return to us your son-in-law,
>Don't mention again the matter of withdrawal. (*She exits.*)

XU ZAN: Come back, my daughter. Come back, my daughter. Ai, the fool!
(*Sings.*)
> The fool stubbornly refuses to retreat.
> Lowering my head and brimming with tears, I am even more disconsolate.
> How can my entire clan escape this alive?
> I call for help from Heaven and earth, but none has given me a response.
>
> (*Speaks.*) What am I going to do? Ah, I know. (*Sings.*)
> I will rush to Prince Xu's residence to plead for his assistance.
> I am willing to give up this old life of mine. (*He exits.*)

Scene 18

EMPEROR: (*Enters and sings.*)
> The Yang family has led an army which besieges the capital.
> We, the emperor, have ordered a minister to effect a retreat,
> But we fear that he might not succeed.
> We have been worrying about it night and day.

ATTENDANT: I report to Your Majesty. Prince Xu has entered into the imperial court with a portrait of the deceased emperor on his head and an imperial ancestral hammer in his hand.[21]

EMPEROR: What are we going to do?

PRINCE XU: (*Enters and sings.*)
> Carrying a portrait of the late emperor on my head, I rush to the golden throne.
> Listening to slander, you silly emperor have killed the loyal and wise.
> With this bronze hammer in my hand, I'll give you a good beating,
> I'll first give the dim-witted emperor a good beating and then exterminate the traitor.

EMPEROR: Why is our imperial elder brother so furious? Please put away the imperial portrait, and we'll discuss whatever is on your mind as emperor and subject.

PRINCE XU: What is there to discuss? An army has besieged the capital all on account of that treacherous scoundrel Yan Song. I want to know whether you are willing to give him up?

---

21. These items apparently enable him to represent the deceased ancestors of the imperial family and therefore become more venerable than the emperor himself.

EMPEROR: We gave our word that we would never execute Yan Song as long as we live. Now that events have reached this stage, we can only take away his ministerial seal, demote him to a commoner and send him home.

PRINCE XU: Then issue the edict immediately.

EMPEROR: Attendants, dispatch our message: send a golden staff and a silver bowl to the Yan residence; order him to return immediately to his native home as a commoner.

PRINCE XU: Your subject is guilty of defying Your Majesty.

EMPEROR: Forget it. What's your crime? Now that I have suspended the prime minister from office, what happens if Yang Hu still refuses to retreat?

PRINCE XU: Don't worry, Your Majesty. Yang Hu has a sister who is talented in both literature and martial arts. We can match her up with the Crown Prince and bestow high posts to everyone in the Yang family. Their army will retreat for sure.

EMPEROR: Our imperial elder brother, please leave the court and deliver the edict for us.

PRINCE XU: I obey the imperial will. (*They exit.*)

Scene 19

YAN SONG: (*Enters and sings.*)
>
> I regret having committed so many crimes while in the court;
> It is only through the protection of Heaven that I got to last for so long.
> Prince Xu applied pressure upon the sovereign, my seal was taken.
> His Majesty has also demoted me to the status of a commoner.
> I brought all this upon myself, whom can I blame?
> What I fear is meeting the Yang army, my life would be in jeopardy.
> Shivering and trembling, I proceed cautiously. (*He exits.*)

YANG SUZHEN: (*Enters and sings.*)
>
> Hearing the news today, my chest is filled with rage.
> Soldiers report that the scoundrel Yan Song was demoted to a commoner.
> Until that rogue is slain, my grievance will not be avenged.
> My only worry is, unable to recognize him, I might kill the wrong man.
> Let me stand by the road and listen to what people say.

(*Off stage: Look, everyone, even the scoundrel Yan got what he deserves today. He won't be able to hurt the loyal and upright at the court any more. His Majesty was too easy on him though—should have killed that trash. Hey! Speak of the devil, here he comes!*)

YANG SUZHEN: I just heard that the scoundrel has arrived. Let me wait for him. (*Yan Song enters.*) Are you Yan Song?

YAN SONG: I am not Yan Song. I am just an innocent passer-by.

YANG SUZHEN: How dare you dispute it! Follow me! (*They exit.*)

Scene 20

XU JINDING: (*Enters with Yang Hu.*) Whenever the scoundrel Yan is mentioned, I get so angry that my teeth grind. Today I will finally avenge my husband's grievous death.

YANG HU: I report to sister-in-law. The scoundrel Yan has been caught.

XU JINDING: Tie up the scoundrel Yan and bring him here. So you are Yan Song. What a treacherous scoundrel! You didn't think you'd come to this, did you? Take my orders.

SOLDIER: (*Enters.*) Yes.

XU JINDING: Take this scoundrel away. Pull out his tongue, gouge out his eyes, and scoop out his heart and liver. Fill his body with oil to make a candle out of him[22] and offer it to your young master's spirit tablet. (*Off stage: An imperial edict has arrived!*) Tell them that I will go greet the messenger. (*She exits and re-enters with Prince Xu.*) Please read the edict, your highness.

PRINCE XU: Here is the edict. The emperor announces, "Yang Long's merit in drawing the bow is as great as Heaven. The wrongful execution of a meritorious subject is our mistake. To rectify the situation, we bestow upon Yang Hu the post of Governor of Nine Gates 九門齊督; Yang Long's wife, Madam Xu, the title of Lady of Military Heroism 英武夫人. We award Xu Zan with the position of Censor 督察尉使 and Yang Suzhen will be married to the Crown Prince." End of the edict.

EVERYONE: Long live the emperor! Long live the emperor! Long live the emperor!

XU JINDING: Your highness, please pardon our offense for not having greeted you sooner.

PRINCE XU: Don't worry about it.

---

22. The idea seems to be to skin the person whole from neck down (or may be only the trunk of the body is used) and fill the cavity with oil and a wick which is then burned. I have read once of the practice of pouring mercury between the skin and the body to help separate them.

XU JINDING: Come, attendants. Set up a banquet at the second hall.
SOLDIER: The banquet is ready. Please attend the banquet, everyone.
XU JINDING: Certainly. If you please.

The End

14: Owner of the trunk at Bidu 必獨, Shanxi. Photo: author.

15: The master puppeteer at Bidu, Shanxi. Photo: Bao Chengjie.

16: The lead drummer at Bidu, Shanxi. Photo: Bao Chengjie.

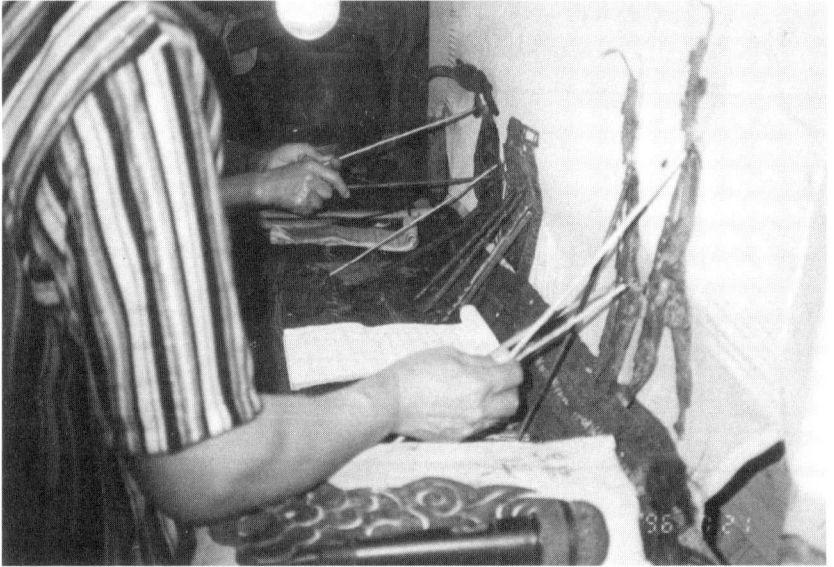

17: Performance of *The Temple of Guanyin*. Photo: Bao Chengjie.

The Temple of Guanyin
觀音堂

Introduction

The *Temple of Guanyin* is an orally transmitted w*anwanqiang* play from Shanxi. Considerably less sophisticated than *wanwanqiang* plays found in Shaanxi where it originated, it seems to be more of a local play with *wanwanqiang* music and style of shadow figures. In preparing this translation, I tried to make a composite version, taking the best from two scripts and from a transcribed performance.[1] In its story *The Temple of Guanyin* presents the masculine side of women—the welcomed helpmate motif—which is not uncommon in popular Chinese culture (Chen 1992). Like many other women warriors in Chinese drama and popular fiction, Hu Yunzhuang, the warrior queen of *The Temple of Guanyin*, seems to reflect a conception of female power and prowess within the popular imagination. Although, his-

---

1. During the 1950s, the local Ministry of Culture of the Lüliang 呂梁 area (where Xiaoyi is located) undertook the project of transcribing recitations of shadow plays by aging performers. Copies of 135 plays have been collected at the Research Institute of Drama (RID) in Taiyuan. Discrepancies between the RID copy of *The Temple of Guanyin* and the ones I translated are even more drastic. The RID version, for example, is at least 50 percent longer. While the lyrics and dialogue are, in many cases, exactly the same and the plots generally conform, the RID version creates more drama and characterization by expanding the interactions among the characters. Artistically speaking, the composite version I present below is slightly inferior, perhaps, but it does have all the essential ingredients of the tale. The protagonists are all consistent and distinctive in their characterization, and the progression of the play is probably already too slow for a contemporary audience. On the rare occasions where the texts disagree (regarding the self-pity expressed by the warrior queen, Hu Yunzhuang 胡云狀, for example, before her impending execution), I have based the composite translation on details as they appear in the RID version.1 I have also added some stage directions in parenthesis as I saw fit.

torically speaking, a warrior queen by the name of Fu Hao 婦好 did lead expeditions for the Shang dynasty king Wuding 武丁 (r. 1339–1280 b.c.), we know very little about her. Tales of her exploits did not enter the world of legend and history. In fact, her existence was not even known until the Shang dynasty oracle bones were deciphered during early twentieth century, and the excavation of her grave in 1976 (Li 1995, 120–121; Institute of Archaeology 1980). Even today only scholars seem to be aware of her existence.

There is no dearth of women warriors in popular Chinese novels (Chen 1992) and traditional dramatic literature (Kaulback 1969; Yang 1991). Characters such as Fan Lihua 樊梨花 and Mu Guiying 穆桂英 continue to delight Chinese audiences. A famous queen of the State of Qi 齊國 during the Warring States period (403–221 b.c.), distinguished by her unusual comeliness, is portrayed as a warrior character in seven *bangzixi* 梆子戲 (clapper operas; Yang 1991, 37–39) and at least one major shadow play.[2] Indeed, a great many of the lengthy shadow plays of the Luanzhou tradition in Hebei province feature talented women warriors. Unlike their human counterparts on stage, the shadow warrior figures, like those in novels, can employ magic weapons, fly, disappear underground, and perform all manner of supernatural feats.

In *The Temple of Guanyin*, Hu Yunzhuang, the queen, is a superior warrior sent by Heaven to aid her husband, the king. As dastardly and gullible as he is, she has to defer to him, defeat invaders of his kingdom, and at the same time contend with another of his wives for his affections. Although formidable on the battlefield, she is helpless when her irrational and insecure husband condemns her to death for alleged treason. She may be protector of his realm, but he has power over her fate. It is not until after her death that her status as a goddess becomes apparent to him. Could this have been a figurative representation of gender relations in the Chinese peasant mentality? One can only wonder. Also of significance is the fact that no matter how wrathful the queen or resentful her rival, Consort Xia Cuiping 夏翠平, the truly evil schemer in *The Temple of Guanyin* is ultimately shown to be a man: the Grand Tutor.

The unlikely portrayal of Guanyin 觀音, one of the most popular Chinese Buddhist deities, in the guise of Hu Yunzhuang, as well as the way in which this is abruptly revealed at the end of the play, seem puzzling.[3] Indeed, the

---

2. The warrior queen Wuyan, 無鹽/無豔 is featured prominently in the shadow play *Wanbaozhen* 萬寶陣 (Strategy of Ten Thousand Magic Weapons) of the Luanzhou tradition. Consisting of nine hand-copied volumes, a copy of this play from Chengde 承德, Hebei, is in my own collection.

3. In all fairness, the creator of the play did try to hint at her godliness earlier in the play by having a dragon appear above her head during one battle scene and by comparing her to

concept of "goddess-as-warrior queen" is divorced entirely from any of the common characteristics attributed to Guanyin (Yü 1979, 221–286; Xu 1994, 4-40; Dai 1982, 266–267). Hu Yunzhuang is not merciful, nor does she possess prodigious magical powers to subdue demons who are devastating the mortal realm.

In fact, as I discovered almost by accident, she is the protagonist of a *qinqiang* 秦腔 clapper opera, *Qingshiling* 青石嶺 (Azure Rock Mountain)—which originated in Sichuan.[4] In this human actors' opera, the warrior queen's name is Su Yunzhuang 蘇云狀 rather than Hu Yunzhuang, but the names of her rival consort and the male warriors are identical. The plot is also basically the same. Su Yunzhuang subdues the warriors Wang Hong 王洪 and Meng Xi 孟喜, who surrender to her. She returns to court and almost dies because of schemes hatched by Cuiping and her father, but is saved by Wang and Hong. She fights for her husband, the king, again. But this second time she dies in battle. The main difference between this character and Hu Yunzhuang is her fully mortal condition. Su Yunzhuang claims no connections to Guanyin at the end of the play. There is no apotheosis for her after her death, and the king neither orders the building of temples in her honor nor commemorates the nineteenth of the Second Month every year. Was there a reason for the appropriation of Guanyin by the shadow theatre opera? The answer, I believe, is yes.

As the nineteenth day of the Second Month was traditionally celebrated as Guanyin's birthday, Su Yunzhuang's story was probably appropriated to fulfill a function related to the performance of shadow plays. As a consequence, this basically nonreligious play was linked with Guanyin and performed on the goddess's designated holiday every year. At the same time it fulfilled a sacred need and provided secular entertainment. The owner of the trunk at Bidu told me that *The Temple of Guanyin* had not been performed for a long, long time. He kept nodding when I asked, "How long? Twenty years? Thirty years?" Given the "religious" nature of *The Temple of Guanyin*, this shadow play may never be sponsored again.

Guanyin in another. But these scenes appear to be weak attempts at incorporating Guanyin into an existing play. The connection between Guanyin and Hu Yunzhuang is at most very tenuous.
4. See Yang (1991, 55–56) for synopses of this play and others about Su Yunzhuang.

Cast

ATTENDANT: *a palace attendant.*

BEI YIWANG 北易王: *vassal king to Zhou Yiwnag and king of the North Sea[5] region.*

CAIHUA ZHANG YUN 采花張云: *a warrior in Bei Yiwang's service.*

CELESTIAL OFFICIALS (zhongxingsu 眾星宿): *Celestial Officials of the Constellations.*

CONSORTS: *consorts of Zhou Yiwang.*

DONG 東: *consort of Zhou Yiwang; consort of the Eastern palace.*

GRAND MASTER HUNYUAN: *celestial tutor of Wei Tianbao.*

GRAND TUTOR (XIA HOULI 夏厚禮): *Consort Xia Cuiping's father.*

GUANYIN: *a goddess,[6] Hu Yunzhuang after her apotheosis.*

HU YUNZHUANG: *queen of Zhou Yiwang; a woman warrior.*

LI BEIHAI 李北海: *a warrior under Hu Yunzhuang's command.*

MENG XI: *a celestial warrior.*

MINISTER LI 李臣: *a minister of Zhou Yiwang's court.*

SOLDIERS

THE TUTELARY GOD (Tudi 土地)

WANG HONG: *a celestial warrior.*

WARRIOR: *the executioner.*

WEI TIANBAO 魏天保: *a celestial warrior under Hu Yunzhuang's command; a disciple of Grand Master Hunyuan (Hunyuan Laozu 渾源老祖).*

XIA CUIPING: *consort of Zhou Yiwang; consort of the Western palace.*

ZHANG TINGLAN 張廷蘭: *a warrior under Hu Yunzhuang's command.*

ZHAO CHUN'EN 趙春恩: *a warrior under Hu Yunzhuang's command.*

ZHOU YIWANG 周易王: *a fictitious king, presumably of the Zhou dynasty (1122–255 b.c.).*

---

5. The North Sea refers to a nebulous, distant region to the north of China.

6. The normal rendering of Guanyin as the "Goddess of Mercy" is not used in this translation since Hu Yunzhuang is a fictional character totally divorced from the Bodhisattva Guanyin of the Buddhist tradition. The placement of Hu Yunzhuang into a fictitious reign of the Zhou dynasty and her subsequent transformation into Guanyin among Daoist immortals reflect not only the conflation of Daoist and Buddhist deities in popular culture but also the ornamental use of historical setting in popular literature and theatre for dramatic effect. Unlike many fictional historical novels and plays, however, none of the characters in this drama has any historical basis. Buddhism and its deity, Guanyin, the Bodhisattva Avalokitesvara, were not even known in China during the Zhou dynasty.

Scene 1

(*A large, ornate scene of a palace decorates the stage; percussion music is played.*)

ZHOU YIWANG: (*Enters and recites.*)

> I wear a flying dragon hat,
> And don an imperial dragon robe. (*He sits on the throne and continues.*)
> On the scaffold, the golden rooster crows,
> Down below, a tide rises in the sea.
> When we ascend the golden court,
> Military and civil officials attend court early.

(*Speaks.*) We are the reigning king, Zhou Yiwang.[7] Ever since we ascended the throne, the weather has been seasonable and the state and its people stable. It has truly been a time of peace except for the fact that the evil Bei Yiwang desired to snatch our realm and dispatched several declarations of war to us. Fortunately, Consort Hu led an army against him personally. She has just returned from the pacification. We have not yet celebrated her victory. We are presently holding an early court. Palace attendant!

ATTENDANT: Yes!

ZHOU YIWANG: Have a feast prepared in the palace to celebrate the victory of the queen!

ATTENDANT: Yes!

ZHOU YIWANG: (*Sings.*)

> A feast will be prepared in the imperial harem,
> We will return there and greet our consort with felicitations.
> Hurriedly, we command the court attendant to prepare the imperial carriage,
> The king will celebrate the consort's meritorious victory and congratulate her. (*They exit.*)

Scene 2

(*Meng Xi and Wang Hong enter.*)

MENG XI: We possess unmatched military prowess.

WANG HONG: We are heroes capable of making kings.[8]

MENG XI: I am the Great General, Meng Xi.

---

7. The Chinese royal "we" is used by the kings.
8. Contenders to thrones have always relied on the assistance of powerful warriors.

WANG HONG: I am the Lesser General, Wang Hong.

MENG XI: We brothers are in fact celestials from the mountains and have mastered all eighteen styles of the military arts. We have just left the mountains. We brothers heard that Bei Yiwang has just brought out some recruitment banners in order to recruit the heroes under Heaven.

WANG HONG: My elder brother!

MENG XI: Why don't we two go eat his soldiers' rations and earn an official title or two? It just might be a break for us!

WANG HONG: It's all up to you, elder brother.

MENG XI: Then let's go. (*Sings.*)

> Thus we brothers made our decision,
> We'll join the military and eat the rations. (*Meng Xi and Wang Hong exit.*)

BEI YIWANG: (*Enters and sings.*)

> The words are different, the language is different, but the characters are the same,
> We both are the roots and seeds of Yao 堯, Xun 舜, Yu 禹, and Tang 湯.[9]
> Should the north and south become divided,
> From one tree different flowers could sprout.

(*Speaks.*) We are the king, Bei Yiwang. Zhou Yiwang is superior; our state is inferior. Hence we pay tribute and homage to his state yearly. When we missed paying tribute for one year, Hu Yunzhuang invaded with her army and rampaged until I refused to leave my camp. I can think of no better way now than hoisting a banner of recruitment to attract the heroes under Heaven. So this is my strategy. Soldiers!

SOLDIERS: Present!

BEI YIWANG: Hoist the banner of recruitment!

SOLDIERS: Yes! Hoist the banner of recruitment!

MENG XI: Take away the banner!

SOLDIERS: Your highness, two men have arrived to eat our army rations.

BEI YIWANG: Oh wonderful! Order the eaters of army rations to follow the red banner into our camp!

SOLDIERS: Eaters of army rations follow the red banner into our camp!

MENG XI: Coming! We ration-eaters kowtow to your highness.

BEI YIWANG: Ah! Where are you from? What are your names? What kind of military skills do you two have that you dare to eat our nation's army rations?

MENG XI: Your highness, we two brothers are celestials from the mountains. My name is Meng Xi.

---

9. Referring to the founding kings of the dynasties before the Zhou.

WANG HONG: I am the Lesser General Wang Hong.

MENG XI: We have mastered all eighteen weapons of the military arts.[10] When two states clash, we simply use magic to capture the enemy.

BEI YIWANG: How wonderful, using magic to capture the enemy. Come here, we will give you both the title of Commanding Generals of All Under Heaven. Meng Xi, you will lead an army of fifty thousand to guard Azure Rock Mountain. Wang Hong will lead an army of fifty thousand to guard Jiamen Pass 賈門關. Go, generals!

MENG XI: Thank you, your highness.

WANG HONG: Thank you for the imperial favors. (*They exit.*)

BEI YIWANG: We've just recruited two superior generals. Soldiers!

SOLDIERS: Present!

BEI YIWANG: Prepare the writing equipment for your lord. We, Bei Yiwang, hold the brush in our hand. We write: "Zhou Yiwang, dreadful Barbarian Zhou . . ."[11] Soldier!

SOLDIER: Present!

BEI YIWANG: Take this letter to the Zhou court, hurry!

SOLDIER: Yes. (*He exits.*)

BEI YIWANG: Let us tell you, Zhou Yiwang, Barbarian Zhou, we are not a man if we don't create trouble in your realm. (*Sings.*)
> Dispatching our message to the land of the Zhou dynasty,
> We only await a good fight in the morrow. (*He exits.*)

MENG and WANG: Oh, ho, ho, ho! Oh, ho, ho, ho! Hei, hei!
> The lord has issued his orders,
> Meng Xi and Wang Hong will embark on the expedition.
> We only await a good fight tomorrow,
> We will conquer for our lord. (*They exit.*)

Scene 3

ZHOU YIWANG: (*Enters and speaks.*) Aiya! (*Sings.*)
> We the king and our civil and military officials are just enjoying our drinks,
> Our spy rushes into the court to report.

---

10. According to *Shuihuzhuan* 水滸傳, these eighteen subjects are the "lance, the hammer, the bow, the crossbow, the jingal, the iron whip, the iron truncheon, the two-edged sword, the chain, the whip, the ax, the battle-ax, the *ke* halbert, the *chi* halbert, the shield, the cudgel, the spear, and the rake." (Chang 1990, 88).

11. Since the Song Dynasty, the term "*manzi*" 蠻子, southern barbarian, has come to be used as a derogatory appellation for people residing south of one's state. Hence, while the Chinese called people south of the Chinese borders *manzi*, the Jurchens to China's north called the Chinese *manzi* in many traditional popular novels.

When he says that Bei Yiwang invades the border for the
  second time,
All the civil and military officials freeze in astonishment.
Hurriedly, we bid farewell to the officials and leave the banquet
To return to the palace to discuss the matter with our consort.
Arriving at the Phoenix Pavilion, we disembark from the
  imperial carriage.

CONSORTS: (*Continue the song.*)
Consorts of the three palaces welcome our lord, the king.
(*Speaks.*) Your humble consorts greet Your Majesty. Long live
  the king![12]

ZHOU YIWANG: Consorts, rise. Lead us into the palace.

CONSORTS: Your humble consorts greet our king. (*They bow and
exit; return; and are seated within the palace.*)[13]

ZHOU YIWANG: Consorts, do take the seats. Oh, oh, oh . . .

CONSORTS: What is bothering Your Majesty?

ZHOU YIWANG: Consorts, please sit still and listen carefully to us
while we relay it to you. (*Sings.*)
Our consorts in the Morning Sun Palace[14] 昭陽宮, please sit
  down,
Let us relay to you all the details.
Bei Yiwang invades again with a large army,
All the civil and military officials quiver with fright.

HU YUNZHUANG: Ai, evil thief! (*Sings.*)
When I, Hu Yunzhuang, hear the news, I yell, "Evil thief!"
Who told you to stir up trouble again with a large army?
I have a mind to lead a large army to go fight once again,
But is it possible that within our court there is none loyal
  and virtuous?
(*Speaks.*) Ah, Your Majesty! You should lead the army person-
ally to pacify them.

ZHOU YIWANG: Ah, our consort! See how our entire court is filled with
useless ministers. We would like to have you lead our army again. How
do you feel about it?

---

12. Literally, "Ten thousand years and a hundred thousand years!"
13. The shadow figures leave the stage to indicate traveling and are then placed with their legs
bent to suggest sitting down.
14. This is apparently the main building of the women's quarters where the queen resides.

HU YUNZHUANG: Ah, Your Majesty! See how I've been fighting continuously until now. Both my horse and I are exhausted. I really can't go!

XIA CUIPING: Ah! I know why the queen won't go!

HU YUNZHUANG: What do you know?

XIA CUIPING: Your Majesty the queen won't go because she fears defeat!

HU YUNZHUANG: Ah, ah! How dare you evil consort be so rude! Well, if I return defeated from the war, I am willing to surrender the seal of the queen to you. What do you, evil consort, dare to wager?

XIA CUIPING: Who's afraid of making a wager?

HU YUNZHUANG: Evil consort, do you dare to make a bet?

XIA CUIPING: Then we'll strike hands as a deal. One, two. (*They gesture with their hands.*)

ZHOU YIWANG: Oh, consorts, you shouldn't be doing this. We are almost losing our realm and here you are making such a racket in the palace. Ah, ah, ah, ah!

HU YUNZHUANG: Palace lady, hold the ink well for me. (*Sings.*)

> Within the palace I wage a bet and strike hands with the evil consort,
> His Majesty ought to support this matter.
> Should I return defeated from pacifying the North Sea,
> I would be willing to surrender the queen's seal to the evil consort.

XIA CUIPING: (*Sings.*)

> Within the palace I wage a bet and strike hands with the queen,
> I, Xia Cuiping, want His Majesty to support it.
> Should the queen return defeated,
> She will surrender the queen's seal to me.
> Should the queen return victorious,
> Aiyo! I would be willing to surrender this head of mine to the queen!

HU YUNZHUANG: I, Hu Yunzhuang, hurriedly sign my name.

XIA CUIPING: I, Xia Cuiping, sign my name and I shake with fright.

HU YUNZHUANG: I should take this document.

XIA CUIPING: I should take the document.

DONG: Wait a minute. How about letting me take the document? I'll carry both your fates in my palm. What do you think?

HU YUNZHUANG: I can feel safe now with our imperial sister taking it.

XIA CUIPING: Your Majesty the queen, allow me to bid farewell.

HU YUNZHUANG: Ah, evil consort! Do you expect me to see you off?

XIA CUIPING: Ah, our queen. (*Sings.*)

> I, Xia Cuiping, hurriedly bid farewell from the palace.
> The honorable queen's handling of this matter is truly mad.
> I will return to the palace to talk it over with the Grand Tutor;

I'll make sure that you'll have trouble returning from pacifying the North Sea. (*She exits.*)

DONG: Ah, evil consort! (*Sings.*)

Ah, evil consort!

I bow in the palace and bid farewell to His Majesty,

I look forward to the safe return of our honorable queen from the expedition. (*She exits.*)

ZHOU YIWANG: (*Sings.*)

We will stay at the Morning Sun Palace for the night.

When morning comes, our army will destroy the rebel king. (*He exits.*)

Scene 4

WANG HONG: (*Enters.*) Ah! I am the great general, Wang Hong. I descended from the mountains to partake of the soldiers' rations at Bei Yiwang's camp. He granted me the title of Commanding General of All Under Heaven. His lordship has ordered me to guard Jiamen Pass. Soldiers, let's go to Jiamen Pass! (*They exit.*)

SOLDIERS: Oh, ho, ho! Oh, ho, ho, ho! Hei!

HU YUNZHUANG: (*Enters with army and sings.*)

Three cannon balls,[15] I lead the cavalry, the mountains and earth shake,

Their flying tiger banner blocks the sun,[16] and light disappears.

Hoisting the banner of a commanding general with my name on it,

I, Hu Yunzhuang, lead a great army northward once again.

I, the queen, issue the orders in haste while riding on my horse,

Listen attentively, warriors of my three armies, every one of you.

As long as you achieve merit when the two armies meet,

Upon our return, my three armies, high official ranks will be bestowed.

I, the queen, lead the cavalry straight ahead,

I hear members of the three armies reporting to me.

SOLDIER: I report to the queen.

HU YUNZHUANG: What is it?

SOLDIER: We have arrived at Jiamen Pass. Wang Hong blocks us on horse.

---

15. This part is not clear. She probably had three cannon balls shot.
16. The sun frequently alludes to the reigning emperor; here it probably alludes to Zhou Yiwang.

HU YUNZHUANG: My three generals, you fight first. Order Wang Hong to come meet his maker! (*Sings.*)

> Pitching our camp upon the head of a black dragon,
> On the second day, when dawn breaks, battles are fought. (*She exits.*)

WANG HONG: Who's here?

THREE GENERALS: Ah ha! I am your lord Zhang Tinglan, followed by Li Beihai and Zhao Chun'en. You, riding on the horse, are you Wang Hong?

WANG HONG: Yes, I'm your lord Wang Hong. (*They fight to percussion music.*)

WANG HONG: Aiya! The three generals fight ferociously! When they come again I'll use my magic hammer on them. Ah, ha! Ah, ha! Heavens, the three generals fell from their horses. Aiya, how exhilarating! (*Sings.*)

> During the first round Zhang Tinglan lost his life,
> Everyone who approached me died from my hammer,
> Winning the battle truly fills me with great delight.

SOLDIER: I report to the queen.

HU YUNZHUANG: What is it?

SOLDIER: The three generals have fallen from their horses.

HU YUNZHUANG: Oh no, oh no! (*Sings.*)

> The three armies report that the three generals have lost their lives,
> General Wei, come over, listen to me carefully.
> The three generals from our court have all met with disaster,
> You should leave the camp and charge with your horse.

WEI TIANBAO: (*Continues the song.*)

> I beg of you, our queen, don't you worry,
> When I go, I will definitely have him end up in hell. (*He exits.*)

HU YUNZHUANG: (*Sings.*)

> General Wei left the camp in too much of a hurry,
> It makes me, the queen, worry greatly. (*She exits.*)

Scene 5

GRAND MASTER HUNYUAN: (*Enters and sings.*)

> In the Heaven beyond the Thirty-three Heavens,[17]
> A grass hut is built on top of a black dragon.

---

17. According to Liu Ts'un-yan in *Buddhist and Taoist Influences on Chinese Novels*, "This... [Thirty-three Heavens] is the *Trayastrimsa* or the Indra Heaven, the second of the six heavens of form" (Liu 1962, 167).

One hears people talking in the grass hut,

And finds them to be a couple of celestials giving sermons on the Dao.

(*Speaks.*) I am a Daoist priest by the name of Grand Master Hunyuan. Just now I cast a divination in my grotto and discovered that my pupil, Wei Tianbao, will encounter disaster in battle. Let me descend from the mountain to save him and bring him back up. He will destroy Caihua Zhang Yun in the future. Let me close the gate to my grotto. I must get underway. (*Sings.*)

I, the indigent priest, leave my thousand-year-old grotto.

Watch me, the indigent priest, perform my magic skills.

Exhaling one deep breath into the air,

Leisurely, I now float right up to the sky.

I push aside a cloud and look with my eyes,

I see everything clearly on all eight sides.

When I look eastward, the east has its own scenery,

The old dragon king is meditating in his crystal palace.

When I look westward, the west has its own scenery,

An old Buddha in Western Paradise sits where thunders are created.

When I look southward, the south has its own scenery,

The scholar of the South Sea meditates in the Purple Bamboo Grove.

When I look northward, the north has its own scenery,

Bao Xuantian[18] 報宣天 of the north is found right in the middle of it.

Looking up, I see the Spiritual Cloud Palace of the Heavenly Jade Emperor,

Looking down, I see the eighteen levels of Hell.

I seat myself, meditating style, securely on a cloud,

Intending to rescue my pupil back to the mountains and woods.

WEI TIANBAO: (*Enters and sings.*)

I, Wei Tianbao, get my order from the camp in a hurry,

When I go, I can assure you that you'll end up in Hades.

Here I arrive at the gate of Jiamen pass,

I yell for Wang Hong, the devil of a thief.

(*Speaks.*) Come out and fight, you infant Wang Hong!

WANG HONG: Here I come.

WEI TIANBAO: Is this Wang Hong before my horse?

---

18. The identity of this deity is not clear.

WANG HONG: Yes. I'm your lord Wang Hong. Are you Wei Tianbao on the horse?

WEI TIANBAO: So I am! Wang Hong, little boy, how dare you invade us? Don't go! Watch my broadsword! (*They fight. Wang is defeated.*)

WANG HONG: Aiya! Wei Tianbao is a ferocious fighter. Let me use my magic hammer to win again. Ha! One swing of my hammer and he's knocked off his horse. A violent wind blows and he disappears without a trace. How suspicious! (*Sings.*)

> I knocked him off his horse but then he disappeared without a trace;
> This matter truly causes me great concern. (*He exits.*)

SOLDIER: I report to the queen.

HU YUNZHUANG: What is it?

SOLDIER: Wei Tianbao got knocked down and then disappeared.

HU YUNZHUANG: Get my horse and spear ready. You, the stinky imp approaching on horse, are you Wang Hong?

WANG HONG: Are you Hu Yunzhuang on the horse?

HU YUNZHUANG: Don't leave! Watch my spear!

WANG HONG: Hu Yunzhuang fights ferociously. I'll use my magic hammer again. (*They fight, she falls and faints; the shadow of a large black dragon appears over her head. He sings.*)

> I, Wang Hong, while riding, stare fixedly with my eyes.
> I see emerging from the head of Hu Yunzhuang a real dragon!
> Could it be that Zhou Yiwang is blessed with both greatness and fortune,
> That Heaven has sent Hu Yunzhuang to help him with the expeditions?
> Quickly, I wield my magic hammer,
> But why am I hurting myself rather than her?
> I, Wang Hong, get off my horse at once and kneel:
> I awake her ladyship in order to surrender to her.

(*Speaks.*) Your ladyship, please wake up!

HU YUNZHUANG: (*Sings.*)

> The magic hammer has made me very dizzy,
> My three souls float away but are returning.
> In a daze, in a dream,
> I seem to hear a voice calling into my ears.
> I force myself into opening my eyes,
> He knocked me down from my horse, why didn't he kill me?

WANG HONG: (*Continues the song.*)

> Pray, your ladyship, please do not be alarmed,
> I am willing to surrender to the Zhou and help preserve its state.

HU YUNZHUANG: (*Continues the song.*)

Surrender to the Zhou dynasty! What proof do I have from you? You tricked me down from my horse, but couldn't you kill me?

WANG HONG: (*Continues the song.*)

> I, Wang Hong, kneel before your horse and quickly make a vow:
> I surrender to the Zhou. Any change of heart, may Heaven strike me with thunder.

HU YUNZHUANG: (*Continues the song.*)

> As soon as I see General Wang make a vow,
> I, the queen, am filled with great delight.
> Three of my generals have lost their lives,
> I will make you my foster son and junior minister.
> Three of my generals have lost their lives,
> I will make you my foster son and junior minister.

WANG HONG: Thank you, my lady. Ah, Your Majesty, your subject has already surrendered, but I have an elder brother, Meng Xi, who will be invading from Azure Rock Mountain. His magic, the Three Parts of True Fire 三分真火, has hurt many.

HU YUNZHUANG: What would you suggest?

WANG HONG: I suggest that Your Majesty avoid his Three Parts of True Fire. I will hoist a flag of truce over the fort. Who'll fear that he won't surrender then?

HU YUNZHUANG: Very good. Warriors, let's all ride to Azure Rock Mountain. (*They exit.*)

Scene 6

MENG XI: (*Enters and sits down.*) I have studied the military arts in an immortal mountain since childhood. An old female celestial taught me the secrets of the Dao. I descended from the mountain in order to install a king. My brother and I both guard the passes. I, General Meng Xi, descended from the mountain with my brother to surrender to Bei Yiwang. He has given us the title of Commanding General of All Under Heaven. That little brother of mine helps guard Jiamen Pass. I guard Azure Rock Mountain. Today is a propitious day. Let me look up above my tent. Ha! I see my banners flutter without wind; some military event is afoot.

SOLDIER: I bring a report. The second lord has come to our pass.

MENG XI: Welcome, welcome! (*They greet each other.*) My dear little brother, why did you come to my pass today? Why? Tell me, tell, tell.

WANG HONG: (*Sings.*)

> Oh, my big brother!
> My big brother, please don't get angry.

Let me, your little brother, explain it to you.

Losing the pass was a minor matter;

Losing your little brother would not do.

MENG XI: My dear little brother, if such were the case, you rest at the pass first. Wait for me to block the attack for a while.

WANG HONG: Do be very careful!

MENG XI: No need to worry. Come! Soldier! Get me my horse and whip. You, approaching on horse, are you the little girl Hu Yunzhuang?

HU YUNZHUANG: (*Enters.*) Your ladyship sure is. You, the ugly demon coming toward my horse. Are you Meng Xi?

MENG XI: Yes, I am the great general Meng Xi. Watch my whip! (*They fight; Meng loses.*) Hu Yunzhuang's skills are ferocious. Let me employ my weapon, the Three Parts of True Fire. (*He releases the fire but loses; sings.*)

Ah, what impressive fighting skills!

I, Meng Xi, take a good look at her from my horse,

I see Hu Yunzhuang, as beautiful as a fairy.

It is as if Guanyin has appeared,

Holding a silver spear, steadfast in her carved saddle.

HU YUNZHUANG: (*Sings.*)

Meng Xi, you thief, you don't need to steal glances at me,

Listen to me, the queen, I'll tell you in clear terms.

Get off your horse right away and surrender to me.

If you don't, I'll make sure that you'll lose your life in front of my horse.

MENG XI: My dear brother, open the pass right away; your big brother has been defeated.

WANG HONG: My big brother! Your little brother has already hoisted the flag of truce. I suggest that you surrender too.

MENG XI: Impossible! You go ahead and surrender yourself. (*He fights Hu again and loses again.*)

HU YUNZHUANG: Meng Xi, are you going to surrender or not?

MENG XI: Hold your hand, your ladyship. I'll surrender! I'll surrender!

HU YUNZHUANG: Since you are willing to surrender, I'll grant you the title of Junior Guardian of the Crown Prince. Stand aside.

MENG XI: My gratitude to the queen.

SOLDIER: I report to the queen. Bei Yiwang has dispatched two generals with a letter of surrender. He will never invade again.

HU YUNZHUANG: That's good. Accept the letter of surrender. Wang Hong, Meng Xi, listen to my orders: return to the court with me. (*They exit; Meng Xi tries to sneak away but is prodded on by Wang Hong behind him.*)

Scene 7

MINISTER LI: I am Minister Li. Just now a spy has reported that our queen has returned victorious from her expedition to the North Sea. Let me go to the court and memorialize it to my lord.

ZHOU YIWANG: Our consort has led an army, but she has not returned.

MINISTER LI: (*Enters.*) I bow to His Majesty the king. Long live the king!

ZHOU YIWANG: Our dear minister, please rise.

MINISTER LI: My gratitude for the imperial favor.

ZHOU YIWANG: Our dear minister, why did you come to our court?

MINISTER LI: Ah, Your Majesty. Our queen has returned victorious from her second expedition to the North Sea. She now awaits your decree at the imperial gate.

ZHOU YIWANG: Wonderful! Pass along our decree; we will have an audience with the queen.

MINISTER LI: His Majesty has issued a decree. The queen will attend court.

HU YUNZHUANG: I accept the decree. I prostrate myself before Your Majesty the king.

ZHOU YIWANG: Come here, our consort. Please rise.

HU YUNZHUANG: My gratitude for the imperial favor.

ZHOU YIWANG: Our consort, how did your expedition go?

HU YUNZHUANG: Your Majesty, during this second expedition led by your humble consort, I brought back two powerful warriors, Wang Hong and Meng Xi. Your Majesty, please award them with titles at this court.

ZHOU YIWANG: Our consort, stand behind me.

HU YUNZHUANG: Yes, Your Majesty.

ZHOU YIWANG: Palace attendant, have Wang Hong and Meng Xi enter the court!

ATTENDANT: Yes, Your Majesty! Wang Hong and Meng Xi, enter the court!

MENG XI and WANG HONG: (*Enter.*) We accept the decree. We, Meng Xi and Wang Hong, prostrate ourselves before Your Majesty. Long live the king!

ZHOU YIWANG: Are you Wang Hong and Meng Xi?

MENG XI: Yes, we are.

ZHOU YIWANG: Now that you two have joined our court, we grant Meng Xi the title of Junior Guardian of the Crown Prince, and we grant Wang Hong the title of the Royal Foster Son. Change into the regalia of our court. You may take the decrees and leave. (*Meng and Wang exit.*) Palace attendant, we will go to the Phoenix Pavilion.

HU YUNZHUANG: Please wait, great king. Ah, Your Majesty, do you still remember the wager I made with Xia Cuiping before the expedition?

ZHOU YIWANG: How could we have forgotten? We'll let you take care of it.

HU YUNZHUANG: Your humble consort will be audacious then. Palace attendant, summon Xia Cuiping to the court!

ATTENDANT: The queen has issued a decree. Lady Xia should enter the court!

XIA CUIPING: I accept the decree. I prostrate myself before the queen. The queen must have endured much hardship during the expedition to the North Sea.

HU YUNZHUANG: Oh you evil consort. Do you remember the wager we made?

XIA CUIPING: How could I have forgotten it? That was a shortsighted mistake I made.

HU YUNZHUANG: You don't need to say anything more. Warrior, enter the court!

WARRIOR: I bow to the queen.

HU YUNZHUANG: Take the evil consort and execute her!

XIA CUIPING: Oh no!

WARRIOR: Let's go!

MINISTER LI: Ah, ah! Hold the knife! Please don't do it, our queen. Don't do it, our queen. I realize that Consort Xia has committed a crime and should be executed. But considering that I, an old minister, will act as her guarantor, please excuse her.

ZHOU YIWANG: Ah, that's right. Considering that the military advisor will act as her guarantor, and also as a favor to us, you should excuse her.

HU YUNZHUANG: Well, all right. Considering that the military advisor will act as her guarantor and as a favor to His Majesty, I, the queen, will excuse the evil consort. Military advisor, you may leave the court.

MINISTER LI: The queen is most merciful. (*He exits.*)

HU YUNZHUANG: Palace attendant, relay my decree: order Xia Cuiping released.

ATTENDANT: Lady Hu has issued a decree: release Lady Xia.

XIA CUIPING: I accept the decree. I accept the decree. My gratitude to the queen for the favor of not executing me.

HU YUNZHUANG: All right, you evil consort. If you cross me again, I'll have you killed for certain. You may leave the court.

XIA CUIPING: The queen is most merciful. (*She begins to leave.*) But let me say, Hu Yunzhuang, you bitch of an evil consort, I'll show you that a spear in the open is easy to dodge, but an arrow shot behind one's back is difficult to defend against. Ah, what suffering will occur! (*She exits.*)

ZHOU YIWANG: Our consort returned victorious as promised. How glorious along the way! Palace attendant, get our carriage to return to our palace. (*They exit.*)

Scene 8

XIA CUIPING: (*Enters and sings.*)
> I, Xia Cuiping, return to the palace. I sadly sit on my bed,
> Hu Yunzhuang has been insane in handling this matter.
> She wanted me beheaded right in front of the court,
> But thanks to Minister Li's intercepting as guarantor, I avoided a calamity.
> Returning to the palace, I will discuss the matter with the Grand Tutor.
> I'm going to assure you, Hu Yunzhuang, that you will have no peace.
> Depressed and worried, I meditate at the back of the Western Palace,
> I'll summon the Grand Tutor to the palace and then we will scheme.

(*Speaks.*) Palace attendant, summon the Grand Tutor to the palace!

ATTENDANT: Lady Xia has issued an order. Summon the Grand Tutor to the palace!

GRAND TUTOR: When entering the palace, I will perform the greetings of a minister before recognizing our father-daughter relationship. My lady, I, Xia Houli, prostrate myself.

XIA CUIPING: The Grand Tutor is here. Please sit down.

GRAND TUTOR: Thank you, my lady, for allowing me to sit down.

XIA CUIPING: I prostrate myself before you, my father!

GRAND TUTOR: Don't stand on ceremony, my child. Please sit down and talk.

XIA CUIPING: Your child thanks you for allowing me to sit down.

GRAND TUTOR: How is my lady?

XIA CUIPING: Never mind. And how are you, Grand Tutor?

GRAND TUTOR: Your humble minister thanks you for the inquiry. Ah, what military problem did my lady summon me here to discuss so early in the evening?

XIA CUIPING: Grand Tutor, you wouldn't have known, but Hu Yunzhuang has returned victorious to the court from her second expedition. She nearly had me executed because of our bet.

GRAND TUTOR: Who was the guarantor that saved you from death?

XIA CUIPING: Thanks to the military advisor's guarantee, I was released. But I can't bear the anger and resentment. I want to destroy—

GRAND TUTOR: Shush! (*Looks around the door.*)

XIA CUIPING: Palace attendants, leave, all of you.

GRAND TUTOR: My lady, destroy what?

XIA CUIPING: I want to destroy her. But I don't have a scheme.

GRAND TUTOR: My lady, I, your minister, do have a clever scheme!

XIA CUIPING: What clever scheme do you have?

GRAND TUTOR: My lady, you can put a plate under the king's bed and place a poisonous snake on it. When His Majesty goes to bed, he'll be frightened. At that moment you arrive and say that Hu Yunzhuang came back from the North Sea expedition with all sorts of evil demons in order to murder His Majesty so that she can become a female emperor.[19] When the king has heard your story, you can be certain that the evil consort Hu Yunzhuang will end up dead.

XIA CUIPING: Good. What an excellent scheme! Please, leave the palace now.

GRAND TUTOR: Thank you, my lady. (*He exits.*)

XIA CUIPING: Palace attendant, go to the main palace and see if Lady Hu is there.

ATTENDANT: Yes, my lady. (*He exits and returns.*) I report to my lady. The queen has not yet returned from a banquet in the Eastern Palace.

XIA CUIPING: Leave. I don't need your services now.

ATTENDANT: Yes.

XIA CUIPING: Ah, how joyous! (*Sings.*)

> Fortunately, Hu Yunzhuang is not at the Main Palace,
> It's worked out perfectly for me to make the arrangements tonight.
> I place the plate securely under the royal bed,
> When His Majesty arrives, it will be right there to shock him.

ZHOU YIWANG: (*Enters and sings.*)

> I, the king, had a banquet with our civil and military officials,
> In unison, all our civil and military officials sang her praises.
> Accomplishing distinguished meritorious service, Consort Hu wins
> our affections,

---

19. Female emperor is used here because the word "empress" usually refers to the wife of an emperor which is different from what is described here. The Chinese words used literally means "woman emperor" and were used in regard to an actual ruler, Empress Wu Zetian 武則天 (r. 690–705), after she ascended the throne.

We bid farewell to our officials and rush back to our palace.

ATTENDANT: I report to His Majesty. We have arrived at the Morning Sun Palace.

ZHOU YIWANG: We don't need your services. Leave. (*The palace attendant leaves.*) Happily we approach the royal bed of the main palace. Let us, the king, rest on our bed. Ah! How it scares me to death! (*A new shadow figure of the king with disheveled hair displaces the original one instantaneously. He sings.*)

> An evil thing appears from under the royal bed and scares the king terribly,
>
> But we fail to recognize what it is that hides under our bed.
>
> Fortunately, Consort Hu has not yet arrived,
>
> If the king were hurt, upon whom could she then depend?

XIA CUIPING: (*Enters.*) I greet His Majesty the king.

ZHOU YIWANG: Strike the evil spirit, strike the evil spirit, strike, strike, strike the evil spirit!

XIA CUIPING: Your Majesty, it is I, your humble consort.

ZHOU YIWANG: Oh, it's only you, Consort Xia. Do raise yourself.

XIA CUIPING: Why is Your Majesty not resting on your royal bed?

ZHOU YIWANG: Consort Xia, you wouldn't have known. We just came back from giving a banquet in the Eastern Palace. We were just going to rest on our royal bed when something strange scared us terribly.

XIA CUIPING: Your Majesty wouldn't have known, but our queen came back from the North Sea expedition with all sorts of evil demons in order to kill Your Majesty so that she can become a female emperor.

ZHOU YIWANG: Was it she? Consort Xia, are you telling the truth?

XIA CUIPING: How would your humble consort dare to lie?

ZHOU YIWANG: For the time being, leave.

XIA CUIPING: My gratitude to his Majesty. Ah, the scheme has worked! (*She exits.*)

ZHOU YIWANG: Hu Yunzhuang! Oh, you evil consort! (*Sings.*)

> Evil bitch consort! Born with the heart of a wolf and lungs of a dog,
>
> Why should you have tried to harm us so ruthlessly?
>
> Angrily, we, the king ascend the imperial carriage and the throne,
>
> And order our attendant to summon the evil consort to court.

(*Speaks.*) Palace attendant, summon Hu Yunzhuang to the court immediately!

ATTENDANT: Lady Hu is summoned to the court!

HU YUNZHUANG: (*Enters and sings.*)

> In the Eastern Palace, while partaking a banquet with my imperial sister,

A palace attendant announces an imperial summons and I rush back immediately.

I, Hu Yunzhuang, approach the throne and prostrate myself,
I ask His Majesty why he has summoned his humble consort.
(*Speaks.*) I prostrate myself before His Majesty the king.

ZHOU YIWANG: Is the person prostrating herself Hu Yunzhuang?

HU YUNZHUANG: Yes, it is your humble consort.

ZHOU YIWANG: Tell us, do you admit that you are guilty of your crime?

HU YUNZHUANG: Your humble consort knows not which law she has infringed!

ZHOU YIWANG: You will be executed whether you admit to being guilty or not. Warrior, come to the court and tie up Hu Yunzhuang for me. (*She prostrates herself and is instantaneously displaced by a different figure in plain black robe with disheveled hair.*)

WARRIOR: Yes.

HU YUNZHUANG: How it scares me to death! (*Sings.*)
Seeing this situation, I, Hu Yunzhuang, am terrified
And I ask His Majesty, for what will I be executed?
(*Speaks.*) Ah, Your Majesty, Your Majesty! Please explain this to your humble consort!

XIA CUIPING: Ah, you evil consort! When you returned from the expedition to the North Sea, you brought back two rebel generals and a host of evil demons so that you could kill the king and become a female emperor. How can you still pretend that you know nothing of it?

HU YUNZHUANG: Ah, how I would take care of you, you evil consort! (*Sings.*)
I, Hu Yunzhuang, scream vehemently at you in the court,
I'm sure it was the secret scheming of you and your father.
Should I live, I'll have you hacked into ten thousand pieces;
Should I die, I'll wait for you, my enemy, at the court in Hell.
Hu Yunzhuang weeps until her face is covered with tears,
I entreat His Majesty on the throne, please, to listen to me.
Killing me is as easy as cutting a blade of tiny grass,
But if Bei Yiwang should rebel again, who will be there to block him?

ZHOU YIWANG: Who needs you to say more? Put her under custody for execution!

HU YUNZHUANG: Ah, I'm in deep trouble now! (*She exits with the warrior.*)

MINISTER LI: Ah, ah, ah! Hold the knife. I'll go memorialize to the throne. Your Majesty must not do it! My king, you must not do it! Although the queen, Lady Hu, has committed a crime and should be executed, considering the service she has rendered leading the two expeditions to the North Sea. One should therefore excuse her.

ZHOU YIWANG: Oh, as for this—

XIA CUIPING: Ah, Your Majesty! She must not be excused! She must not be excused!

ZHOU YIWANG: Who needs you to say more? Palace attendant, chase him out of the court!

ATTENDANT: Hurry, hurry, hurry! Do leave the court!

MINISTER LI: Yes, Your Majesty! Oh, heavens! What can I say? Our Lady Hu has been indicted. My guarantee didn't help. How can I save her? Oh, yes! I'll have to report to their excellencies, Wang Hong and Meng Xi, about it. (*He exits.*)

GRAND TUTOR: (*Aside.*) Ah! I am a great evil minister. (*To the king.*) Your minister, Xia Houli, prostrates himself before Your Majesty.

ZHOU YIWANG: Grand Tutor, what do you wish to memorialize?

GRAND TUTOR: Ah, Your Majesty, Lady Hu has committed a crime. Who will supervise the execution?

ZHOU YIWANG: Do you, our minister, desire to supervise the execution?

GRAND TUTOR: Your minister accepts the imperial wish. (*He murmurs and gestures to Xia Cuiping.*)

XIA CUIPING: What are you saying?

GRAND TUTOR: Hm, hm, hmmmmm . . . (*He murmurs and gestures more.*)

XIA CUIPING: I understand. (*Grand Tutor exits.*) Ah, Your Majesty, when the queen dies, who will preside over Morning Sun Palace?

ZHOU YIWANG: Do you mean for us to give the title to you?

XIA CUIPING: My gratitude to our lord for this imperial favor.

ZHOU YIWANG: For what imperial favor are you thanking me?

XIA CUIPING: I thank Your Majesty for granting me reign over Morning Sun Palace.

ZHOU YIWANG: We were just joking.

XIA CUIPING: A king never jests.

ZHOU YIWANG: Ah, all right, so a king never jests! Take us back to the palace. (*Sings.*)

> Today the evil consort will lose her life,
> Today the deed is done, we'll grant you reign over Morning Sun
> Palace. (*They exit.*)

Scene 9

WANG HONG and MENG XI: (*Enter.*) Hm! Your Excellency!

MINISTER LI: I don't know what crime the queen has committed, but she is bound at the execution ground.

MENG XI: Oh, who will supervise the execution?

MINISTER LI: Xia Houli will supervise the execution.

WANG HONG: I see. I say, Your Excellency Minister Li, our dear military advisor, with the two of us brothers as guarantors, there should be no problem. Please go home. Thank you, Your Excellency. (*Minister Li exits.*)

MENG XI: Ah, my dear little brother, the queen has been indicted. I, your big brother, have absolutely no idea what to do.

WANG HONG: Big brother, don't worry, I plan to issue a false—

MENG XI: Shush! (*He checks the door.*) My dear little brother, a false what?

WANG HONG: I, your little brother, plan to issue a false decree.

MENG XI: I, your big brother, intend to disrupt the execution. Brother, let's go. (*Sings.*)

> The brothers discussed and made plans
> To save the queen from the pit of fire. (*They exit.*)

HU YUNZHUANG: (*Enters and sings.*)

> I, Hu Yunzhuang, have arrived at the execution ground; I lower my head.
> I can't help but be confused, my mind is a mass of tangled hemp.
> That day, when I invaded the North Sea, my merit was ever so great,
> Yet today, I don't know what law I have infringed.
> Hu Yunzhuang can only weep until tears drop like rain,
> I turn around and inquire of the Grand Tutor the root of the problem.

(*Speaks.*) I say, Grand Tutor.

GRAND TUTOR: What do you wish to ask?

HU YUN ZHUANG: When I, the queen, was indicted, the civil and military officials of the entire court tried to act as my guarantor. Why didn't I see you guaranteeing for me? How did you become the execution supervisor so suddenly?

GRAND TUTOR: I, your minister, guaranteed you for three days.

HU YUNZHUANG: If you've been guaranteeing me for three days, then why must I die?

GRAND TUTOR: I guarantee you'll join your maker in three days![20]

HU YUNZHUANG: Ah, how I will take care of you, you evil thief! (*Sings.*)

---

20. Literally, you'll ascend the "Homeland Lookout" (*wangxiangtai* 望鄉台) in purgatory.

Here at the execution ground, I, Hu Yunzhuang, curse vehemently,
I curse you, evil thief; how you've ruined me.
If I don't die, I will have you hacked into ten thousand pieces,
If I do die, I will wait for you at the gates of the three passes for
   ghosts.
I, Hu Yunzhuang, weep until my tears fall like rain.
(*Speaks.*) Here at the execution ground, I cry first for Wang Hong, then
for Meng Xi. I, the queen, brought you two brothers back to my court
to share its luxuries and wealth. Today, I, the queen, have been in-
dicted. The civil and military officials of the entire court guaranteed for
me, but I didn't see you two brothers guarantee for me. Where did you
two go? (*Sings.*)
I cry, Wang Hong and Meng Xi, where on earth are you?
Why are you not at the execution ground to save your queen?
I, Hu Yunzhuang, cry until tears cover my face,
But I hear a guard making a report.
SOLDIER: I report to Grand Tutor. I bring an edict from the king.
GRAND TUTOR: What? An edict from the king? Ai, you son of a bitch!
   Just like a fly, if there's a smell, he's bound to be here. Leave for now.
SOLDIER: Yes. (*He exits.*)
GRAND TUTOR: Come. Here I was just going to supervise the execution
   of this evil consort and he has to arrive. Come! Guard the evil consort
   over there. Let's receive the king's edict first.
SOLDIER: Here! The imperial edict will be received. His Excellency is
   here. Read the edict.
WANG HONG: I will read the edict. Grand Tutor, listen to the edict.
GRAND TUTOR: Here I am.
WANG HONG: His Majesty issued this edict. The queen has been indicted
   and should have been executed, but considering her great contribution
   in leading the North Sea expeditions, she can only be pardoned, she
   must not be executed. I, Wang Hong, read the edict. Meng Xi, receive
   the edict.
MENG XI: Just say you brought it. Ha, ha, ha, ha!
GRAND TUTOR: Ah! What's going on today? Why this commotion at the
   execution ground today? Let me ask. Hey you! Your Excellency
   Meng!.
MENG XI: Ho!
GRAND TUTOR: Ah, Your Excellency Meng, please lower your voice; do
   lower your voice. Your Excellency, the execution ground is full of confusion today. Why did he read the edict and you receive it? What kind
   of a protocol is this?
MENG XI: This is my protocol, the protocol of this dark old father of
   yours. This is the protocol I use. Ah, ha, ha, ha, ha!

GRAND TUTOR: Ha! Ah! What a lot of confusion. What an unreasonable man. I say, Your Excellency Meng.

MENG XI: Ho!

GRAND TUTOR: Ah, Your Excellency, please lower your voice. Do lower your voice. The way I see it, this edict today is probably false.

MENG XI: What? False? Of course it is not. But even if it is false, what can you do about it? What can you do about it? Ah, ha, ha, ha, ha!

GRAND TUTOR: Ah! How truly unreasonable! How utterly unreasonable! Your Excellency!

MENG XI: Ho!

GRAND TUTOR: Ah! Your Excellency, please lower your voice. Do lower your voice! Is it possible that you new officials to our court have no knowledge of the laws of our court?

MENG XI: What's that? Laws? Laws? Laws are your mother's dog fart! You watch how your dark old father here will take off my court robe and black gauze hat, and beat you son of a bitch to death! (*A figure of Meng Xi with disheveled hair and simple clothing displaces the original figure instantly.*)

GRAND TUTOR: Ah, ah, ah, ah! General Meng, Your Excellency, this is a rebellion!

MENG XI: If you say that it's a rebellion, then it is a rebellion. Have a taste of three slashes of my whip first. Ha, ha, ha! My dear brother.

WANG HONG: What?

MENG XI: Stay here and keep the queen safe. Wait for your big brother to fight my way into the court! (*Sings.*)

> At the execution ground, I kill the dog of an evil thief!
> Proceeding to the court, I will now kill the dog of a muddled king.

(*He exits.*)

Scene 10

ZHOU YIWANG: (*Enters and sings.*)

> We, the king, are at the palace, we think to ourselves,
> Executing our Consort Hu seems somewhat unjust.
> We, the king, ascend the golden throne of our court.

MENG XI: (*Calling backstage.*) You, muddled-headed king!

ZHOU YIWANG: We hear General Meng rebelling and entering the court. (*Meng Xi enters fighting.*)

TUTELARY GOD: Ah, ah, ah, ah, ah. Goodness gracious, goodness gracious. I am Zhou Yiwang's tutelary god. See how the little boy Zhou Yiwang has crossed the hot-headed Meng Xi. He's going to beat up the kid king, beat up the kid king. I'm going to have to defend him. Hai, ah, ah, ah! Look, he's not stupid—he had the gate closed. But I think I still have to defend it for him. If I don't defend it well, it will cost the kid his life. I'd better defend it well. (*He kneels with his head against a chair which symbolizes the gate. Zhou Yiwang is on the other side of the "gate."*)

MENG XI: Let's go! Ha! I arrived a moment too late, the muddle-headed king has got the palace gate closed. You muddle-headed king, open up the gate for me! Open the gate! (*He slashes three times with his whip and hits the tutelary god who is invisible to him.*)

TUTELARY GOD: Ahyoyo, ahyoyoyo! (*He rubs his buttocks and straightens his back while still kneeling against the "gate."*) Meng Xi, you hotheaded kid, the three slashes on my head are easy to defend, but those striking at my waist are simply too awesome![21] Aiya, you've cracked this old grandpa's waist. Old grandpa dares not fool around and talk rubbish. If I can, I'll have to defend this gate. If I can't take it, I'll still have to defend this gate. (*He bends his back and butts his head against the "gate" again.*)

ZHOU YIWANG: General Meng, why are you angry with us?

MENG XI: You muddle-headed king, oh crazy muddled-headed king! Lady Hu brought us brothers to your court from the Northern country so that your land could be as secure as an iron chain. I don't know what crime Lady Hu has committed, but you immediately wanted her tied up; you immediately wanted her executed. How many heads does a person have growing out of her neck to be chopped off—to be hacked by you? You think when you want to chop, you could just have people chop, chop, chop? (*He slashes with his whip again.*)

TUTELARY GOD: Yoyoyoyoyo! (*He rubs his buttocks and straightens his back.*) Meng Xi baby, you hothead, I've already told you, the three slashes on my head are bearable but those striking at my waist are simply too awesome. Here you go again. I think you've broken this old grandpa's back! But persist I must. I'll have to defend this gate even if my back is broken. If I can defend it, I'll have to; if I can't defend it, I'll still have to. (*He butts his head against the "gate" again.*)

ZHOU YIWANG: General Meng! That was a temporary mistake we made.

MENG XI: Ah, muddle-headed king. So you say that it was a mistake? If you admit that it was a mistake then it's easy to deal with. Open the palace gate and come out; I'll give you three slashes with my whip and say that I've made a mistake too! (*He slashes with his whip again.*)

TUTELARY GOD: Yoyoyoyoyo! (*Rubbing his buttocks.*) I say, Meng Xi, my child, I've already told you, the three slashes are bearable, but

---

21. A modern slang is used here which I have tried to reproduce.

you're going to kill this old grandpa. I think you've smashed my brain! Whew, it's still there. But what a lot of work, I'll have to defend this if I can, I'll have to defend this if I can't. I prop it with my head. I'm propping it. (*He butts his head against the "gate."*)

ZHOU YIWANG: General Meng, we will release her from the execution.

MENG XI: So you'll release her from the execution? Muddle-headed king, open the door and then you can talk about releasing her from the execution!

HU YUNZHUANG: (*Enters.*) Leave!

MENG XI: Ah, you've arrived, my lady! This infuriating muddle-headed king is getting off easy. Ahyo! What a secure palace gate this was!

TUTELARY GOD: Ah hm! Go ahead and strike. Old grandpa's head is propping the door all the way down onto the floor. Are you going to strike again? Are you going to strike again? The kid is not talking. (*He looks.*) Ah, no wonder he's not striking any more, the honorable one[22] has arrived! (*He stands up.*) Your humble celestial greets you with a bow and a kowtow to thank you, honorable one. If you, honorable one, had come sooner, your humble celestial wouldn't have had to go through so much beating and pain. Now that you are here, my business is finished. Come, old grandpa will leave. But how will I leave? Oh yes! I'm a god after all. How will I leave? Come! I'll ride on a cloud. Now, heaven oh heaven, earth oh earth, one kick on the ground, up into the sky I fly. (*He flies on a cloud.*) Ho, ho, ho! Up rises the mist, I'm floating in mid-air. Should anyone ask me, I am a god. I'm flying, I'm flying!

MENG XI: Aiya, you muddle-headed king!

TUTELARY GOD: Aiya! Oh, the kid! Old grandpa was just riding on a cloud when the kid yelled and made me reveal myself. I don't dare fly again. Ah, I know. There is a stream down there. Let old grandpa return by disappearing through the water opening. (*He dives and disappears.*)

SOLDIER: I report to the queen. Caihua Zhang Yun is invading us with an army of four hundred and fifty thousand.

HU YUNZHUANG: Leave for the time being.

MENG XI: Good for the rebels!

WANG HONG: Bravo for the rebels!

HU YUNZHUANG: Listen, you muddle-headed king, Caihua Zhang Yun is invading with an army of four hundred thousand, you should personally lead an expedition against him.

---

22. Literally, the term used is "the old one," indicating respect. Here the tutelary god uses it to refer to Hu Yunzhuang because of her higher original (celestial) status.

ZHOU YIWANG: It's best that you, Consort Hu, should lead the expedition. When you return, we will apologize to you.

WANG HONG: I won't go.

MENG XI: Nor will I.

HU YUNZHUANG: Well, as a favor to your father, the deceased king, I'll keep you, the muddle-headed king around. Here is my precious sword which I leave to you at the court. When I return from the expedition, if Xia Cuiping is cut down then all will be well. If she's not killed, I promise that I'll even the score with you. Wang Hong and Meng Xi, listen to my commands!

MENG XI and WANG HONG: Present!

HU YUNZHUANG: Leave with the army immediately!

MENG XI and WANG HONG: She's too much!

ZHOU YIWANG: Consort Hu, we will apologize to you when you return from the expedition. I think she has left. Let me open the palace gate.

ATTENDANT: Eeee!

ZHOU YIWANG: Oh no, she's still here! She's still here!

ATTENDANT: Eeee!

ZHOU YIWANG: You're here too!

XIA CUIPING: Here I come. Aiya, Your Majesty! Meng Xi has killed my father at the execution ground. Please do something about it for your humble consort!

ZHOU YIWANG: Hm. Ah, you evil consort, watch my sword! (*Her head drops off.*) Palace attendants, take the corpse away and throw it in the ditch. (*Sings.*)

> Today the evil consort has lost her life,
> Our realm will now have peace. (*They exit.*)

GRAND MASTER HUNYUAN: (*Sings.*)

> Here I am in my ancient grotto making prognostications,
> This very day five celestials should return to the Heavens.

(*Speaks.*) I, an indigent Daoist priest, am Grand Master Hunyuan. I have just made a prognostication in my grotto. Caihua Zhang Yun is attacking the Middle Kingdom[23] with a force of four hundred and fifty thousand. I'll have to summon my disciple Wei Tianbao and have him go down the mountains to defeat Zhang Yun. Come here, my disciple Wei Tianbao.

WEI TIANBAO: I'm a mere child living deep within a mountain; my master transmits the Dao to me. I, Wei Tianbao, bow to my master.

GRAND MASTER HUNYUAN: No need to bow, my pupil.

---

23. *Zhonghua* 中華, literally "the Beautiful Middle Kingdom," is a modern (probably used no earlier than the twentieth century) term for China; it is used here anachronistically to denote the legitimacy of Zhou Yiwang's reign.

WEI TIANBAO: My master, did you summon me at such a time to transmit to me the Dao?

GRAND MASTER HUNYUAN: No, I'm not going to preach an important sermon on the Dao. My pupil, you wouldn't have known, but Caihua Zhang Yun is leading an army of four hundred and fifty thousand against the Middle Kingdom. I'd like to have you, my disciple, descend the mountain to destroy Zhang Yun. How do you feel about it?

WEI TIANBAO: Your pupil is willing to descend the mountain.

GRAND MASTER HUNYUAN: Since you are willing to go, here is a fiery gourd. Take it with you. It contains a seven-star precious sword. Call for it, and it will shoot out. Stand firmly in this ancient grotto and listen to your master. (*Sings.*)

> Zhou Yiwang has ascended the throne, he is blessed with regulated wind and rain,
> Heaven has sent a bodhisattva[24] to assist him with the two expeditions.
> I command you to descend the mountain in order to destroy Zhang Yun.
> Zhang was originally a golden-winged peng-bird on the Buddha's head.[25]

WEI TIANBAO: (*Continues the song.*)

> My master has made it crystal clear at his grotto,
> I now realize that everything in the universe is predestined.
> I kowtow to thank my master and hurry out of the ancient grotto,
> Blowing a puff of air, I ride on a cloud and rise into the sky.

GRAND MASTER HUNYUAN: (*Sings.*)

> Now that my disciple has left,
> I, the old celestial, begin to worry.[26]
> Caihua Zhang Yun, you are in trouble,
> My pupil will never let you off. (*He exits.*)

WEI TIANBAO: I will ride on an auspicious cloud and descend from the mountaintop. I climb onto an auspicious cloud, and look down beneath. I ride on the cloud and speed away.

CAIHUA ZHANG YUN: (*Enters.*) Hm! I am Caihua Zhang Yun. I left the mountains and surrendered to Bei Yiwang, who has given me the title of Commanding General of All Under Heaven. I have just heard that the Zhou dynasty has dispatched an army here. Soldiers, surround the Zhou army and kill everyone. (*He exits.*)

---

24. In popular religion, Buddhist and Daoist deities co-exist and are often conflated.
25. The Garuda.
26. Although all is in order for victory, as a Daoist master he is saddened by the prospect of bloodshed.

Scene 11

WANG HONG: I'm Wang Hong!

MENG XI: I'm Meng Xi! I have been commanded by Lady Hu to fight Zhang Yun. Let's charge!

ZHANG YUN: Is it Wang Hong on the horse?

WANG HONG: Is it Zhang Yun on the horse? Watch my broad knife, little devil. Ah! Wang Hong fights ferociously. Watch my flying knife!

WEI TIANBAO: I am Wei Tianbao. I see Lady Hu. Let me spur on and charge. Is it Zhang Yun on the horse?

ZHANG YUN: What is your name, general?

WEI TIANBAO: I'm your young lord, Wei Tianbao. Watch my sword!

ZHANG YUN: Ha! Wei Tianbao fights ferociously. Watch my flying knife too!

WEI TIANBAO: Ah! Zhang Yun's fighting skills are exceptional. He travels so fast. Let me open my gourd. Aiya! I killed Caihua Zhang Yun. What do you know, my master is sending me a message. He wants me to go up to the Heavenly Platform to take a look. Let me go up to the Heavenly Platform to take a look. (*He exits.*)

Scene 12

MINISTER LI: Hm, I am old Minister Li. Our queen has not yet returned from the expedition to the North Sea. I exit from my gate this morning. Aiya, a letter floats down from the sky. I don't dare open it myself. I'll go the court and report it to the king. (*He exits.*)

ZHOU YIWANG: (*Enters.*) My consort has left with the army, but we have not seen her return.

MINISTER LI: I enter the court. I prostrate myself before Your Majesty. Long live the king!

ZHOU YIWANG: Rise, my dear minister.

MINISTER LI: My gratitude for the imperial favor.

ZHOU YIWANG: We did not summon you. Why did you come to court?

MINISTER LI: Your Majesty, you wouldn't have known, but when I, your minister, got up this morning, I picked up a letter from the sky. I dared not open it myself. I report it to Your Majesty personally.

ZHOU YIWANG: Where is it?

MINISTER LI: It is in your minister's sleeve.

ZHOU YIWANG: Place it on the dragon desk. Let us take a look at it. Oh no, the consort whom we'll never see again!

MINISTER LI: Don't weep so hard, Your Majesty. What if you should injure the imperial body from crying so hard? Tell me why. Explain it all to your minister.

ZHOU YIWANG: My dear minister, what you don't know! Your queen has expired during this third expedition to the North Sea.[27]

MINISTER LI: Oh no, our dear queen!

ZHOU YIWANG: My dear minister, don't cry so hard. Announce an edict for us. Tell all the civil and military officials of the entire court to take all our carriages to accompany us to the Temple of Guanyin to present a robe and pay our debts.

HU YUNZHUANG: (*In the form of Guanyin. Sings.*)
> I wear a headgear of dainty pagoda,
> And tread on a lotus flower of a thousand petals.
> If you want to know from which dynasty I came,
> I was originally the Bodhisattva Guanyin.

(*Speaks.*) I am the Nanhai Dashi 南海大士,[28] today is the nineteenth day of the Second Month. Zhou Yiwang has come here to present a robe and pay his debts. Celestial Officials of the Constellations!

CELESTIAL OFFICIALS: The benevolent goddess!

GUANYIN: Erect the statue of the goddess! Minister Li and the king are entering the temple to pay their respects to the goddess.

MINISTER LI: Ah, Your Majesty! A letter floats down from the sky. Please take a look, Your Majesty.

ZHOU YIWANG: Let us take a look at it. It says,
> "The river and mountains of the Zhou dynasty are prosperous,
> The old mother[29] has stabilized heaven and earth.
> The four directions are filled with tranquility,
> The eight directions enjoy great peace."

Oh no! Our suffering consort! Oh no, our Lady Hu!

MINISTER LI: Please do not weep so hard, Your Majesty. What if you should injure those imperial eyes!

ZHOU YIWANG: My dear minister, announce an edict for us. Tell all under Heaven to build a temple to Guanyin outside the southern gate of all the cities and make offerings on every nineteenth day of the Second Month. Have the carriages take us back to the palace.

GUANYIN: Celestial Officials of the Constellations!

CELESTIAL OFFICIALS: The benevolent goddess!

GUANYIN: Remove the goddess statue. (*They all exit.*)

---

27. For some reason, her death was not dramatized in any of the versions available to me.
28. Another name for Bodhisattva Guanyin.
29. This may be a reference to Guanyin.

Bibliography

A. Chinese Shadow Theatre and Cited Sources In European Languages

And, Metin. 1979.
Karagoz: Turkish Shadow Theater. Istanbul: A Dost Publication.

Ankerson, W. A. 1946.
"The Chinese Shadow Play." *Journal of North China Royal Asiatic Society* LXXII: 46-54.

Baird, Bill. 1973.
The Art of the Puppet. New York: The Macmillan Co., a Ridge Press Book.

Benton, Pauline. 1940.
The Red Gate Players. Peking: Lotus Court Publications.

Berliner, Nancy. 1986.
"Depictions of Hell in Chinese Painting and Shadow Puppets." *Orientations*, April, 42-49.

Blackham, Olive. 1960.
Shadow Puppets. London: Barrie and Rockcliff.

Bordat, Benis and Francis Boucrot. 1956.
Les Theatres D'Ombres: Histoire et Techniques. Paris: L'Arche Rue Saint Andre des Arts, au 17.

Breton, M. 1824.
"Puppet-show" in *China: Its Costume, Arts, Manufactures* Vol. IV: 127-132. London: Howlett and Brimmer.

Broman, Sven. 1995.
Chinese Shadow Theatre Libretti. Stockholm: Etnografiska Museet Monograph Series No. 17.

_____. 1983.
"Notes on Chinese Puppetry." *Bulletin of the Museum of Far Eastern Antiquities* 55.

_____. 1981.
Chinese Shadow Theatre. Stockholm: Etnografiska Museet, Monograph Series No. 15.

254

Chang, Lily. 1982.
The Lost Roots of Chinese Shadow Theatre: A Comparison with the Actors' Theatre of China. Ph.D. dissertation. Los Angeles: University of California.

Chang, Shelley Hsueh-lun. 1990.
History and Legend: Ideas and Images in the Ming Historical Novels. Ann Arbor: University of Michigan Press.

Chen, Fan Pen. Forthcoming.
The Chinese Shadow Theatre and Popular Religion and Women Warriors. Montreal and Manoa: McGill and Queens Universities Press and the University of Hawaii Press.

_____. 1999.
"The Temple of Guanyin: a Chinese Shadow Play." *Asian Theatre Journal,* 16:1, 60-106.

_____. 1999.
"Shadow Theatre Research 1998." *News From the Joyous Dragon,* 6 (Autumn). The Gold Mountain Institute for Traditional Shadow Theatres.

_____. 1998.
"Second Shadow Theatre Research Trip to China." *News From the Joyous Dragon,* 3 (Spring). The Gold Mountain Institute for Traditional Shadow Theatres.

_____. 1992.
"Female Warriors, Magic and the Supernatural in Traditional Chinese Novels" in Arvid Sharma and Katherine K. Young eds., *The Annual Review of Women in World Religions volume II: Heroic Women,* 91-109. Albany: State University of New York Press.

_____. 1997.
"Shadow Theatre Research in China." *News From the Joyous Dragon,* 1 and 4 (Winter). The Gold Mountain Institute for Traditional Shadow Theatres.

Chen, Jack. 1954.
"Shadow Theatre" in *Folk Art of New China,* 14-16. Peking: the Foreign Language Press.

Chen Lin-jui. 1954.
"Chinese Shadow-Plays." *China Reconstructs* 3-4: 23-27.

Chin Chen-an (Qin Zhen'an). 1993.
The Mainstay of the Chinese Shadow Show—the Lanchou Shadow Show. Taipei: The Student Book Co. (This is a translation of his book in Chinese).

Dandelet, Lucile Fessenden. 1976.
"Shadow Woman." *NRTA Journal,* March-April: 51.

Dolby, William. 1981
"The Origins of Chinese Puppetry." *Journal of the School of Oriental*

and African Studies 41.1:97-120.

Du Halde, P. 1736.
The General History of China (translated from *Description Géographique, Historique, Chronologique, Politique, et Physique de L'empire de la Chine*) Vol. 2. London: printed by and for John Watts at the Printing office in Wild-Court near Lincolns-Inn Fields.

Einstein, Susan. 1979.
Asian Puppets: Wall of the World. Los Angeles: Museum of Cultural History, University of California at Los Angeles.

Erda, Bettie. 1979.
Shadow Images of Asia. Katonah: the Katonah Gallery.

Gardiner, Bertha A. 1939.
"Chinese Shadow Plays with an American Accent." *Players* 12:2:9-10.

Grube, Wilhelm and Emil Krebs. 1915.
Chinesische Schattenspiele. Munchen: Koniglich Bayerischen Akademie der Wissenschaften.

Hardiman, Richard and Liu Deshan. 1995.
Chinese Shadow Puppets. Beijing: China National Publishing Industry Trading Co.

Hatchelder, Marjorie H. 1947.
Rod-Puppets and the Human Theatre (Chapter III). Columbus: The Ohio State University Press.

Hejzlar, Josef. 1967.
"The Magic of Coloured Shadows." *New Orient* (Prague), 38-41.

Hirsch, Mary. 1998.
Chinese Shadow Theater Playscripts: Two Translations. M.A. thesis. University of Washington.

Humphrey, Jo. 1983.
"The Chinese Shadow Theatre Today." *CHINOPERL Papers* 12:112-129.

_____. 1981.
"The Yueh Lung Shadow Theatre: An Example of Cultural Preservation." *CHINOPERL Papers* 10:141-164.

_____. 1980.
Monkey King: A Celestial Heritage (Chapter VIII). Catalogue from exhibit, Chung Cheng Art Gallery. New York: St. John's University.

_____. n.d.
"Asian S1hadow Theatre." New York: Gold Mountain Institute for Traditional Shadow Theater. (Slide lecture notes, 4 pages.)

Jacob, Georg and Hans Jensen. 1933.
Das Chinesische Schattentheater. Stuttgart: Verlag Von W. Kohlhammer.

Jacob, Georg. (1925). 1972 reprint.

Geschichte des Schattentheaters im Morgen—und Aberdland. Biblio Verlag. Osnabrück.

Jones, Kenneth Lee. 1995.
"Sichuan Shadows." *Puppetry Journal.* Summer, 2-4.

Kaulback, Barbara M. 1969.
"The Woman Warrior in Chinese Opera: An Image of Reality or Fiction?" *Fu Jen Studies: Literature and Linguistics* (Taiwan) 15:69-82.

Laufer, Berthold. 1923.
Oriental Theatricals. Field Museum of Natural History.

_____. 1901.
Peking and Shanghai Shadow Puppet Opera. 38 cylinder recordings deposited with the Archives of Traditional Music (accession # Pre-'54 [150]). Indiana University.

Li, Xiaolin. 1995.
Women in the Chinese Military. Ph.D. dissertation, University of Maryland. (UMI microform 9607792)

Liu Jilin. 1988.
Chinese Shadow Puppet Plays. Beijing: Morning Glory Publishers.

Liu, T'sun-yan. 1962.
Buddhist and Taoist influences on Chinese Novels: The Authorship of the Feng Shen Yen I. Vol. I. Wiesbaden: Kommissionsverlag.

Mair, Victor H. 1988
Painting and Performance: Chinese Picture Recitation and Its Indian Genesis. The University of Hawaii Press.

March, Benjamin. 1938.
Chinese Shadow-figure Plays and Their Making. Detroit. n.p.

_____. 1931.
"The Peiping Shadow Drama." *Puppetry, a Yearbook of Puppets and Marionettes* 2: 64-71.

_____. 1930.
"A Chinese Puppetman." *Puppetry, a Yearbook of Puppets and Marionettes,* 36-42.

Meander, Deborah. 1938.
"The Revival of the Art of the Chinese Shadow Theatre." *The School Arts Magazine,* Nov.: 85-86.

Mills, Winifred H. 1937.
Marionettes, Masks and Shadows. New York: Doubleday, Doran and Co., Inc.

Minnesota Museum of Art. 1970.
Shadow Figures of Asia From the Collection of Pauline Benton.

Miyao Jiryo. 1976.
"Pei Kau Hi: The Taiwanese Shadow Theater." *East Asian Cultural Studies* XV: 1-4, 61-66.

Miyazaki Ichisada. 1976.
China's Examination Hell: The Civil Service Examination of Imperial China. Translated by Conrad Schirokauer. New York and Tokyo: Weatherhill.

Needham, Joseph. 1962.
"Shadow-Play and Zoetrope" in *Science and Civilization in China.* London: Cambridge University Press, Vol. 4. 1:26, 122-125.

Obraztsov, Sergei. 1961.
The Chinese Puppet Theatre. Translated by J.T. MacDermott. London: Faber and Faber.

Phillips, Henry A. 1934.
"China's Vanishing Shadow Show." *Asia,* July, 412-415.

Ransome, Grace Greenleaf. 1931.
Puppets and Shadows: A Bibliography. Boston: F.W. Faxon Co.

Reiniger, Lotte. 1970.
Shadow Theatres and Shadow Films. New York: Watson-Guptill Publication.

Severn, Bill. 1959.
Shadow Magic: The Story of Shadow Play. New York: David Mckay Company, Inc.

Simmen, René. 1972.
The World of Puppets. New York: Thomas Y. Crowell Co.

Simon, Rainald. 1986.
Das Chinesische Schattentheater: Katalog der Sammlung des Deutschen Ledermuseums. Offenbach am Main.

Somderdruck. 1971.
Mitteilungen au den Museum Für Volkerkunde. Hamburg N.F. (Pp.111-118 for a list of the Beijing shadow plays in their collection).

Stalberg, Roberta H. 1984.
Puppetry of China. Catalogue of Exhibition with the Center of Puppetry Arts. Atlanta, GA.

_____. 1984.
China's Puppets. San Francisco: China Books.

_____. 1983.
"Berthold Laufer's China Campaign." *Natural History* 2:34-36.

Taiwan's Government Information Office. n.d.
"Puppetry—Shadow Theater." At the web address: http://www.roctaiwan.org/info/culture /cultur30.html.

Van der Loon, Piet. 1979.
"Chu Wen: a Play for the Shadow Theatre." *Occasional Papers: European Association of Chinese Studies* 2:75-92:i-xxxii.

Werle-Berger, Helga and Eversberg, Gerd. 1992.
"Ombres Chinoises" Schattentheater in Eurasien: Kataloge der

Museen in Schleswig-Holstein 2. Husum: Husum Druck- und Verlags-gesellschaft.

_____. 1987.

"Migration Theories on Asian Shadow figures." Unpublished notes from the symposium, "Comparison of Luanchou and Chaochou Shadow Traditions" organized by the Gold Mountain Institute for Traditional Shadow Theatre, 1. Held at the Taipei Theatre, New York City.

Werle, Helga. 1973.

"Swatow (Ch'aochow) Horizontal Stick Puppets." *Journal of Royal Asiatic Society, Hong Kong Branch* 1:73-84.

Whanslaw, H.W. 1950.

Shadow Play. Redhill, Surrey: Wells Gardener, Darton and Co., Ltd.

Wimsatt, Genevieve. 1936.

Chinese Shadow Shows. Cambridge: Harvard University Press.

_____. 1955.

"Finger Masks, Shadow Shows and Silhouettes" in *A Griffin in China*, 35-41. New York and London: Funk and Wagnalls Co.

Young, Conrad Chun Shih. 1971.

The Morphology of Chinese Folk Stories Derived from Shadow Plays of Taiwan. Ph.D. dissertation. Los Angeles: University of California.

Yu, Chunfang. 1979.

"Images of Kuan-yin in Chinese Folk Literature." *Hanxue yanjiu* 8:1, 221-286.

Yu Feng. 1963.

"The Shadow Theatre and Shadow Puppets." *Chinese Literature* 6, 78-83.

B. Selected and Cited Sources in Chinese

Dun Gen 鈍根. n.d.

"Limao huan taizi" 狸貓換太子 (Exchanging the Crown Prince with a Raccoon) in *Xikao daquan* 戲考大全 (A Complete Study of [Peking/Beijing] Operas), Vols. 33-36. Shanghai: Shanghai shudian. (This book is also edited by Liu Zhengyi 劉爭義 and reprinted in 1990 by the same publisher; but the 1990 recension only contains 2 of the four volumes/acts.)

Gu Jiegang 顧頡剛. Ca. 1944. (1983 reprint).

"Zhongguo yingxi lueshi jiqi xianzhuang" 中國影戲略史及其現狀 (A Short History of the Chinese Shadow and Its Present Situation). *Wenshi* 19:1,109-136. According to the appendix of the reprint, this article was written more than ten years after his 1934 "Luanzhou yingxi."

Guan Junzhe 關俊哲. 1959.

Beijing piyingxi 北京皮影戲 (The Shadow Theatre of Peking). Beijing: Beijing chubanshe.

Huan Zhi 驩之. 1992.
"Huabu taidou—yiweida de xiqujia Li Fanggui" 花部泰斗——一偉大的戲曲家李芳桂 (Shining Star of the *huabu* Opera Traditions—A Great Playwright, Li Fanggui). *Weinan shizhuan xuebao* 渭南師專學報 2:92.

Institute of Archaeology. 1980.
Yinxu Fuhao Mu 殷墟婦好墓 (The Tomb of Fuhao at the Ruins of Yin.) Beijing: Beijing Cultural Relics Publishing House.

Jiang Guoqing 江國慶. 2000.
"Jiang Guoqing lun piying" 江國慶論皮影 in *Shaanxi Guanzhong piying wangluo bowuguan* 陝西關中皮影網絡博物館 (Shaanxi Guanzhong Shadow Play Web Museum; original translation). Xi'an. This is a CD which can be obtained from the author at jgq@xaonline.com.

Jiang Yuxiang 江玉祥. 1999.
Zhongguo yingxi yu minsu 中國影戲與民俗 (The Chinese Shadow Theatre and Local Customs). Taipei: Suxiang chubanshe. (The first two-thirds of the book is the same as *Zhongguo piyingxi*).

_____. 1992.
Zhongguo Yingxi 中國影戲 (Chinese Shadow Theatre). Chengdu: Sichuan renming chubanshe.

Ke Xiulian 柯秀蓮. 1977.
"Piyingxi de yishu xingshi jiqi jiazhi" 皮影戲的藝術型式及其價值 (The Artistic Form and Value of the Shadow Theatre), *Huagang bowuguan guankan* (Taiwan) 5:156-166. (The two articles are recensions of her M.A. thesis.)

_____. 1977.
"Taiwan piyingxi de jiyi ji yuanyuan" 臺灣皮影戲的技藝及淵源 (The Technique and Origins of Piyingxi in Taiwan). *Zhonghua wenhua fuxing yuekan* (Taiwan) 10:1, 79-92.

_____. 1976.
Taiwan piyingxi de jiyi yu yuanyuan 臺灣皮影戲的技藝及淵源 (The Techniques and Origins of the Shadow Plays in Taiwan). M.A. thesis, Zhongguo wenhua xueyuan yishu yanjiusuo.

Liu Qingfeng 劉慶豐. 1986.
Piying shiliao 皮影史料 (Historical Materials on the Shadow Theatre). Harbin: Heilongjiangsheng yishu yanjiusuo.

Liu Rongde and Shi Yuzhuo 劉榮德 石玉琢. 1991.
Leting yingxi yinyue gailun 樂亭影戲音樂概論 (Overview of the Music of Leting Shadows). Beijing: Renmin yinyue chubanshe.

Liu Ruihua 劉銳華. n.d.
"Jidong piying" 冀東皮影 (The Jidong (Eastern Hebei; Luanzhou)

Shadow Theatre) in *Tangshan piying shiliao* 唐山皮影史料 (Historical Materials on Tangshan Shadows), 311-327. An internal publication.

Lü Sushang 呂訴上. 1969.
Taiwan piyingxishi 臺灣皮影戲史 (The History of the Shadow Theatre in Taiwan). Taipei: yinghua chubanshe.

_____. 1961.
Taiwan dianying xiju 臺灣電影戲劇 (Cinema and Theaters of Taiwan). Taipei: The Orient Cultural Service.

Qin Zhen'an 秦振安 (Chin Chen-an). 1991.
Zhongguo piyingxi zhi zhuliu: Luanzhou yinxi 中國皮影戲之主流：灤州影戲 (Main Stream of the Chinese Shadow Theatres: The Luanzhou Shadow Theatre). Taipei: Taiwan xuesheng shuju.

Shaanxisheng Wenhuaju 陝西省文化局 ed. 1980.
Shaanxi chuantong jumu huibian jumu jianjie 陝西傳統劇目彙編劇目簡介 (Abstracts of Plays in the Collection of Traditional Operas of Shaanxi). Xi'an: Shaanxisheng wenhuaju.

Shaanxi donglu Huaxian piying 陝西東路華縣皮影 (The Eastern Style Shadow Theatre of Shaanxi at Huaxian). 1991.
Hansheng (Taipei) 44: Special Edition.

Sun Kaidi 孫楷第. 1965.
"Jinshi xiqu de changyan xingshi chuzi kuileixi yingxi kao" 近世戲曲演唱形式出於傀儡戲影戲考 (Study of the Derivation of the Style of Performance of Chinese Operas from the Puppet and Shadow Theatres) in *Changzhouji* 滄州集 3:238-307. Beijing: Zhonghua shuju.

_____. 1965.
"Kuileixi yingxi buzai" 傀儡戲影戲補載 (Addendum to [My Study on] the Puppet and Shadow Theatres) in *Changzhouji* 滄州集 1:308-316. Beijing: Zhonghua shuju.

_____. 1952.
Kuileixi kaoyuan 傀儡戲考源 (A Study of the Sources of the Puppet Theatre). Shanghai: Shanza chubanshe. Also reprinted in *Minsu Quyi* (Taiwan) 23-24 (1983):141-214.

Tong Jingxin 佟晶心. 1937.
"Da Wu Xiaoling xiansheng guanyu 'yingxi' yu 'baojuan' de wenti" 答吳曉鈴先生關於影戲與寶卷的問題 (A Reply to Mr. Wu Xiaoling Concerning the Shadow Theatre and Precious Scrolls). *Geyao* 2:40, 2-3.

_____. 1937.
"Tanlun 'baojuan' zai suwenxue shangde diwei 談論寶卷在俗文學的地位 (An Exploration of the Importance of the 'Precious Scrolls' in the Study of Popular Literatures). *Geyao* 2:37, 1-2.

_____. 1934.
"Zhongguo yingxikao" 中國影戲考 (Examination of the Chinese

Shadow Theatre). *Juxue yuekan* 3:1, 1-19.

Tsao Pen-yeh (Cao Benye) 曹本冶 ed. 1987.

Xianggang de mu'ou piyingxi jiqi yuanliu 香港的木偶皮影戲及其源流 (The Puppet and Shadow Theatres in Hongkong and Their Origins). Hong Kong: The Museum of Hong Kong.

Wang Guangyue 王光越 ed. n.d.

Zhongguo yingxi yanjiu zhuanti wenxian xuanbian 中國影戲研究專題文獻選編 (Selected Documents for the Research of the Chinese Shadow Theatre). 57 volumes. Beijing: Quanguo Ming Qing dang'an ziliao zhongxin. (The only copy can be found at the University of Hawaii at Manoa).

Wang Peilun 王沛綸 ed. 1975.

Xiqu cidian 戲曲辭典 (A Dictionary for Chinese Operas). Taipei: Taiwan Zhonghua shuju.

Wang Zhaowen 王朝文 ed. 1995.

Zhongguo minjian meishu quanji 12: youyibian—mu'ou yingxi juan 中國民間美術全集 12: 木偶影戲卷 (The Complete Collection of Chinese Folk Art: Entertainment 12—the Volume on Puppet and Shadow Theatres). Jinan: Shandong jiaoyu chubanshe.

Wei Gexin 魏革新. 1990.

Leting piying 樂亭皮影. Hebei: Letingxian wenjiaoju.

Wu Cun 吳村. 1990.

Erbaizhong zhongguo tongsu xiaoshuo shuyao 200 種中國通俗小說述要 (Synopses of Two Hundred Traditional Chinese Popular Novels). Taipei: Hanxin wenhua shiye youxian gongsi.

Wu Tiantai 吳天泰. 1983.

Piyingxi juben de wenhua fenxi 皮影戲劇本的文化分析 (A Cultural Analysis of Shadow Playscripts). M.A. thesis, Taiwan National University, Department of Anthropology.

Xu Jianhua 徐建華 et. al. 1994.

Zhongguo fohua 中國佛話 (Chinese Buddhist Tales). Shanghai: Shanghai wenyi chubanshe.

Yang Mengheng 楊孟衡 et. al. 1991.

"Qingshiling" 青石嶺 (Mount Azure Rock) in Shanxi, Shaanxi, Henan, Hebei, Shandongsheng yishu yanjiusuo ed., *Zhongguo bangzixi jumu dacidian* (Encyclopedia of Abstracts on the Chinese Clapper Opera), 55. Taiyuan: Shanxi renmin chubanshe.

Yao Zongyi 堯宗頤. 1979.

"Chaoben Liu Longtu xiwen ba" 鈔本劉龍圖戲文跋 (Postface to the Hand-Copied Playscript *Liu Longtu*). *European Association of Chinese Studies* 2:73-74.

Yu Xun 魚訊 and Jiao Wenbin 焦文彬. 1983.

Shaanxi xiqu juzhongzhi 陝西戲曲劇種志 (Types of Traditional Operas in Shaanxi). Xi'an: Shaanxi juzhongzhi.

Zang Jinshu 藏晉叔 (1550-1620) ed. 1983 reprint.

Jinshuiqiao Chen Lin baozhuanghe zaju 金水橋陳琳抱粧盒雜劇 (The Yuanzaju Play, Chen Lin Carries a Box at the Bridge of the Golden River) in *Yuanquxuan* 元曲選 (A Selected Collection of Yuan Dramas), Vol. 4. Taipei: Taiwan Zhonghua shuju (reproduced from a Ming dynasty edition in the *jibu* 集部 of *Sibubeiyao* 四部備要).

Zhang Fuguo 張榑國. 1997.

Piyingxi—Zhang Decheng yishi jiachuan ying'ou tulu 皮影戲一張德成藝師家傳影偶圖錄 (Shadow Figures of the Performing Artist, Zhang Decheng's Family Collection). Taipei: Jiaoyubu.

_____. 1996.

Piyingxi—Zhang Decheng yishi jiachuan jubenji 皮影戲一張德成藝師家傳劇本集 (Playscripts of the Performing Artist, Zhang Decheng's Family Collection). Taipei: Jiaoyubu.

Zhang Yimou 張藝謀, director. 1994.

Huozhe 活著 (To Live). The video and DVD of this film with English subtitles are distributed through Mgm/Ua Studios.

Zhao Jianxin 趙建新. 1995.

Longdongnan yingzixi chubian 隴東南影子戲初編 (A Preliminary Study of the Shadow Theater of Southeastern Gansu). Taipei: Shi he Zheng minsu wenhua jijinhui.

Zhou Wei 周衛 and Hu Rong 胡蓉 ed. 1996.

Dongbei minzhu minjian meishu zongji: piyingjuan 東北民族民間美術總集皮影卷 (A Complete Collection of Folk Art Among the Northeastern Nationalities: Volume on the Shadow Theatre). Shenyang: Liaoning meishu chubanshe.

Zhou Yibai 周貽白. 1983 reprint.

"Zhongguo xiqu yu kuileixi yingxi—dui Sun Kaidi xiansheng *Kuileixi kaoyuan* ishu zhi shangque" 中國戲曲與傀戲影戲一對孫楷第先生傀儡戲考源一書之商榷 (Chinese Opera and the Puppet and Shadow Theatres: an Evaluation of Mr. Sun Kaidi's *Source Studies on the Puppet Theatres*). *Minsu quyi* (Taiwan) 23-24:215-255.

_____. 1953.

"Kuileixi yu yingxi" 傀儡戲與影戲 (Puppet and Shadow Theatres) in *Zhongguo xijushi* 中國戲劇史 (A History of Chinese Drama), 124-140. Shanghai: Zhonghua shuju.

CORNELL EAST ASIA SERIES

Order online: www.einaudi.cornell.edu/eastasia/CEASbooks, or contact Cornell East Asia Series Distribution Center, 95 Brown Road, Box 1004, Ithaca, NY 14850, USA; toll-free: 1-877-865-2432, fax 607-255-7534, ceas@cornell.edu